NEW YORK GENEALOGICAL

RESEARCH

by

George K. Schweitzer, Ph.D., Sc.D.
407 Regent Court
Knoxville, TN 37923

Typed by

Anne M. Smalley

ISBN 0-913857-11-4

TABLE OF CONTENTS

Abbreviations

A	Agricultural Census
AGLL	American Genealogical Lending Library, Bountiful, UT
C	Union Civil War Veteran Census
CH	Court House(s) and County Archives
DAR	Daughters of the American Revolution
E	Early Pre-1790 Census-Like Lists
FHC	Family History Center(s), Genealogical Society of UT
FHL	Family History Library, Genealogical Society of UT, Salt Lake City, UT
I	Industrial Censuses
LGL	Large Genealogical Libraries
LL	Local Library(ies) and Other Local Repositories
M	Mortality Censuses
NA	National Archives, Washington, DC
NAFB	National Archives Field Branch(es)
NYSA	New York State Archives, Albany, NY
NYGB	New York Genealogical and Biographical Society, New York, NY
NYHS	New York Historical Society, New York, NY
NYPL	New York City Public Library, New York, NY
NYSL	New York State Library, Albany, NY
P	Pensioner Census, Revolutionary War
R	Regular Federal Censuses
RL	Regional Library(ies)
S	NY State Censuses

Chapter 1

NEW YORK BACKGROUND

1. New York geography

The state of New York (hereafter abbreviated NY), one of the thirteen original colonies, is located in the north central region of the eastern seaboard of the US. In shape it resembles a triangle with the long side on the east, with the point on the west cut off, and with a southward protrusion in the southeast. The state is about 332 miles broad from east to west and its greatest width, which it shows in the east, is about 312 miles. At the southeastern extreme are several islands, a small one occupied by Manhattan (New York City), and the largest, Long Island, extending eastward for about 118 miles. NY is bounded on the north by Lake Ontario, the St. Lawrence River, and Canada, on the east by VT, MA, and CT, on the south by the Atlantic Ocean, NJ, and PA, and on the west by PA, Lake Erie, and the Niagara River. Across Lake Ontario, the St. Lawrence River, Lake Erie, and the Niagara River rests Canada. The capital of the state is located at Albany in the east central region, and the state is divided into 62 counties. The major cities of NY (with their approximate populations in thousands) are New York City (7071K) in the southeast, Buffalo (358K) in the northwest, Rochester (242K) in the northwest, Yonkers (195K) in southeast, Syracuse (170K) in the central area, Albany (102K) in the central east, Town of Tonawanda (78K) in the northwest, New Rochelle (71K) in the southeast, and Schenectady (68K) in the central east.

An understanding of the progressive settlement of the state and the genealogies of its early families is greatly enhanced by an examination of its major geographic regions and features. These are pictured in Figure 1. The first region consists of the Atlantic Coastal Plain (AC), made up of Long Island and Staten Island in the southeastern corner of NY. The terrain is low and level, and the soil is good for farming, but Staten Island and western Long Island are now highly populated parts of New York City. The second region is the New England Upland (NE), a narrow strip of hills and

6

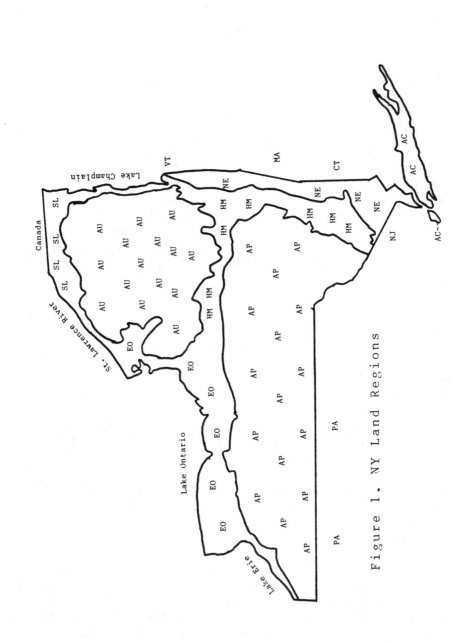

Figure 1. NY Land Regions

low mountains running along NY's southeastern border from lower VT down through Manhattan Island (New York City). The third region is the Hudson-Mohawk Lowland (HM), a narrow band (10-30 miles wide) of low-lying fertile valley land. It runs along the Hudson River from just west of Manhattan Island to above Albany, then connects with lowland leading into VT. There is also a lowland entry into the Hudson Valley on the CT border. Just north of Albany the lowlands turn westward and follow the Mohawk River to the region around Rome. The soil along the rivers is excellent for farming and falls along the rivers provide abundant water power. The fourth region is the Adirondack Upland (AU), which occupies most of northeastern NY. This is a hill and mountain region with poor soil, but with timber and mineral resources. Just north and east of this region is the fifth region, the St. Lawrence Champlain Lowland (SL), which is a strip of gently rolling land 10-20 miles wide on the south side of the St. Lawrence River and on the west side of Lake Champlain. The sixth region is the Erie-Ontario Lowlands (EO), a low plain with fertile soil which rests south of Lakes Erie and Ontario. The remainder of the territory in NY, which makes up its largest region, is the Appalachian Plateau (AP) which covers southwestern and south central NY. As one moves southward and eastward in the area the terrain gets more rugged with the Catskill Mountains occupying the eastern portion. The best farming section rests in the north central part of the region.

Figure 2 depicts the major waterways of NY. It is important to have a good perception of them because they provided the main early transportation and communication routes of NY. The patterns of settlement therefore centered around them and the valleys which run along them. The state has three sets of waterways according to their drainage: those that drain into the Hudson, those that drain northward or westward into Lakes Erie and Ontario and the St. Lawrence River, and those that drain southward into PA. The major rivers of NY are the Hudson and its main tributary the Mohawk, which drains central NY. Western NY is drained by the Allegany River which flows into PA, the Cattaraugus and the Tonawanda Rivers which empty into Lake Erie, and the Genesee River which discharges its water into Lake Ontario. To the east of the Genesee River another river flows into Lake Ontario,

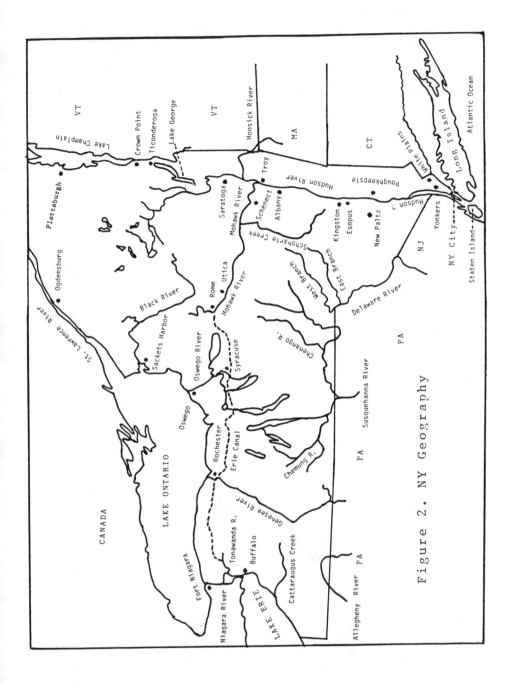

Figure 2. NY Geography

the Oswego, which receives water from the Finger Lakes. The land south of the Finger Lakes is drained by the Susquehanna River system which flows into PA. Water falling on territory south of the Mohawk River empties through the Delaware River which moves south or Schoharie Creek which flows north into the Mohawk River. In northeastern NY, your attention needs to be called to the Black River which empties into Lake Ontario, the St. Lawrence River which drains the northern section, and Lakes George and Champlain along the NY-VT border, with Lake Champlain extending into Canada.

The importance of the Hudson-Mohawk Lowland region (Figures 1-2) and the continuation of lowlands along the Erie-Ontario Lowland region cannot be overemphasized. The route from New York City up the Hudson Valley to Albany, then west along the Mohawk Valley, then further westward to the far western end of NY state is the major migration route that facilitated the populating of much of the northern US. Please notice that people migrating from New England could also enter into this route easily. This is all due to the fact that the Mohawk Valley is the only sizable break in the Appalachian Mountains in the northeastern US. Other than this, the mountain range blocks access to the west all the way from Canada to southern PA, where the next available gateway presents itself (to Pittsburgh). This gateway is not nearly as good as the Mohawk Valley, which is the lowest pass through the Appalachian Mountains between ME and GA. Through the Mohawk Valley and across the Erie-Ontario Lowland, NY built the Erie Canal in the 1820s. This fantastically enhanced the movement to and from the west, a movement which was further facilitated when NY's principal railroad lines were laid along the same route. All these linked New York City to the Great Lakes and hence to the northern tier of the growing Midwest.

2. The Dutch period, 1609-64

The territory which is now NY State was inhabited in 1600 by about 40,000 Indians belonging to many tribes and gathered into two major groups. The Iroquois were tightly organized and inhabited central and western NY. The Algonkins were more loosely affiliated and lived in eastern NY. The area had been visited by early explorers sailing on behalf of England, France, and the Netherlands, all of which claimed the land. The year 1609 saw two very important events with regard to NY. The first of these was an action by the French who had set up a colony in Canada for fur trading with the Indians. Their leader Champlain and his soldiers joined the Huron Indians and invaded NY to attack the Iroquois who were interfering with the fur trade. The French soon would explore much of central, west, and south NY, would increase their fur trading there, would send missionaries among the Indians, and later would build several forts in the NY back country. The second of the important events of 1609 was the sailing of Hudson into the NY harbor, then his proceeding up the river (now called the Hudson) until it became too shallow for his ship. He had arrived at the site of Albany. Hudson was exploring for the Dutch East India Company, and upon his return to the Netherlands, his favorable reports caused the Dutch to begin to develop the fur trade up and down the river. In 1614, they built Fort Nassau on an island near Albany to serve as the headquarters for the trade activity. Three years later, a replacement fort was constructed nearby at a place just below Albany.

In 1621, the Dutch Republic granted a charter to the Dutch West Indies Company for a 24-year trade monopoly in the Americas. In 1624, as part of a colonization plan, they sent out settlers, some of them stopping at the mouth of the Hudson (New Amsterdam), but most going up river to Fort Orange (Albany). More settlers came the following year and New Amsterdam at the southern tip of Manhattan Island became the headquarters of New Netherland. A director-general (governor) was given practically exclusive power to govern as he saw fit. The village grew slowly, its population in 1630 being about 300, in 1650 about 1000, and in 1660 over 2000. The major activities in the colony were fur trading and lumbering, these being so profitable that few settlers chose to farm. People of many nations came to New Netherland from the outset. In addition to the Dutch and the Walloons who came earliest, there were British, French, Finns, Swedes, Flemish, and others. To counteract the slow growth and the lack of laborers and farmers, the Company introduced several measures: the importation of black slaves, the offering of land to persons who would cultivate it, the encouragement of importation of indentured servants, and the granting of patroonships. This latter

plan gave a large tract of land to anyone who brought
over 50 adults within four years. The tract would extend
24 miles along one river bank or 12 miles on both banks.
A number of men tried the scheme but only Van Rensselaer
succeeded as a patroon. His patroonship, called Rennse-
laerwyck, covered most of the area now occupied by Albany, Rensselaer, and Columbia Counties. The patroon
brought tenant farmers over, supplied them with tools and
buildings, leased them the land, and required an annual
rent. The tenant could never purchase the land; it
remained the property of the patroon. The majority of
farmers in this period, however, were owners of the lands
they cultivated.

As the population of the colony slowly inched up,
the Dutch government in 1653 made New Amsterdam into a
chartered city. It continued to develop with many new
brick houses, shops, offices, wharves, warehouses, and a
church being built. Other settlements began to rise
around New Amsterdam, especially on Long Island. New
Englanders started coming into the eastern end of the
island before 1640, and a treaty was drawn up in 1650
between New Netherland and New England dividing the
island between them, only the far western part going to
New Netherland. By about 1650 a settlement called Beverwyck had grown up around Fort Orange. The year 1653
brought a new settlement at Esopus (Kingston), and the
movement of Dutchmen into the Mohawk Valley began in
1661. The Dutch fostered education and religion in the
colony by the requirement of schools in the settlements
and by the establishment and support of the Dutch Reformed Church.

Relationships with the Indians were usually friend-
ly, although there were some periods when the Indians
attacked the colonists and spread terror in outlying
settlements. Most of these hostilities were provoked by
greedy trade practices or by ill-advised policies or
aggressive actions by Dutch leaders on defenseless Indian
villages. Toleration of diverse religious practices was
fairly good until 1656, when the director-general (governor) prohibited any worship except that of the Dutch
Reformed Church. When Quakers in Flushing protested, the
Dutch West India Company upheld them and countermanded
the governor's action. In September 1664, English vessels with armed forces aboard came to New Amsterdam and

demanded surrender of the colony. The English King had
decided to make good a long-standing claim of his country
to the area. The governor surrendered, and New Netherland became the English colony of NY, except for a few
months during 1673-4 when Dutch control temporarily
returned. About 8000 Dutch citizens in small settlements
on NY Bay and the Hudson River became subject to British
rule.

3. The English period, 1664-1775

The takeover of the New Netherlands by the English
was provoked by the granting by King Charles II of a
large tract of land in America to James, Duke of York and
Albany. This piece of territory included all of the area
claimed by the Dutch. The seizure of New Netherland
added to the British possessions the only non-English
territory between New England and VA. The colony of New
Netherland became NY, the town of New Amsterdam became
NY, and the village of Beverwyck became Albany. The
Dutch were allowed to keep their lands, businesses,
religion, and many of their local laws. The colony
continued its slow growth, the population rising as
follows: 1703 (20,000), 1723 (40,000), 1737 (60,000),
1756 (99,000), 1771 (168,000), 1775 (200,000). In 1775,
about half of the population was English, many of them
having come in from New England. Other sizable groups
were Scottish, Irish, French, and German, plus about
20,000 black slaves.

Among the reasons for the slow population growth
were the threat of hostile French and Indians on the
frontier, English regulations forbidding settlement of
central and western NY, and the corrupt land grant practices of many of the English governors. These governors,
deviously getting around the law, granted very large
tracts of land to friends and groups of rich merchants.
These landholders then often did one of two things with
their land. They either simply leased it out or held it
for a while as a speculative investment (making it un-
available for settlement or sale), or they established
manors. The manors were patterned after the patroonship
Rensselaerwyck, which the English had approved and continued as a manor, in that the owners refused to sell the
land to farmers, but leased it out, making sure that they
continued to own it. Among the manors of the colonial

period of NY (with the dates) are: Rensselaerwyck (1630/7), Gardner's Island (1639), Fox Hall (1667), Livingston (1668), Plumme Island (1675), Philipsborough (1680), Bentley or Billop (1687), Casiltown (1687), Pelham (1687), St. George (1693), Cortlandt (1697), Morrisania (1697), Scarsdale (1701). Among other larger grants of the early years of this period were: Great Nine Partners (1697), Beekman (1703), Waywayanda (1703), Minnisink (1704), Hardenbergh (1708), Kayaderosseras (1708), plus many more later. Many of these are pictured in Figure 3, and a complete listing will be found in J. H. French, GAZETTEER OF THE STATE OF NY, Freidman, Port Washington, NY, 1860, pages 46-53. It must not be believed that small grants were not made to others since this was by no means the case. Many were made. However, the manor owners became an aristocratic landed gentry class of NY, and along with the prosperous merchants effectively controlled the colony. Few people wanted to immigrate to NY only to become tenant farmers, especially when good land was for sale elsewhere.

In spite of the aristocratic control of much land in the southeast and the hostile French and Indians in the central area, the population rose slowly, towns grew, and new settlements were established. New villages were set up between New York and Albany, then settlements began to spread into other river valleys, particularly the Mohawk. Notable among early immigrant groups were the French Huguenots who established New Paltz (1677) in present-day Ulster County and New Rochelle (1689) in Westchester County. Then in 1708-10, Germans from the Pfalz (Palatines) came first to the Hudson Valley, then moved on into the Schoharie and Mohawk Valleys. Settlement in the Susquehanna Valley began about 1740, but the groups were few, small, scattered, and threatened by the French and Indians. Most settlements north of Albany were chiefly forts for defense. In 1768, the Treaty of Ft. Stanwix forbid settlers to move into Iroquois territory which was defined roughly as anything west of a line drawn directly south of where Rome is today. The major peoples who had come to NY in the 1600s were Dutch, English, New Englanders, and French Huguenots.

In late 1683, NY was divided into twelve counties: New York, Kings, Queens, Richmond, Suffolk, Orange, Westchester, Dutchess, Ulster, Albany, Dukes, and Cornwall.

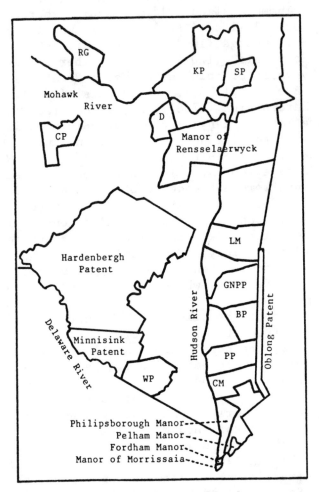
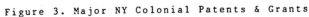

Figure 3. Major NY Colonial Patents & Grants

BP   = Beekman Patent
CM   = Cortlandt Manor
CP   = Croghan Patent
D   = Duanesburg
GNPP = Great Nine Partners Patent
KP   = Kayadrerosseras Patent
LM   = Livingston Manor
PP   = Philipse's Highland Patent
RG   = Royal Grant
SP   = Saratoga Patent
WP   = Waywayanda Patent

In 1768, Cumberland County was set up, in 1770 Gloucester County was established, and in 1772 Tryon and Charlotte Counties were created. After the Revolution, Dukes was annexed to MA, Cornwall was attached to ME, Tryon was renamed Montgomery, and Charlotte was renamed Washington, all in 1784. In 1790, Cumberland, Gloucester, and eastern Charlotte Counties were officially recognized as being in VT. NY and the colonies on its east, CT and MA, disagreed continuously over the location of the border. CT and MA claimed it ran 20 miles east of the Hudson River and NY insisted it was much farther east. At times armed raiding broke out in the disputed area. The territory that is now VT was also argued over, both NH and NY asserting ownership. Both colonies made land grants in the region, and a Royal Council upheld NY. However, NY did not press its claims and the settlers of the VT region began to set up their own government in 1770.

During the colonial period, NY inhabitants in the rural areas made their living by farming, lumbering, fur trapping and trading, and iron mining and refining. The town dwellers engaged in crafts, trades, professions, and in commerce. New York City very early became a business center, exporting colonial products and importing goods from abroad. The merchant class grew and prospered, many wealthy large land owners becoming merchants, and many wealthy merchants becoming large land owners. Together they tended to dominate the colonial government. British policy controlled the trade since the colonies were intended to enrich England. The colonists were instructed to send raw materials only to England and to buy manufactured products only from English factories. The colonists disobeyed these laws by smuggling, by sales to other countries, and by manufacturing enterprises. They and England were continually in conflict over these trade laws.

The two most important churches in the colonial era were the Dutch Reformed and the Anglican (Episcopalian, Church of England). Neither ever completely became the official or the established church. The NY aristocracy (government officials, wealthy merchants, large land owners) usually were Anglicans, the center of Anglican activity stemming from the parent church, Trinity, in New York City. As Scottish, Scotch-Irish, and German settlers came in, they brought with them their Quaker,

Presbyterian, and Lutheran faiths. The oldest Jewish congregation in North America was the one in New York City. Because of the French-English conflicts throughout this era, Catholics were not generally welcome in the colony. Printing was among the earliest businesses in New York City, this activity beginning in 1693, and the first newspaper (the NY Gazette) dates back to 1725. By about 1755, New York City was becoming a large metropolis with ferries connecting the sections, with fire, water, sanitation, and crime problems, with taverns, coffee houses, musical and theater performances, a college (King's College, later Columbia), and both public and private schools.

At the beginning of the English period, the chief officer of the colony was the governor, who was appointed by the Crown, and who was assisted by four councillors and a secretary. They regulated the finances, established the courts, set up a jury system, made land grants, provided for the military, and appointed town and local officials. In 1665, in response to Long Islanders who were used to more local control, the governor drew up a set of laws (the Duke's Laws) for them which were gradually extended to the whole colony. These laws contained a civil code, a criminal code, a court system, a military system, taxation regulations, arrangements for record keeping, and provisions for local government. Unfortunately, many of the colonial governors were incompetent and corrupt. They illegally gave large land grants, profiteered from their positions, and mismanaged the colony's affairs, particularly Indian relations. In 1689, Jacob Leisler led a revolt and took over the government, but he ended up being arrested and put to death. However, as a result of his cause, an Assembly of freeholders was established. The Assembly over the years slowly wrested power away from the governor, such that by 1720, it controlled the finances of NY and had become the law-making body. With these advantages, the Assembly could control the governor and his policies. In these governor-Assembly conflicts, the governor was generally supported by the merchants and large landowners, and the Assembly by the craftsmen, laborers, small shopkeepers, and farmers. The English government in London, of course, opposed the growing independence of the Assembly.

During most of the NY colonial period England and France were at war with each other. NY figured very strongly in these conflicts because of her strategic geographical position. The French were active in Canada, and in what is now northern NY, and they controlled the MS River plus the back country between the river and the northern colonies. They wanted to control and sustain the profitable fur trade which the westward-pressing English farmers threatened. The four wars between England and France which affected the colonies were King William's War (1689-97), Queen Anne's War (1701-13), King George's War (1744-8), and the French and Indian War (1756-63). None of the wars settled anything, except the last. Some Indians sided with the English, and some with the French. The two warring nations built forts at strategic sites, including many places in NY. From these forts, the French and their Indian allies launched attacks on English frontier settlements, some of them being wiped out. The major French forts were Fort Niagara (1726), Crown Point on Lake Champlain (1731), and Ticonderoga on Lake George (1755). Standing over against them, the English built numerous defense posts north and west of Albany. In the early years of the French and Indian War (1756-8), the French registered several victories, capturing English forts and repulsing English attacks on their forts. However, the tide turned in 1759, and the English took Ticonderoga, Crown Point, Niagara, Oswego, and Quebec, then in 1760 captured Montreal. This latter event essentially ended the war and left Britain in control of Canada and the country behind the colonies. The French had been removed from the NY frontier, but things were not well between England and her colonies as the feeling grew in the colonies that they should be governed by their Assemblies rather than by Parliament, and that they should not be taxed without participation in the government.

4. The Revolutionary period, 1763-1783

Following the termination of the French and Indian War (1763), Britain found herself severely in debt, and began to tighten up her trade and taxation policies in the American colonies. Having become used to an independence fostered by British disinterest, the colonies strongly resented the new taxes and the restrictive trade regulations. In addition, the British government had forbidden settlers from moving into west central NY. New York City merchants, businessmen, and lawyers joined with working men to organize rallies and protest groups, and to boycott all businesses which dealt with England. In 1765, a group called the Sons of Liberty began public protest rallies, opposing the British policies and the quartering of British troops in private homes. Several clashes between the Sons and the soldiers occurred, a particularly bloody one in early 1770. In defiance of the Tea Tax, which the British used to insist on their right to tax, and following the example set in Boston, in April 1774 the Sons of Liberty dumped a load of tea from a British ship into the harbor. The British Parliament passed retaliatory acts against the colonists, and the NY Assembly appointed a committee to correspond with the other colonies about their mutual problems. This committee was the state counterpart to many county, town, and district committees of protest which had been coming into existence all over NY.

In October 1774, a Continental Congress met at which the colonies agreed to boycott English trade unless their rights were respected. News of the outbreak of hostilities at Lexington on 19 April 1775 led to the collapse of the Royal government in NY, the NY Provincial Congress taking over. And with that and similar incidents elsewhere, a full-blown war began, a war of the 13 colonies against Britain. In July 1776, a Continental Congress (all 13 colonies) met in Philadelphia, and wrote the Declaration of Independence, which NY approved on 09 July. The new state of NY was very important to the war, almost one-third of all the battles being fought there because of the strategic importance of the Hudson River Valley. Further, the people of NY were sharply divided into those who remained loyal to England (Loyalists, Tories) and those who opposed England (Patriots). NY probably had a higher percentage of Loyalists than any other colony; Patriots were never in the majority, even though they had taken over the government. Loyalists fought with both the British army and with local Loyalist units. In areas under Patriot control, their property was confiscated. There was much Loyalist-Patriot strife in NY throughout the war. The major sites of the war are depicted in Figure 2.

The state of NY sat between New England and the southern colonies, and both sides knew that whoever controlled NY could control the colonies. Early on, in May 1775, VT forces captured the British Fort Ticonderoga on Lake Champlain. Two days later, New Englanders took Crown Point. These forts were used as bases to invade Canada, Montreal being captured on 12 November 1775, but an assault on Quebec failed, and the Americans returned to NY. Now the Patriots of NY faced three threats: (1) the Loyalists in their midst, (2) the British-supplied and inspired Indians on the frontier, and (3) the British ships loaded with soldiers ready to invade. After Washington drove the British from Boston, he immediately began to fortify New York City. On 30 June 1776, Howe landed 10000 British troops on Staten Island, and by 01 August reinforcements gave him 31000. He defeated the Americans at Brooklyn Heights on 26-27 August, moved to Manhattan on 15 September, and forced Washington's troops to retreat at Harlem Heights the next day. Then on 28 October, the British suffered many losses but pushed the Americans back at White Plains, forcing Washington to retreat into NJ. The British held New York City and used it as their headquarters for the rest of the war. Many Loyalists moved into the city, and the British brought prisoners of war there.

In 1777, the British attempted to implement a three-pronged attack to take NY state: (1) General Burgoyne moving south from Montreal down Lake Champlain and then the Hudson River toward Albany, (2) Colonel St. Leger moving southwest from Montreal down the St. Lawrence River to Lake Ontario and then turning east through the Mohawk Valley toward Albany, and (3) General Howe moving north from New York City toward Albany. Burgoyne set out with a large force of British regulars, German mercenaries, Indians, Canadians, and some Tories. They took Fort Ticonderoga readily, then defeated the Patriots again at Hubbardton, VT, and then took Forts George, Ann, and Edward, the latter on 30 July 1777. Burgoyne was deep in New York territory with long supply lines, and a growing shortage of food. A contingent was sent to Bennington, VT, to attempt to capture American supplies, but the troops were defeated by American forces. Meanwhile, St. Leger had arrived at the western end of the Mohawk Valley, and began to lay seige to Fort Stanwix (Rome). On their way to relieve the beleaguered fort, American General Herkimer's men were ambushed at Oriskany (east of Rome), but fought ferociously, causing St. Leger's Indians and then his British troops to retreat. St. Leger gave the campaign up and returned to Canada, permitting the Patriot forces to go to stand over against Burgoyne. Howe, instead of advancing up the Hudson River as the third part of the plan called for, set sail with his troops to take Philadelphia, leaving Henry Clinton to go to Burgoyne's aid. Clinton moved his British forces up the Hudson River, taking forts, then reaching Kingston, where the new state government had been organized. The British burned the city, then went back downstream, apparently not aware that Burgoyne waited for them to reinforce him.

As Burgoyne waited on help, American forces were gathering, so he decided he had better attack, which he did on 19 September. The armies fought to a stand off in this battle, which was called the First Battle of Saratoga. In the Second Battle of Saratoga on 07 October, Burgoyne was dealt a stunning defeat and surrendered his entire force. The campaign to split NY and divide the colonies had failed. The French, who now came to believe the colonies might win, joined the Patriots against the British. And the British turned their major efforts to conducting the war in the southern colonies in the hope that success could be had there. In the year after Saratoga, Indian and Tory groups conducted brutal raids all along the frontier murdering civilians and burning settlements. To counteract this, American Generals James Clinton and Sullivan combined forces to invade the heart of the Indian country. They destroyed the food supplies of the Indians and demolished many Indian villages. Indian raids, however, started up again and became particularly bad in the Mohawk and Delaware Valleys.

In the south, the tide of war went very much in Britain's favor as they took Savannah, GA, on 29 December 1778, secured the rest of the state of GA by the following February, then captured Charleston, SC, on 12 May 1780. That fall Cornwallis led a British invasion of NC, but was stopped at Kings Mountain on 07 October 1780. In a second invasion of NC, Cornwallis met American forces at Guilford Court House, NC, on 15 March 1781. Though the British won the field, they were so weakened they had to fall back to their supply base on the coast, Wilming-

ton, NC. From there Cornwallis moved into VA, finally
ending up at Yorktown where he was bottled up by the
French fleet and surrounded by American and French forces
under Washington's command. Cornwallis surrendered on 19
October 1781, and Washington returned to NY, where his
troops camped outside New York City to watch the British.
On 03 September 1783 a peace treaty was signed and on 25
November 1783 the British left New York City. The new
state was left in terrible shape: many dead, destroyed
settlements, damaged property, unstable currency, run-
away inflation, and hatred for Loyalist sympathizers.
There were some bright aspects, however: many hostile
Indians had gone to Canada, the war had stimulated manufacturing, and the old colonial aristocracy had been
greatly weakened.

5. Early statehood, 1783-1825

Early in the War for Independence, the NY provincial
congress in Kingston drafted and on 10 April 1777
approved a constitution for the new state. This document
provided for three branches of state government: execu-
tive (governor and his staff), legislative (a Senate and
an Assembly), judicial (judges and courts). The constitution provided that all white men owning property worth
20 pounds or paying 40 shillings annual rent could vote,
and guaranteed rights to impeach, to due process, to
trial by jury, and to freedom of worship. The new legislature passed a code of laws, including the repeal of
primogeniture (inheritance by the eldest son) and entail
(land could not be sold, only inherited). Later in 1799,
acts to gradually end slavery were enacted. During the
early war years, the Continental Congress (all 13 colonies) drew up Articles of Confederation as its frame of
government. After the war, these articles were too weak
to give the central government power to solve its many
problems. The leaders of some states, including NY,
preferred to maintain this situation, and opposed the
replacement of the Articles by a US Constitution which
would give a strong central government. The aristocratic
and wealthy people of NY (merchants, landowners, lawyers)
generally favored the Constitution, but the small businessmen, laborers, and farmers opposed it, fearing for
their freedoms. After considerable controversy and one
rejection of the Constitution, NY finally ratified the
document on 26 July 1788 in Poughkeepsie. New York City

became the new capital of the US, Washington was installed as first president, the government was organized, and the Bill of Rights was approved. Then, in 1790, the government returned to Philadelphia.

Before the Revolution, most NY people lived on Long Island or close to the Hudson and Mohawk Rivers. No sooner had the war ended, than the settlement began to spread into the central, western, and northern parts of the state. As previously mentioned, the war began and ended with there being 12 counties in what is now NY: Suffolk, Queens, Kings, Richmond, New York, Westchester, Orange, Ulster, Dutchess, Albany, Tryon, and Charlotte (Washington). The eastern border of NY was long disputed, the line 20 miles east of the Hudson River being agreed upon with CT (1731) and MA (1773), and such a line moving north through Lake Champlain being agreed upon with VT (effectively 1777, officially 1790). The vast Indian lands in central and western NY were claimed after the war, which opened the entire area up for settlement. In 1786, the NY Land Commissioners began selling land, over 5.5 million acres being disposed of by 1791. Many small plots were sold, but most of the land was bought as large tracts by NY, New England, Dutch, English, and French speculators. These speculators had the land surveyed and then sold small plots to individuals, many plots being sold on credit. NY State also offered bounty land to its Revolutionary veterans. Lands in the Old Military Tract in northeastern NY (Now Clinton, Essex, and Franklin Counties) were first made available, but few ex-soldiers wanted them. Then in 1788-9, land in the New Military Tract was offered. This tract was what is now Cayuga, Cortland, Onondaga, and Seneca Counties. Each private received 500 acres; those of higher rank received more. Some moved onto the land, but most sold it. This area, along with others mentioned below, is depicted in Figure 4.

The land in western NY was claimed by both NY and MA, both referring to their charters. In 1786, it was agreed to give MA a large part of the land, but NY would retain political control of it. MA, in need of money, sold its land, which ended up after several land purchases and transfers as three large speculator tracts: the Holland Land Purchase (present Niagara, Erie, Chautauqua, and Cattaraugus Counties plus the western

23

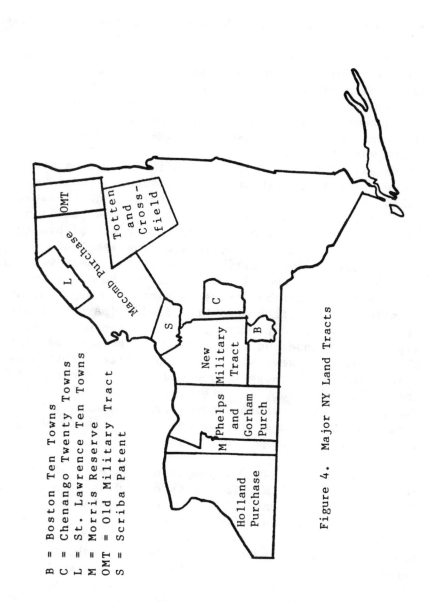

B = Boston Ten Towns
C = Chenango Twenty Towns
L = St. Lawrence Ten Towns
M = Morris Reserve
OMT = Old Military Tract
S = Scriba Patent

Figure 4. Major NY Land Tracts

portions of Allegany, Wyoming, Genesee, and Orleans Counties), the Morris Reserve (eastern portions of present Orleans, Genesee, Wyoming, and Allegany Counties and western portions of present Monroe and Livingston Counties), and the Phelps and Gorham Purchase (eastern portions of present Monroe and Livingston Counties, all of present Ontario, Steuben, and Yates Counties, and western portions of present Wayne and Schuyler Counties). There were several smaller tracts adjacent and within these major ones. Land sales offices were maintained by these speculators within their tracts. There were also sales of large tracts to speculators in northeastern NY, in particular Macomb, who by 1792 owned 4 million acres (all of present Lewis County, almost all of present St. Lawrence, Franklin, and Jefferson Counties, and parts of present Oswego and Herkimer Counties). There were other somewhat smaller speculator tracts in the area, including the tracts of Scriba (parts of present Oswego and Oneida Counties), and Totten and Crossfield (parts of present Herkimer, Hamilton, Essex, and Warren Counties). See Figure 4. These northeastern NY tracts passed through the hands of several other speculators, but proved a disappointment because they could not compete with the much richer lands in the central and western regions. The lands in all these tracts were rapidly divided and distributed to small individual owners, there being only remnants of the large tracts by 1840.

By 1825, the 340,000 people of NY in 1790 had grown to 1,614,000 with New York City expanding from 33,000 to 166,000. Fewer than 15% of the population lived in centers larger than 3000 people. Even so, the major NY cities had been established, practically all of them along the trade waterways. The remarkable population expansion was partly due to a high birth rate, but chiefly to immigration. Some of this was from Europe (French to the Black River, Welsh to Oneida County, Germans to cities and the Genesee Valley, a few Scots, and a few Irish). But most of the large numbers of immigrants came in from New England, beginning about 1783, pouring into the Hudson Valley, turning both up and down the valley, moving up the Mohawk Valley, then fanning out into central and western NY. By 1825, New Englanders were in every county, town, and city of NY. They simply overran the state, most of it becoming as Yankee as CT, MA, NH, VT, RI, and ME. These immigrants brought with them

Yankee hard work and ingenuity. They established their churches and schools, developed farms, expanded the trade, provided ministers, lawyers, physicians, and teachers who had been trained in New England colleges, rapidly took over the mercantile and shipping businesses, and developed New York City into the leading port of the US. In all this, they gradually overshadowed the old NY aristocracy, as they brought to NY their love for democratic freedom.

All this development experienced one major interruption, the War of 1812. As of this date, England and France were once again deeply involved in war. The US was trading with both, and both stopped American ships trading with the other. The British activity of this sort was greater, and in addition, Britain was encouraging and supplying Indians who were attacking US frontier settlements. NY opposed any military action against England because of the profitable trade, but most states west and south of NY were strongly in favor of it. Further, there were broadspread desires for the US to capture both Canada and FL. These states predominated and the US declared war on England on 18 June 1812. Three attacks on Canada were set in motion, two of them launched from NY. US General Hull was to invade Canada from Detroit, General Van Renssalaer was to invade Canada from around Buffalo, and General Dearborn was to move north from Plattsburgh and capture Montreal. All three campaigns ended in failure, as British forces repelled and/or defeated the US troops, in the last two actions the failures being largely due to refusals of NY militia to leave the state. American troops, however, were able to fight off British assaults on Sackets Harbor and Ogdensburg on 19 July and 04 October.

In February of 1813, the British destroyed much property of Ogdensburg, but in April, an American expedition crossed Lake Ontario, burnt York, then landed men at Niagara and captured the British garrison at Fort George. In May, NY militia successfully defended Sackets Harbor against a naval attack, and in July a British foray into the Niagara area was driven back. In the same month, a British naval squadron took Lake Champlain and burned US barracks at Plattsburgh. The month of September saw a crushing US naval victory on Lake Erie, securing the lake, and in October, US troops defeated the major Brit-

ish army in the west. A November campaign by the US down
the St. Lawrence to take Montreal met defeat before they
got to the city. In December, the US lost Fort George,
then the Canadian forces invaded NY at Niagara, then laid
waste the area all along the Niagara River, burning Black
Rock and Buffalo.

In 1814, in spite of the reinforcement of British
troops with soldiers who had beaten Napoleon, the US
captured Fort Erie (Niagara), won a battle at Chippewa,
then one at Lundy's Lane. But a real threat to NY was
the British force which began to move down the Lake
Champlain route. In September, the British land troops
were forced to retreat at Plattsburgh when their fleet
was severely beaten on the lake. The war was essentially
over in NY, the peace was signed in Europe in December
1814, but before the news reached New Orleans, British
invaders were dealt a stunning defeat in early January.
During the war British forces had burnt Washington and
invaded Baltimore, so New York City remained constantly
alert and prepared for an attack. Such never came. The
war ended with few changes in boundaries, but with re-
duced Indian threats in the southwest and the northwest,
and with the northwest securely in US hands.

During this period (1783-1825), three major developments occurred in the state: the development of farming,
the development of lumbering, and the development of the
NY business empire. The majority of the many immigrants
into rural NY had come to the state to farm. The amount
of developed farmland increased from about 1 million
acres to almost 6 million acres, as settlers pushed to
and beyond the western and northern boundaries of NY. As
the farms increased, the amount of food raised and mar-
keted increased, which caused the development of better
transportation routes for shipping to both domestic and
foreign markets. There was also demand in these markets
for the lumber which NY had in abundance, so this commodity came to be broadly exported. The chief agricultural crops came to be wheat, corn, oats, and pota-
toes, and there was the production of large quantities of
dairy products, and the raising of much livestock. Many
sawmills were set up to process the lumber. As life
became more settled, special occupations to serve the
farm population arose in the developing towns: black-
smiths, tinsmiths, storekeepers, coopers, cobblers,

carpenters, cabinetmakers, tanners, gunsmiths. All of this economic activity filled the wharves of New York City to brimming as trading escalated rapidly. By 1825, New York City was handling 50% of US imports and about 24% of exports. As a result wholesaling, retailing, banking, investing, insurance, and manufacturing grew in New York City in proportion.

Transportation within NY during 1783-1825 remained largely waterborne as it had been before. However, beginning about 1800, roads began to be built connecting settlements with waterways, and turnpikes (toll roads) were built between major towns. By 1825, over 4000 miles of roadway had been set up. Albany became a hub for turnpikes, eight of them emanating as spokes in a wheel. Wagons, stagecoaches, herds of livestock, peddlers, artisans, and settlers moved along these roads, whose roadsides were dotted with taverns and inns. But the turnpikes and the rivers could not provide enough cheap transportation for the vast quantities of heavy goods which had to move to and from New York City and between towns. The rivers might have met the need if they had not been partially blocked by rapids, waterfalls, and long stretches of shallow water. These problems could be solved by canals built in, adjacent to, feeding into, and connecting the rivers. Some small stretches of canal were built early, and then in 1800, a proposal was made to connect New York City to Lake Erie by a cross-state canal (the Erie Canal) from the Hudson River to Buffalo. After being delayed by the War of 1812, construction began in 1817, and the exceptionally arduous task was completed in 1825. The cheap transportation caused a literal explosion in the economy of NY, and produced boom towns along the canal: Rochester, Buffalo, Syracuse, Utica. The position of New YOrk City as the leading port of the nation was resoundingly assured. And the canal opened up the upper mid-west by providing cheap transportation to and from it. The opening of the canal was followed quickly by the construction of numerous feeder canals. The two major groups in the amazing growth of NY during 1783-1825 were the pioneer farmers and the many sorts of merchants. The farmers turned NY into a highly productive agricultural state, and the merchants brought to New York City the internal, coastal, and transatlantic trade of the US. NY was now first among the US states in population, agriculture, and trade. The old colonial

aristocracy was gone, and had been replaced by a democratic state of hard-working farmers and aggressive
businessmen.

6. The national period, 1825-61

Shortly after the success of the NY canal system,
railroad construction began in the state in 1831 between
Albany and Schenectady. A revolution in transportation
ensued as the Hudson-Mohawk-Erie lowland received rail
service, which was then rapidly expanded into the southern and northeastern counties. By 1850, 30 separate
railroads with about 1400 miles of track were operating
in the state, and in 1853 eight of them were combined to
give unified service from Albany to Buffalo. By 1861, NY
railroads were handling large amounts of passenger travel
and freight service, causing abandonment of turnpikes and
of some canals. All of this transportation further
enhanced the progress of NY as an agricultural, industrial, and mercantile state.

The growth in agriculture and transportation facilitated new means of production which caused industry to be
rapidly developed as mills and factories were set up.
These factories, with machines designed for mass production and assembly-line operation, increased production,
employed increasing numbers of workers, and resulted in
the organization of large business corporations. These
corporations could raise capital for building factories
by selling stock. Industrialization increased rapidly
during this period, the major facilities which grew being
grist mills, saw mills, cotton factories, woolen factories, fulling mills, carding factories, mines, foundries,
tanneries, distilleries, and breweries. The major com-
modities which were manufactured were textiles, food,
wood, and metals, with large concentrations of factories
and workers swelling the cities. The excellent port
facilities of New York City made it the leading port of
the US, and with excellent transportation systems connecting it with the interior, it became the leading
commercial and financial city.

The astonishing industrial growth in NY was accompanied by a rapid increase in population, most of which
was due to immigration. The immigrants early in the
1800s were largely New Englanders, but during this

period, they were chiefly Europeans, the largest groups being Irish and German. Over 3.7 million Europeans arrived at New York City during 1820-60. Population figures (in thousand, K) during this period were 1825-(1614K), 1830(1913K), 1835(2175K), 1840(2429K), 1845-(2604K), 1850(3097K), 1855(3466K), 1860(3881K). These figures are remarkable considering that over a million NY natives had left the state by 1860, most moving west. The population increase was accompanied by a centralization of people in the cities, which means that the cities grew very fast, and as a result, developed many problems: sanitation, fire protection, police protection, traffic, slums.

The changes in industry, commerce, transportation, agriculture, and urbanization during 1825-61 brought several problems to NY, and general conditions in the US brought others. NY politics during this time were very complicated, quite turbulent, and often corrupt. The two-party system broke down several times as the major parties split, and some older parties died out with newer ones being formed. The principal issues were the governmental relations to canals, railroads, banks, immigrants, prohibition, and slavery. In spite of all this dissension, numerous humanitarian reform movements had success or partial success, including ones relating to education, penology, mental care, temperance, women's rights, and slavery. In 1821, a new constitution had given the vote to practically all white men over 21, but farmers living on leased land on manors felt they were not free under the system, since they could never own the land. In the 1840s, they started the anti-rent movement, rebelled against the system, and agitated for change, which ended in a 1846 constitution which terminated the lease system. State aid to education increased during 1825-61, but it was not until 1867 that free education through high school was available to all. By the end of the period, NY had 22 colleges, including ones for medicine, teacher training, and engineering.

During the 1830s a religious movement which had been sweeping NY reached its peak. Many unchurched people joined up, and church members and their leaders participated in various reform movements. The leading Protestant groups (in order of size) were: Methodist, Presbyterian, Baptist, Congregational, and Episcopalian. The fastest growing denomination, the Roman Catholic, was fed by the numerous Irish and German immigrants who were members of the faith. Not many of NY's people in 1860 were Jewish, most of those of this belief living in NY City. Numerous new religious groups also developed in NY during this time: Anne Lee's Shakers, Jemima Wilkinson's followers, Noyes' Oneida community, Spiritualist groups, the Millerites, and the Church of Jesus Christ of Latter Day Saints (the Mormons, founded by Joseph Smith near Palmyra). In 1848, NY became the first state to permit women to own property, and in that year, a women's rights convention met in Seneca Falls. Susan B. Anthony and Elizabeth C. Stanton led a movement which secured many rights for females, including rights to go to universities, enter professions, work for the same wages as men, and make contracts. Women were very active in the major reform movements of this time: temperance, peace, treatment of prisoners, treatment of the mentally ill, and anti-slavery.

Along about the middle of this period, the state of TX was annexed to the US. Some time thereafter Mexican troops crossed into TX, bombarded Fort Taylor, and on 12 May 1846, the US declared war. The Mexican troops were driven back into Mexico, Santa Fe was captured, and CA switched over to American rule. In February 1847, the Mexican forces were defeated at Buena Vista, and the final campaign of the war began in March of that same year. US troops landed at Vera Cruz and a drive on Mexico City began. The city was taken on 14 September 1847, and the peace treaty of 02 February 1848 provided for Mexico's session of two-fifths of its land to the US. NY was remote from the battle areas and had no vital interests in the conflict, but even so, the state furnished soldiers who fought valiantly. The war did not severely tax the resources of the US, and therefore NY was asked for only nominal support to the war effort.

Slavery had ended in NY in 1827, and it had ended also in the other northern states, but it persisted in the southern states, where slave laborers had become built into much of the agricultural system. US law required that slaves who ran away from the south into the north be returned to their owners. Some people in NY, in opposition to this law, aided slaves to escape to Canada. Further, there were very strong anti-slave societies

operating in NY. In the last half of the 1850s, a critical question came to the forefront of national politics.
The question was whether slavery should be permitted in
the territories in the west and in the states that were
gradually being formed out of them. This issue served as
a focus for the slowly worsening relations between the
northern and the southern states. When the Republican
Party met in 1860, the two major candidates were Seward
of NY and Lincoln of IL. After three ballots, Lincoln
was chosen, his opposition to slavery in the territories
being well known. When the Democratic Party split into
three separate groups over the slavery issue, Lincoln's
election was assured. And with Lincoln's election,
secession of at least some southern states became in-
evitable. The north and south differed not only over
slavery; they differed in that the north was industrial
with the south being agricultural, the north had a growing population which accepted immigration while the south
had a steady population and opposed immigration, and the
north favored centralized national government with the
south preferring decentralization.

7. The Civil War, 1861-5

Prior to 1860, compromises between the many differences which separated the northern states and the
southern states were worked out. However, these arrangements became increasingly unsatisfactory as the 1850s
wore on, and conflict loomed large. After Lincoln's
election but before his inauguration, SC seceded from the
Union on 20 December 1860, and by 01 February 1861, they
had been joined by AL, FL, GA, LA, MS, and TX. On 12
April, US Fort Sumter in Charleston harbor fell to Confederate attackers, and Lincoln called for troops to
defend the North. By the end of May, four other southern
states had refused to answer Lincoln's call and had
seceded (NC, VA, AR, TN) to join the Confederacy. The
two sides, Union and Confederate, mobilized their men and
resources, and four years of horrible conflict began. We
will now summarize the War, and then we will look at NY's
part in a bit of detail.

The intention of the Union came to be defeat of the
Confederacy by invasion and subdual. Five strategies
were to be pursued: (1) the blockading or capture of
Southern ports to cut off supplies, (2) the taking of the

Confederate capital Richmond by attack from the north,
(3) the splitting of the Confederacy by driving down and
pushing up the MS River, (4) the further splitting of the
Confederacy by driving from the northwest corner of TN
down the TN and Cumberland Rivers to Nashville to Chattanooga to Atlanta to Savannah, and then (5) the pushing
north from Savannah into SC, then into NC, and finally
into VA to assault Richmond from the south.

Strategy 1, the sea blockade, was accomplished early
in the War with most Atlantic and Gulf ports blocked or
captured by the end of 1862. Strategy 2, the drive
against Richmond from the north, failed again and again,
the Confederacy even making two counter-invasions to
threaten Washington, until success began to be had by
Grant in 1864, Richmond falling on 02-03 April 1865.
Strategy 3, the drives to take the MS River, had been
completed with the collapse of Port Hudson on 09 July
1863. Strategy 4, the drive from northwest TN to Savannah, took 34 months, but ended in the capture of Savannah
on 22 December 1864. Strategy 5, the drive north from
Savannah, was accomplished by the taking of Charleston
and Columbia in February 1865, then pushing into NC where
one of the two remaining major Confederate armies surrendered on 26 April 1865. The other had surrendered at
Appomattox on 09 April 1865.

The state of NY played an exceptionally important
role in the Civil War. Almost 465,000 NY men fought for
the Union cause. Some served 30 days, some served the
entire war, but most spent about three years in service.
The fighting forces of NY participated in about 2000
military actions (battles, engagements, sieges, skir-
mishes) in practically every area of conflict. The state
supplied 293 regiments plus 65 companies of soldiers.
About 51,000 sailors and marines were New Yorkers. Over
50,000 men of NY died during the War either of wounds or
of disease. In addition, the state supplied money to
finance the conflict and materials to equip the armed
forces. A draft law, which was passed in 1863, led in
July to anti-draft riots in New York City. Property was
destroyed, blacks were lynched, and other lives were lost
before Federal troops were called in to restore order.
In spite of strong peace movements throughout the War,
chiefly in New York City, the state of NY provided more
soldiers than any other state, more supplies, and more

money. NY citizens paid the most taxes, bought the most war bonds, and donated the most to war relief and charity organizations.

The internal effects of the War on NY state were quite mixed. The numerous deaths of young men were felt strongly, especially in the rural areas. In general the conflict had stimulated business in NY, but foreign trade was held constant, and the US merchant marine declined severely. Manufactures gleaned large profits, but working people suffered from a rise in the cost of living and inflation. The societal disruption produced by the War resulted in crime, graft, corruption, and profiteering, but many NY residents exhibited generosity and self-sacrifice in providing care for veterans and their needy dependents. Unfortunately, times did not improve for the blacks of NY. Free in principle, they remained outcasts socially and economically. Segregation was the rule, and in 1860 an amendment to grant the vote to blacks was defeated. In many ways, the religious, political, economic, educational, and social lives of NY suffered setbacks during the War, and recovery from many of them was slow.

8. The post-war years, 1866-

In the years following the Civil War, the state of NY was transformed from a predominantly agricultural and lumbering economy into an industrial commonwealth. The chiefly agrarian and rural society rapidly was changed into a manufacturing and urban society. Farms by no means ceased to exist, but their character changed in that they became highly-mechanized, large-sized business enterprises supported by specialized food processing and distribution organizations. As mechanized mass production of food increased, the number of farmers required to run farms decreased, and the 25% of the state's 1870 population that were farmers slowly declined to a few percent. By about 1870, the major timber regions of NY had been cut, so lumbering declined. However, wood product manufacture continued with the raw timber being shipped in. The industrial revolution, which had started in the early 1800s, continued after the Civil War at an ever increasing rate. More and more corporations to sponsor manufacturing were formed, and factories continued to concentrate in the cities, with New York City having the overwhelming majority. The economic and social situation of the factory workers of NY remained dismal for many years, with low wages and long hours. However, in spite of governmental opposition, trade unions finally began to gain enough influence to alter these conditions.

The railroads which had been put in place before 1861 expanded, so that by 1900, over 6000 miles of track were being used. The railroads played a key role in the development of NY's cities, the shipping of raw materials to factories, and the distribution of the finished products to state, national, and international markets. The later coming of automobiles and trucks along with the required highways further increased the passenger and freight traffic of NY State. As time went on, the combined NY economic prowess and working people's demands to share in its results produced sizable alterations in the cultural life of New Yorkers. The middle class increased in size and the time and economic resources for leisure and cultural activity became available to more and more people.

During the decades after the War Between the States, graft, corruption, machine politics, and catering to special interests characterized the political scene on city, county, and state levels. Public outrage around the turn of the century plus some outstanding statesmen resulted in reform programs which regulated corporations, introduced labor laws protecting workers, and took important soil and forest conservation steps. Reforms were also promoted in the areas of education and health which added to the social and economic well-being of the general populace.

Throughout the post-war years, the population of NY continued to increase: 1870(4383K), 1880(5083K), 1890 (6003K), 1900(7269K), 1910(9114K), 1920(10385K). As mentioned before, the years 1840-60 saw the coming to NY of large numbers of Irish and Germans. These two groups continued to be the major immigrants during the period 1870-90, with large numbers of Scandinavians also entering. Then, beginning about 1890, the leading groups entering the port of NY were unskilled peasants and laborers from southern and eastern Europe: Italians, Poles, Russians, Romanians, others from the Austro-

Hungarian Empire, and east European Jews. The period 1861-1900 saw over 14 million immigrants settling in NY state, a large fraction of them in New York City, and during 1901-14, another 13 million came. In the larger cities, especially New York City, immigrants of a particular nationality often formed ethnic neighborhoods. The New York City population after the Civil War followed this trend: 1870(942K), 1880(1206K), 1890(1515K), 1900 (3437K), 1910(3767K), 1920(5620K). Notice that over half the state's population is in New York City as of 1920.

NY earned its position of world leadership in trade and commerce in these years. This leadership was due to the combined effect of many factors: optimum geographical location, large population, excellent transportation, diversity of industry, richness of financial institutions (banking, insurance, underwriting, brokerage, commodity), and numerous service and professional agencies. NY not only became a great export-import center, but it also developed somewhat later into the world's leading market for stock, bond, and security exchange. All the above development was punctuated by the outbreak of the Spanish American War in 1898, a relatively short war with only a few battles.

9. NY counties

The state of NY is divided into 62 counties, 5 of which are unified as New York City (Bronx, Kings, New York, Queens, Richmond). These 5 counties are also known as boroughs of New York City (Bronx = Bronx Borough, Kings = Borough of Brooklyn, New York = Manhattan Borough, Queens = Borough of Queens, Richmond = Borough of Staten Island). The remaining 57 counties are subdivided into densely-populated cities and rural towns, and the cities are generally further subdivided in wards. Villages are areas within towns which are small population clusters. For example, as of 1860 Albany County was divided into the City of Albany and the Towns of Bern, Bethlehem, Coeymans, Guilderland, Knox, New Scotland, Rensselaerville, Watervliet, and Westerlo. Villages within Bern were Bernville, East Bern, Peoria, Reidsville, and South Bern, and the other towns likewise contained villages. It is important to recognize that cities and towns are independent units in counties; they have their own separate governments. Governmental records of importance to genealogists have been kept by the state, counties, cities, towns, and villages, with those of the state, counties, and cities being the most important.

From the original ten counties which were set up in 1683 on land now in NY state, the present 62 counties have developed. These original counties were Albany, Dutchess, Kings, New York, Orange, Queens, Richmond, Suffolk, Ulster, and Westchester. There came to be 12 counties as of 1772, 20 as of 1791, 30 as of 1800, 45 as of 1809, 53 as of 1821, 59 as of 1841, 61 as of 1899, and the last, Bronx County, was established in 1914. The expansion of New York City beyond Manhattan began in 1873 when 13,000 acres of southern Westchester County were annexed. More of lower Westchester County (the villages of East Chester, West Chester, Pelham, and Wakefield) was added in 1895. Then, in 1897, the NY legislature authorized Greater New York City which was made up of a combination of four counties: New York (Manhattan), Kings (Brooklyn), Queens, and Richmond (Staten Island). Finally, in 1914, the northern section of New York County was made into Bronx County.

The development of the counties of NY is depicted in Figures 5 through 14. The present-day counties appear in Figures 11 and 14 with Figure 14 showing the southeastern counties in and around New York City and Figure 11 showing all the rest. The 62 existing counties are abbreviated on the maps as follows, with abbreviations in parentheses and with locations given following the parentheses: Albany(A) central east, Allegany(Al) west, Bronx (B) southeast, Broome(Br) center, Cattaraugus(C) west, Cayuga(Ca) center, Charlotte(renamed Washington in 1784), Chautauqua(Ch) west, Chemung(Ce) center, Chenango(Cn) center, Clinton(Cl) northeast, Columbia(Co) central east, Cortland(Cr) center, Delaware(D) central east, Dutchess (Du) southeast, Erie(E) west, Essex(Es) northeast, Franklin(F) northeast, Fulton(Fu) central east, Genesee(G) west, Greene(Gr) central east, Hamilton(Ha) northeast, Herkimer(H) central east, Jefferson(J) center, Kings(K) southeast, Lewis(L) center, Livingston(Li) west, Madison (Ma) center, Monroe(M) west, Montgomery(Mo) central east, Nassau(N) southeast, New York(NY) southeast, Niagara(Ni) west, Onondaga(Od), Oneida(O) center, Ontario(On) center, Orange(Or) southeast, Orleans(Ol) west, Oswego(Os)

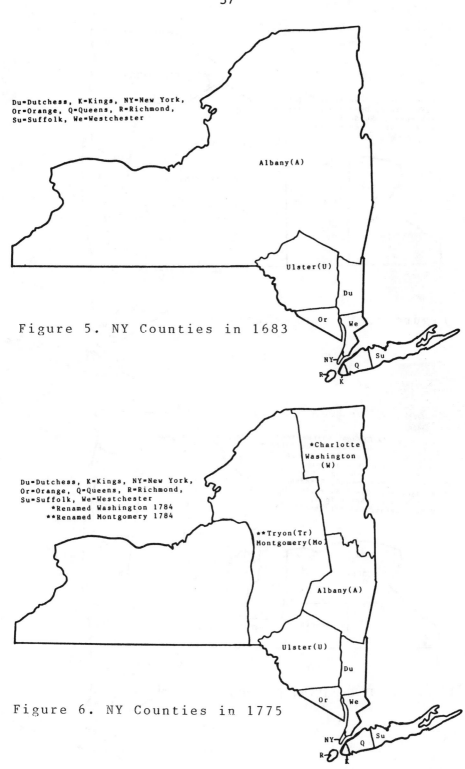

Du=Dutchess, K=Kings, NY=New York,
Or=Orange, Q=Queens, R=Richmond,
Su=Suffolk, We=Westchester

Albany(A)

Ulster(U)

Du

Or

We

NY-

Su

R-

Q

K

Figure 5. NY Counties in 1683

*Charlotte
Washington
(W)

Du=Dutchess, K=Kings, NY=New York,
Or=Orange, Q=Queens, R=Richmond,
Su=Suffolk, We=Westchester
    *Renamed Washington 1784
    **Renamed Montgomery 1784

**Tryon(Tr)
Montgomery(Mo)

Albany(A)

Ulster(U)

Du

Or

We

Figure 6. NY Counties in 1775

NY-

Su

Q

R-

K

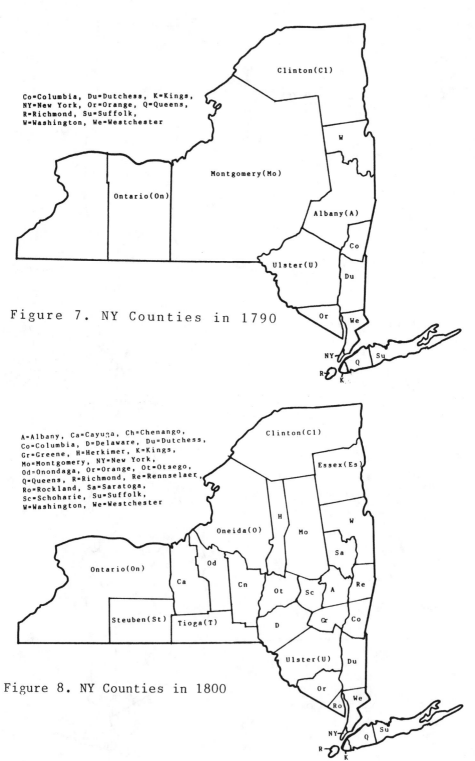

Co=Columbia, Du=Dutchess, K=Kings,
NY=New York, Or=Orange, Q=Queens,
R=Richmond, Su=Suffolk,
W=Washington, We=Westchester

Clinton(Cl)

W

Montgomery(Mo)

Ontario(On)

Albany(A)

Co

Ulster(U)

Du

Or

We

NY

Su

Q

R

K

Figure 7. NY Counties in 1790

A=Albany, Ca=Cayuga, Ch=Chenango,
Co=Columbia, D=Delaware, Du=Dutchess,
Gr=Greene, H=Herkimer, K=Kings,
Mo=Montgomery, NY=New York,
Od=Onondaga, Or=Orange, Ot=Otsego,
Q=Queens, R=Richmond, Re=Rennselaer,
Ro=Rockland, Sa=Saratoga,
Sc=Schoharie, Su=Suffolk,
W=Washington, We=Westchester

Clinton(Cl)

Essex(Es)

H

Mo

W

Oneida(O)

Sa

Od

Re

Ontario(On)

Ca

Cn

Ot

Sc

A

Steuben(St)

Tioga(T)

D

Gr

Co

Ulster(U)

Du

Or

We

Ro

NY

Su

Q

R

K

Figure 8. NY Counties in 1800

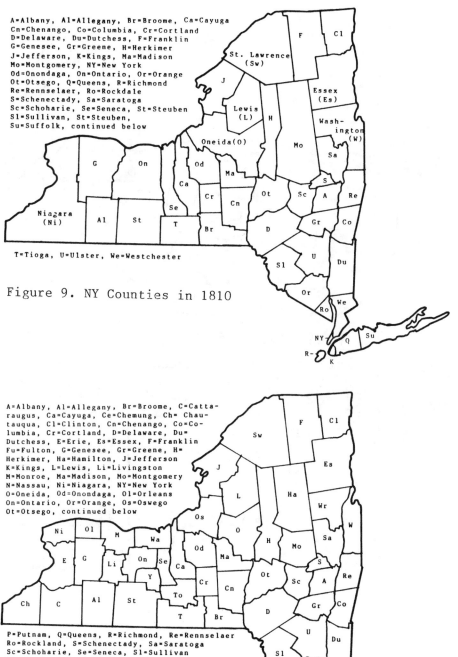

A=Albany, Al=Allegany, Br=Broome, Ca=Cayuga
Cn=Chenango, Co=Columbia, Cr=Cortland
D=Delaware, Du=Dutchess, F=Franklin
G=Genesee, Gr=Greene, H=Herkimer
J=Jefferson, K=Kings, Ma=Madison
Mo=Montgomery, NY=New York
Od=Onondaga, On=Ontario, Or=Orange
Ot=Otsego, Q=Queens, R=Richmond
Re=Rennselaer, Ro=Rockdale
S=Schenectady, Sa=Saratoga
Sc=Schoharie, Se=Seneca, St=Steuben
Sl=Sullivan, St=Steuben,
Su=Suffolk, continued below

T=Tioga, U=Ulster, We=Westchester

Figure 9. NY Counties in 1810

A=Albany, Al=Allegany, Br=Broome, C=Catta-
raugus, Ca=Cayuga, Ce=Chemung, Ch= Chau-
tauqua, Cl=Clinton, Cn=Chenango, Co=Co-
lumbia, Cr=Cortland, D=Delaware, Du=
Dutchess, E=Erie, Es=Essex, F=Franklin
Fu=Fulton, G=Genesee, Gr=Greene, H=
Herkimer, Ha=Hamilton, J=Jefferson
K=Kings, L=Lewis, Li=Livingston
M=Monroe, Ma=Madison, Mo=Montgomery
N=Nassau, Ni=Niagara, NY=New York
O=Oneida, Od=Onondaga, Ol=Orleans
On=Ontario, Or=Orange, Os=Oswego
Ot=Otsego, continued below

P=Putnam, Q=Queens, R=Richmond, Re=Rennselaer
Ro=Rockland, S=Schenectady, Sa=Saratoga
Sc=Schoharie, Se=Seneca, Sl=Sullivan
St=Steuben, Su=Suffolk, Sw=St. Lawrence
Sy=Schulyer, T=Tioga, To=Tompkins
U=Ulster, W=Washington, Wa=Wayne
We=Westchester, Wr=Warren, Wy=Wyoming
Y=Yates

Figure 10. NY Counties in 1830

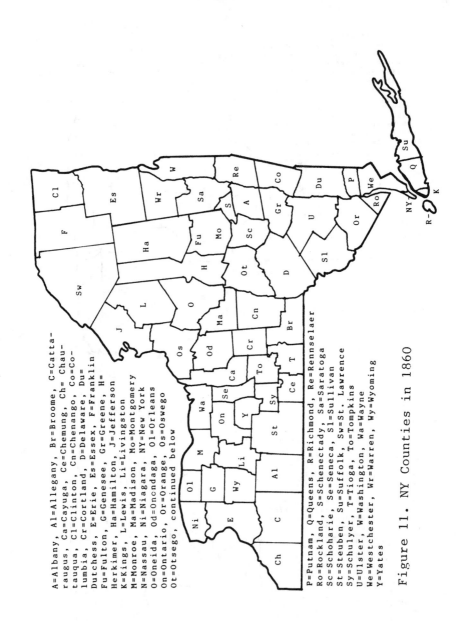

A=Albany, Al=Allegany, Br=Broome, C=Catta-
raugus, Ca=Cayuga, Ce=Chemung, Ch= Chau-
tauqua, Cl=Clinton, Cn=Chenango, Co=Co-
lumbia, Cr=Cortland, D=Delaware, Du=
Dutchess, E=Erie, Es=Essex, F=Franklin
Fu=Fulton, G=Genesee, Gr=Greene, H=
Herkimer, Ha=Hamilton, J=Jefferson
K=Kings, L=Lewis, Li=Livingston
M=Monroe, Ma=Madison, Mo=Montgomery
Ni=Nassau, Ni=Niagara, NY=New York
O=Oneida, Od=Onondaga, Ol=Orleans
On=Ontario, Or=Orange, Os=Oswego
Ot=Otsego, continued below

P=Putnam, Q=Queens, R=Richmond, Re=Rennselaer
Ro=Rockland, S=Schenectady, Sa=Saratoga
Sc=Schoharie, Se=Seneca, Sl=Sullivan
St=Steuben, Su=Suffolk, Sw=St. Lawrence
Sy=Schulyer, T=Tioga, To=Tompkins
U=Ulster, W=Washington, Wa=Wayne
We=Westchester, Wr=Warren, Wy=Wyoming
Y=Yates

Figure 11. NY Counties in 1860

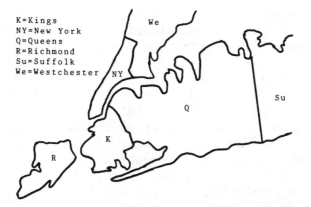

Figure 12. Southeastern NY Counties in 1873

Figure 13. Southeastern NY Counties in 1899

Figure 14. Southeastern NY Counties in 1914

center, Otsego(Ot) central east, Putnam(P) southeast, Queens(Q) southeast, Rennselaer(Re) central east, Richmond(R) southeast, Rockland(Ro) southeast, St. Lawrence(Sw) northeast, Saratoga(Sa) central east, Schenectady(S) central east, Schoharie(Sc) central east, Schuyler(Sy) center, Seneca(Se) center, Steuben(St) center, Suffolk(Su) southeast, Sullivan(Sl) southeast, Tioga(T) center, Tompkins(To) center, Tryon(renamed Montgomery in 1784), Ulster(U) southeast, Warren(Wr) central east, Washington(W) central east, Wayne(Wa) center, Westchester(Wc) southeast, Wyoming(Wy) west, Yates(Y) center. Several points relating to Figures 5-14 need to be made. First, the county abbreviations also accompany the figures. Second, the counties other than those in and around New York City attained their present day form in 1860 (Figures 5-11). The counties in and around New York City, however, did not attain their present-day boundaries until 1914 (Figures 12-14). Third, please note that several county name changes occurred: Charlotte renamed Washington and Tryon renamed Montgomery, both in 1784. Fourth, for more detailed maps showing the towns and cities within each county, consult:

__Genealogical Department of the Church of Jesus Christ of Latter Day Saints, COUNTY FORMATIONS AND MINOR CIVIL DIVISIONS OF THE STATE OF NY, Series B, No. 4, Salt Lake City, UT, 1978.

And for details concerning villages and settlements in each of the towns of the state, look into:

__J. H. French, GAZETTEER OF THE STATE OF NY, Friedman, Port Washington, NY, 1860, reprinted several times.

The counties of NY are very important to genealogical researchers because of the many records they keep. These records refer to individuals who have lived in the county and often give a great deal of detailed information. Important offices in the counties where these records are kept will now be indicated. The office of the county clerk keeps some vital records (birth, marriage, death), civil and criminal court records (Court of Sessions, Court of Common Pleas, Court of Oyer and Terminer, Supreme Court, County Court, Family Court), some federal and state census records, land records (deed, mortgages, surveys), naturalization records, some military service and militia records, assessment records, minutes of county administration, registers of professions, divorce records, coroner's inquests, homestead exemptions, and business licenses. The village, town, and city clerk's offices sometimes hold a few vital records, some court records, some early land records (especially the town clerk), tax records, some naturalization records, a few military records, a few militia records, administrative records, and school records. The office of the county surrogate court keeps records of estates (wills, administrations, proceedings, petitions) and guardianship records. The office of the chief county fiscal officer holds tax and assessment rolls and lists. The office of the county health department maintains vital records. The offices of county, city, town, and village historians must not be overlooked, as is the case for county and city archives, since they often have collections of both governmental and non-governmental records, especially the older ones.

Many of the records mentioned above will be discussed in detail in Chapter 2. You will be told exactly what years they cover, how they may be obtained, what information they contain, and how to discover if they have been published, either in printed or microfilm form. Chapter 3 will inform you about the major genealogical collections (libraries and archives) in and out of NY, and will indicate to you which of the county records are available there. The fourth and fifth chapters list all the NY counties, and tell you what records are available in published form (books and microfilms) for each. In addition, you are told where the county seat is, when the county was created, and the county or counties from which it was formed. These county formation data are very important to you because sometimes you will need to trace an ancestor back into a county out of which a new county came. This occurs when your ancestor lived on a piece of property which was in land split off from an old county to form a new county.

10. Recommended reading

A knowledge of the history of NY and its local regions is of extreme importance for the tracing of the genealogies of its former inhabitants. This chapter has been a brief treatment of that history. Your next step should be the reading of one of the following, relatively short one-volume works:

44

___B. J. Bliven, NY, A BICENTENNIAL HISTORY, Norton and
Co., New York, NY, 1981.
___B. M. Wainger, D. Furman, and E. Oagley, EXPLORING NY
STATE, Harcourt, Brace, New York, NY, 1956.
___M. Glassman, NY STATE (AND CITY) GEOGRAPHY, HISTORY,
AND GOVERNMENT, Barrons, Great Neck, NY, 1965.
After this, it is recommended that you thoroughly read
one of the following volumes. These are larger books
which give much broader coverage of NY history.
___D. M. Ellis and others, A HISTORY OF THE STATE OF NY,
Cornell University Press, Ithaca, NY, 1967.
___B. J. Lossing, THE EMPIRE STATE, American Publishing
Co., Hartford, CT, 1888.
___M. A. Wheeler, NY STATE, YESTERDAY AND TODAY, Scribner,
New York, NY, 1952.
For New York City, good one-volumes histories include:
___C. Rodger and R. Rankin, NY: THE WORLD'S CAPITAL CITY,
Harper and Brothers, New York, NY, 1948.
___B. Still, MIRROR FOR GOTHAM, NY University Press, New
York, NY, 1956.
___J. E. Patterson, THE CITY OF NY, Abrams, New York, NY,
1978.
___M. L. Booth, HISTORY OF THE CITY OF NY, Dutton, New
York, NY, 1880.
If you care to go further, or if you wish to explore a
particular topic or a particular time span in greater
detail, you may wish to employ one or more of the several
multi-volumed histories of NY or New York City. Among
the better ones are:
___A. C. Flick, editor, HISTORY OF THE STATE OF NY, Colum-
bia University Press, New York, NY, 1933, 10 volumes.
___J. R. Brodhead, HISTORY OF THE STATE OF NY, Harper and
Brothers, New York, NY, 1853/71, 2 volumes.
___J. G. Wilson, editor, MEMORIAL HISTORY OF THE CITY OF
NY FROM ITS EARLIEST SETTLEMENT TO 1892, NY History
Co., New York, NY, 1892-3, 4 volumes.
___M. J. Lamb and B. Harrison, HISTORY OF THE CITY OF NY,
Barnes, New York, NY, 1877, 3 volumes.
___J. Sullivan, HISTORY OF NY STATE, Lewis Historical
Publishing Co., New York, NY, 1927, 6 volumes.
___D. Van Pelt, LESLIE'S HISTORY OF GREATER NY, Arkell
Publishing Co., New York, NY, 1898, 3 volumes.

In order to locate books dealing with certain time
periods of NY history, certain regions or counties of NY,

or certain trends, movements, or developments in NY
history, consult the following historical bibliographies:
__C. A. Flagg and J. T. Jennings, BIBLIOGRAPHY OF NY
COLONIAL HISTORY, NY State Library, Albany, NY, 1901.
__H. Nestler, A BIBLIOGRAPHY OF NY STATE COMMUNITIES,
COUNTIES, TOWNS, AND VILLAGES, Kennikat Press, Port
Washington, MY, 1968.
__Bibliographies following chapters in A. C. Flick,
editor, HISTORY OF THE STATE OF NY, Columbia University
Press, New York, NY, 1933, 10 volumes.
__A LIST OF BOOKS RELATING TO THE HISTORY OF THE STATE OF
NY, School Library Division, University of NY, Albany,
NY, 1916.
__RESEARCH AND PUBLICATIONS IN NY HISTORY, State Educa-
tion Department, Albany, NY, 1970.
__See sections on NY in M. J. Kaminkow, US LOCAL HIS-
TORIES IN THE LIBRARY OF CONGRESS, Magna Carta Book
Co., Baltimore, MD, 1975 ff., 5 volumes.
Individual county histories will be listed in Chapters 4
and 5 of this book, and other historical works dealing
with the state, regions, counties, cities, towns, and
villages of NY are listed in:
__M. J. Kaminkow, US LOCAL HISTORIES IN THE LIBRARY OF
CONGRESS, Magna Carta Book Co., Baltimore, MD, 1975
ff., 5 volumes.
__P. W. Filby, BIBLIOGRAPHY OF AMERICAN COUNTY HISTOR-
IES,, Genealogical Publishing Co., Baltimore, MD, 1985.
__NYPL, US LOCAL HISTORY CATALOG, Hall, Boston, MA, 1974,
2 volumes, with BIBLIOGRAPHIC GUIDE TO NORTH AMERICAN
HISTORY, Hall, Boston, MA, annual supplements, 1977-.
The most important of the NY historical periodicals which
you might want to consult because of their excellent
articles on all phases of NY history are:
__NY State Historical Association, NY HISTORY, The
Association, Cooperstown, NY, quarterly, 1919-, Vol.
1-.
__NY Historical Society, NY HISTORICAL SOCIETY QUARTERLY,
The Society, New York, NY, quarterly, 1917-, Vol. 1-.
__NY State Historical Association, NY STATE HISTORICAL
ASSOCIATION PROCEEDINGS, The Association, Cooperstown,
NY, 1901-, Vol. 1-.
__NY Historical Society, NY HISTORICAL SOCIETY COLLEC-
TIONS, The Society, New York, NY, two series, 1809-,
Vol. 1-.

Abbreviations

A	Agricultural Census
AGLL	American Genealogical Lending Library, Bountiful, UT
C	Union Civil War Veteran Census
CH	Court House(s) and County Archives
DAR	Daughters of the American Revolution
E	Early Pre-1790 Census-Like Lists
FHC	Family History Center(s), Genealogical Society of UT
FHL	Family History Library, Genealogical Society of UT, Salt Lake City, UT
I	Industrial Censuses
LGL	Large Genealogical Libraries
LL	Local Library(ies) and Other Local Repositories
M	Mortality Censuses
NA	National Archives, Washington, DC
NAFB	National Archives Field Branch(es)
NYGB	New York Genealogical and Biographical Society, New York, NY
NYHS	New York Historical Society, New York, NY
NYPL	New York City Public Library, New York, NY
NYSA	New York State Archives, Albany, NY
NYSL	New York State Library, Albany, NY
P	Pensioner Census, Revolutionary War
R	Regular Federal Censuses
RL	Regional Library(ies)
S	NY State Censuses

Chapter 2

TYPES OF RECORDS

1. Introduction

The state of New York (NY) is relatively rich in genealogical source material, even though there have been some sizable losses of records, especially in the early years and in a 1911 fire at the State Library in Albany. A great deal of work has been done by many people in accumulating, preserving, photocopying, microfilming, transcribing, abstracting, printing, and indexing records. Among the most important genealogical records of NY are the local county governmental records (court, deed, mortgage, naturalization, probate, tax, town, village, will, some census, and a few birth, death, and marriage). The originals of these records are largely in the county court houses and/or local county archives (CH) and/or local historical society repositories. There are also original records in the offices of town and village clerks, and in the offices of the various agencies of the larger cities of NY State, especially NY City. A number of these records have been microfilmed by the Genealogical Society of UT, and the microfilm copies are available at their main library, the Family History Library, as well as through its over 250 branches (known as Family History Centers) in the US. A number of the original records have also been transcribed and published (books, manuscripts, articles), most being available in large genealogical libraries in NY State and in NY City, and many being available in large genealogical libraries elsewhere.

In addition to the local governmental records (including those of counties, towns, villages, and cities), there are several other categories of records which are of immense use genealogically: state governmental records (birth, census, colonial, court, death, land grant and patent, marriage, military, probate, will), national governmental records (census, immigration, military, naturalization, tax), and private records, both those kept by and those published by private organizations and individuals (Bible, biography, cemetery, church, compilations, directories, gazetteers, genealogies, histories, indexes, manuscripts, mortuary, newspap-

ers, periodicals). Most of the state and national records are available in microfilmed or published form in
large genealogical libraries in NY State and NY City, and
many of them can be found on microfilm at the Family
History Library and its branch Family History Centers.
Private records are available in published, microfilmed,
manuscript, and original forms in these same repositories: large genealogical libraries in NY State and NY
City, and main Family History Library and its branch
Family History Centers. Some of the state, national, and
private records will be available in large genealogical
libraries outside NY, and the national records can be
found at the National Archives and its branches.

The best overall centralized collection of genealogical materials for NY is to be found at the NY State
Library (NYSL) in Albany. The NYSL has an exceptionally
large collection of printed and typescript copies of the
following types of records: atlases, Bible, biography,
cemetery, church, colonial, deed, family histories,
genealogies, histories, immigration, maps, military,
naturalization, town, and will. In addition, the NYSL
has many original manuscripts and microfilm copies of
city directories, federal censuses, newspapers, passenger
lists, some state censuses, and some early NY wills. In
the same building as the NYSL is the NY State Archives
(NYSA), which is the NY agency for the preservation of
official state governmental records. Among their holdings which are of genealogical value are some state
census records, a few local vital records, land grant and
patent files, land survey maps, alien deposition records,
military records, state court records, will and estate
records, and WPA state and local record inventories.
There are several other NY State agencies in Albany which
have state records of genealogical importance. These
include the State Office of General Services (land grant
application files 1803-), Department of Taxation and
Finance (lands sold for tax arrears), State Department of
Health (vital records 1880-), and State Division of
Military and Naval Affairs (military records).

There are in NY City several remarkably good libraries which have extensive collections of NY genealogical materials, chiefly in printed form, but also manuscript materials and some microfilm records and indexes.
The first of these is the NY Public Library (NYPL). In

several of its divisions, you will find records of many
types: atlases, biographies, censuses, city directories,
family histories, genealogical periodicals, local histories, manuscripts, maps, newspapers, passenger lists,
published and typescript records (Bible, cemetery,
church, DAR, estate, land, military, tax, town, vital
records). The second of these is the NY Genealogical and
Biographical Society (NYGB). In its large holdings will
be found records of these sorts: Bible, biography, census
indexes, cemetery, city directories, genealogies, genealogical periodicals, histories, lineage society publications, manuscripts, microfilmed records, NY County estate
and vital record indexes, and volumes on biography,
genealogy, and local history. The third major library in
NY City is the Library of the NY Historical Society
(NYHS), another exceptionally well-stocked repository.
Its holdings, as its name implies, are chiefly historic-
ally oriented, but since genealogy is family history,
these materials are very useful. They include histories
of many sorts (local, state, religious, professional, NY
family), publications of religious and patriotic organizations, an amazingly large collection of newspapers,
many periodicals, an abundance of NY manuscripts, numerous special research collections, and an extensive collection of maps.

There is a sizable collection of books and microfilm copies of NY genealogical materials (especially
county records) in the largest genealogical library in
the world, namely, the Family History Library (FHL) of
the Genealogical Society of UT, which is located in Salt
Lake City, UT. Not only are the materials available at
the library in Salt Lake City, but the microfilms may be
borrowed through the numerous branch libraries known as
Family History Centers (FHC), which are located all over
the US and beyond. Included among these branches are
seven in the state of NY (Albany, Buffalo, Ithaca, NY
City, Plainview, Rochester, Syracuse). Each branch
library has microform copies of the major indexes which
list the holdings of the main library in Salt Lake City,
and from which record microfilms may be borrowed.

Many records pertaining to NY which were accumulated by the federal government are available in the
National Archives (NA) in Washington, DC. These records
include the following types: census, passenger arrival,

naturalization, military (service, pension, bounty land), Indian, Black, land, claims, court, maps. Many of the most useful of these materials have been microfilmed. Some of these microfilms are available in many of the NY libraries mentioned previously, and sizable numbers of them will be found in the eleven National Archives Field Branches (NAFB), one of which is very near NY City, namely, the National Archives NY Branch in Bayonne, NJ. Many may also be borrowed through your local library or individually from AGLL (American Genealogical Lending Library, PO Box 244, Bountiful, UT 84010).

In addition to the above collections, there are NY record collections in a number of large genealogical libraries (LGL) around the country, especially those in states near NY. Other collections, usually with an emphasis on a particular section of NY, are located in several good regional libraries (RL) in NY. Finally, local libraries (LL) in county seats and some other cities have good materials relating to their own areas. These local libraries may be county, city, town, village, or private (such as ones sponsored by local historical or genealogical societies). All of the archives, libraries, and repositories mentioned above will be discussed in detail in Chapter 3.

In this chapter, the many types of records which are available for NY genealogical research are discussed. Those records which are essentially national or statewide in scope will be treated in detail, both governmental and private (non-governmental). Records which are basically county records (both governmental and non-governmental, and including city, town, and village records) will be mentioned and treated generally, since detailed lists of them will be given in Chapters 4 and 5, where the major county (and city, town, village) records available for each of the 62 NY counties will be presented.

2. Bible records

During the past 200 years it was customary for families with religious affiliations to keep vital statistics on their members in the family Bible. These records vary widely, but among them the items that may be found are names, dates, and places of birth, christening, confirmation, baptism, marriage, death, burial, and sometimes military service. Although most Bibles containing recorded information probably still remain in private hands, some of the information has been submitted for publication and some has been filed in libraries and archives throughout NY. You should inquire about such records at every possible library and archives in or near your ancestor's county, especially the RL and LL. These repositories will be listed in Chapters 4 and 5 under the counties.

You should also seek Bible records in the larger archives and libraries in NY: NYSL, NYSA, NYPL, NYGB, NYHS. Also the indexes at FHC(FHL) should be consulted. In these repositories, there may be a special alphabetical Bible record file, or as is more often the case, data from Bibles may be listed in indexes or alphabetical files labelled something other than Bible records. The most likely labels are family records, genealogies, manuscripts, names, surnames. Also do not fail to look in the major card or computer index in each of these repositories for the names you are seeking. It is also important to use the locality and surname indexes at the nearest FHC. The richest collection of NY Bible records is a group of over 230 volumes put together by NY Daughters of the American Revolution:

__DAR of NY, BIBLE RECORDS OF NY STATE, Various Chapters, Various Cities, NY, over 230 volumes, 1924-present.

This voluminous collection is partially indexed (up to 1978) in the following works:

__MASTER INDEX, NY STATE GENEALOGICAL RECORDS, The DAR, Albany, NY, 1971, and MASTER INDEX, SUPPLEMENT, 1972-8, RECORDS AND CORRECTIONS, The DAR, Albany, NY, 1978. Look under name and county. Many names not indexed, so go through county listings in detail.

The indexes and the numerous volumes to which they lead are available in the NYSL and the NYPL. Another index to the records is available in card form:

__SURNAME INDEX, Local History and Genealogy Room, NYSL.

This card index also contains references to other Bible records in the NYSL.

Some other volumes listing and/or indexing NY Bible records have been compiled. Among those that you should examine are the following:

__J. F.-J. Robison and H. C. Bartlett, GENEALOGICAL RECORDS: MANUSCRIPT ENTRIES OF BIRTHS, DEATHS, AND

MARRIAGES TAKEN FROM FAMILY BIBLES, 1581-1917, Genea-
logical Publishing Co., Baltimore, MD, 1917(1972).
Over 3000 names.
__S. V. Talcott, GENEALOGICAL NOTES ON NY AND NEW ENGLAND
FAMILIES, Genealogical Publishing Co., Baltimore, MD,
1883(1973). 18,000 names. Use with care.
__E. K. Kirkham, AN INDEX TO SOME OF THE BIBLE AND FAMILY
RECORDS OF THE US, Volume 2, Everton Publishers, Logan,
UT, 1984.
__J. D. and E. D. Stemmons, THE VITAL RECORD COMPENDIUM,
Everton Publishers, Logan, UT, 1979.
Bible records also appear in genealogical periodical
articles and in published family genealogies. These two
record sources will be discussed in later sections of
this chapter.

3. Biographies

There are several major national biographical works
which contain sketches on nationally-prominent New York-
ers of the past. If you suspect or know that your ancestor was that well known, consult:
__NATIONAL CYCLOPEDIA OF AMERICAN BIOGRAPHY, White Co.,
New York, NY, 1893-present, over 54 volumes, cumulative
index for volumes 1-51.
__DICTIONARY OF AMERICAN BIOGRAPHY, Scribners, New York,
NY, 1928-37, 20 volumes, cumulative index.
__THE 20TH CENTURY BIOGRAPHICAL DICTIONARY OF NOTABLE
AMERICANS, Gale Research Co., Detroit, MI, 1968, 10
volumes.
__AMERICAN BIOGRAPHY: A NEW CYCLOPEDIA, American Histor-
ical Society, New York, NY, 1916-33, 54 volumes, cumu-
lative index for volumes 1-50.
__ENCYCLOPEDIA OF AMERICAN BIOGRAPHY, NEW SERIES, Ameri-
can Historical Co., West Palm Beach, FL, 1934-present,
4 volumes.
__WHO WAS WHO IN AMERICA, 1607-1896, Who's Who, Chicago,
IL, 1967.
Most of these works and about 340 more have been indexed
in a 3-volumed set which gives the sources of over 3
million biographies, all arranged in alphabetical order
of the names:
__M. C. Herbert and B. McNeil, BIOGRAPHY AND GENEALOGY
MASTER INDEX, Gale Research Co., Detroit, MI, 1980, 3
volumes.

For the state of NY (and its regions, counties, cities, towns, and villages) there is a very important privately-held index. This index lists the biographical contents of hundreds of NY biographical and historical works and is indispensible to genealogical searchers.

__G. E. Pohl, BIOGRAPHICAL AND GENEALOGICAL NAME INDEX TO NY BIOGRAPHICAL AND HISTORICAL WORKS, The Compiler, 24 Walden Place, Great Neck, NY 11022.

For a small fee, which is well worth it because of the time it will save, the compiler will check the index for you. Several extensive biographical compilations for the state of NY exist. These volumes list persons who have attained state-wide prominence in the fields of law, agriculture, business, politics, medicine, engineering, industry, science, military, manufacturing, teaching, government, public service, or philanthropy. Included among the better ones are:

__J. W. Barber and H. Howe, HISTORICAL COLLECTIONS OF THE STATE OF NY, Kennikat Press, Port Washington, NY, 1846(1970).

__BIOGRAPHICAL DIRECTORY OF THE STATE OF NY 1900, Biographical Directory Co., New York, NY, 1900.

__B. Blenzer and T. J. Gergel, ENCYCLOPEDIA OF NY, Somerset Publishers, St. Clair Shores, MI, 1982.

__W. J. Comley, HISTORY OF THE STATE OF NY, Comley Brothers, New York, NY, 1877.

__ENCYCLOPEDIA OF CONTEMPORARY BIOGRAPHY OF NY, Atlantic Publishing Co., New York, NY, 1884, 6 volumes.

__C. E. Fitch, ENCYCLOPEDIA OF BIOGRAPHY OF NY, American Historical Society, New York, NY, 1916, 4 volumes. See other editions also.

__GENEALOGICAL AND BIOGRAPHICAL RECORDS OF AMERICAN FAMILIES, NY, States Historical Society, Hartford, CT, 1931-46, 14 volumes.

__M. C. Harrison, NY STATE'S PROMINENT AND PROGRESSIVE MEN, NY Tribune, New York, NY, 1900-2, 3 volumes.

__J. B. Holgate, AMERICAN GENEALOGY, Munsell, Albany, NY, 1851.

__THE MEN OF NY, A COLLECTION OF BIOGRAPHIES DURING THE LAST DECADE OF THE 19TH CENTURY, Matthews & Co., Buffalo, NY, 1898.

__M. A. Hamm, FAMOUS FAMILIES OF NY, New York Evening Post, New York, NY, 1902.

__F. S. Hills, NY STATE MEN, Argus Co., New York, NY, 1906.

__J. R. Simms, THE FRONTIERSMEN OF NY, Riggs, Albany, NY, 1882, 2 volumes.

__J. Sullivan, HISTORY OF NY STATE, Lewis Publishing Co., New York, NY, 1927, 6 volumes, 6th volume biographical.

__WHO'S WHO IN NY CITY AND STATE, Hamersly, New York, NY, 1904-, annual volumes.

In addition to the state-wide biographical works, there are also a number of biographical collections for sections or regions of the state. Among those with the largest number of names are:

__L. R. Doty, HISTORY OF THE GENESEE COUNTRY, Clarke Publishing Co., Chicago, IL, 1925, 4 volumes.

__W. J. Doty, THE HISTORIC ANNALS OF SOUTHWESTERN NY, Lewis Historical Publishing Co., New York, NY, 1940, 3 volumes.

__W. F. Galpin, CENTRAL NY, AN INLAND EMPIRE, Lewis Historical Publishing Co., New York, NY, 1941, 4 volumes, volume 4 biographical.

__N. Greene, HISTORY OF MOHAWK VALLEY, 1614-1925, Clarke Publishing Co., Chicago, IL, 1925, 4 volumes, volumes 3-4 biographical.

__W. E. Lamb, THE LAKE CHAMPLAIN AND LAKE GEORGE VALLEYS, American HIstorical Co., New York, NY, 1940, 3 volumes, volume 3 biographical.

__H. F. Landon, THE [NY] NORTH COUNTRY, Historical Publishing Co., Indianapolis, IN, 1932, 3 volumes, volumes 2-3 biographical.

__H. R. Malone, HISTORY OF CENTRAL NY, Historical Publishing Co., Indianapolis, IN, 1932, 3 volumes, volumes 2-3 biographical.

__L. D. Scisco, INDEX TO PERSONAL NAMES IN VALENTINE'S NY CITY MANUALS, 1841-66, Manuscript, NYGB, New York, NY, 1948.

__B. F. Thompson and C. J. Werner, HISTORY OF LONG ISLAND, Dodd, New York, NY, 1918, 4 volumes, 4th volume biography and genealogy.

__M. R. Wilner, THE NIAGARA FRONTIER, Clarke Publishing Co., Chicago, IL, 1931, 4 volumes.

__L. S. Zimm, SOUTHEASTERN NY, Lewis Historical Publishing Co., New York, NY, 1946, 3 volumes, 3rd volume biographical.

Not only are there national, state, regional, and professional biographical works for NY, there are also numerous local (county, city, town, village) biographical

compilations. This is especially true for NY City, many
of the older ones being listed in;
__R. F. Bailey, GUIDE TO GENEALOGICAL AND BIOGRAPHICAL
  SOURCES FOR NEW YORK CITY, NY, 1783-1898, The Author,
  New York, NY, 1954.
Practically all of the above biographical publications
are available in NYSL, NYPL, NYGB, and NYHS, including
most of the local volumes. The local publications will
also be found in the LL of the places of interest as well
as in nearby RL. When you seek biographical compilations
in a library, look under these headings in their catalogs: US-Biography, NY-Biography, [County Name]-Biog-
raphy, [City Name]-Biography. Listings of biographical
materials for NY will be found in the following sources.
These will be especially helpful for what is available at
the local level, where you are most likely to find references to your ancestor.
__M. J. Kaminkow, US LOCAL HISTORIES IN THE LIBRARY OF
  CONGRESS, Magna Carta, Baltimore, MD, 1975, 5 volumes.
__CATALOGS (CARD, COMPUTER, PRINTED) IN NYSL, NYPL, NYGB,
  AND NYHS, Albany and New York City, NY.
__F. Rider, AMERICAN GENEALOGICAL [-BIOGRAPHICAL] INDEX,
  Godfrey Memorial Library, Middletown, CT, 1st series,
  1942-52, 48 volumes; 2nd series, 1952-, in progress,
  over 140 volumes so far.
Biographical information is also sometimes found in
ethnic publications, genealogical compilations, genealogical periodicals, manuscripts, military records, newspapers, published genealogies, regional records, and historical works (state, regional, local). All of these sources will be discussed in sections to follow.

4. Birth records

During the period of Dutch control (1609-64), the
New Netherland government did not keep official civil
birth records, leaving this task to the church. Many of
these records will be found in:
__T. G. Evans, RECORDS OF THE REFORMED DUTCH CHURCH IN
  NEW AMSTERDAM/NEW YORK CITY, BAPTISMS, 1639-1800, NY
  Genealogical and Biographical Society, New York, NY,
  1901-2, 2 volumes.
When the English took the colony over (1664), they had a
law requiring ministers of parishes and clerks of towns
to record births, but the colony never systematically
enforced the regulation, and only a few records were

kept. Early records of births were included in the town minutes for a number of NY towns, especially those on Long Island, where this New England custom was practiced. This town record keeping did not spread, but declined. The situation of practically no birth recording continued until 1847 when a law requiring birth registration in towns was passed. Fair conformity to the law was seen during 1847-49/50, but the system largely failed thereafter. Many of the fragmentary records mentioned above will be found in town and county records, many have been published in NY genealogical periodicals (Tree Talks, NY Genealogical and Biographical Record), some have been microfilmed by the FHL, and a few are at NYSL and NYSA. Listings of a number of those available will be found in:

___ J. D. and E. D. Stemmons, THE VITAL RECORD COMPENDIUM, Everton Publishers, Logan, UT, 1979.

___ A. H. Eakle and L. R. Gunn, DESCRIPTIVE INVENTORY OF THE NY COLLECTION, University of UT Press, Salt Lake City, UT, 1980.

___ Historical Records Survey, GUIDE TO PUBLIC VITAL STATISTICS IN NY STATE, INCLUDING NY CITY, WPA, Albany, NY, 1942, 1st volume.

Shortly after the midpoint of the 19th century, some larger NY cities began keeping birth records: NY City (1847-52 some, then 1853-), Brooklyn (some 1866-), Albany (1870-), Syracuse (1873-), Utica (1873-), Rochester (1875-), Yonkers (1875-), Buffalo (1878-). Then in 1880 a state law mandating registration was passed, and compliance gradually increased to 50% by about 1900 and 90% by about 1915, when a more stringent law came into effect. The records are available as follows. For NY County (1847-), Kings County (some 1866-, 1880-), Queens County (1847-9, 1880-), Richmond County (some 1847-52, 1880-), Bronx County (1914-), Albany (1870-1914), Syracuse (1873-80), Utica (1873-80), Rochester (1875-80), Yonkers (1875-1914), and Buffalo (1878-1914), records should be sought in the county or city offices for the dates indicated. For Albany (1915-), Yonkers (1915-), Buffalo (1915-), and all the rest of the state (1880-) except the 5 counties of NY City, write or visit:

___ NY State Department of Health, Bureau of Vital Records, Tower Building, Empire State Plaza, Albany, NY 12237. Records indexed.

Public access to birth records prior to 1913 is available, but those after are restricted.

Since NY is so short on official birth records
before 1880 (1853 for NY City), other types of records
often have to be consulted. Among the better ones are
Bible, biography, cemetery, census, church, death, genealogical periodicals, manuscripts, marriage, military,
mortuary, naturalization, newspaper, and published genealogies. All of these are treated in other sections of
this chapter. Numerous non-official sources of this sort
are listed in the two books by Stemmons and Eakle cited
in the first paragraph of this section. When you are
seeking birth date and place information in archives and
libraries, be certain to explore all the above mentioned
sources, and do not fail to look under the county listings and the following heading in library catalogs:
Registers of births, etc.

5. Cemetery records

If you know or suspect that your ancestor was
buried in a certain NY cemetery, the best thing to do is
to write the caretaker of the cemetery, enclose an SASE
and ask if the records or tombstone inscriptions show
your forebear. Gravestones often display names, ages,
dates of death and birth, and sometimes family names of
wives. Tombstones of children often bear the names or
initials of the parents. In order to locate the caretaker, try writing the local county historian, the local
historical society, the local genealogical society, or
the LL. If you do not find that your ancestor is buried
there, then you should ask the above organizations about
records for other cemeteries in the area. The addresses
of these organizations will be given in Chapters 4 and 5.
As you consider possible burial sites, please remember
that most early cemeteries were in conjunction with
churches. Therefore, if you know your progenitor's
religious affiliation, this could be of help.

Another important cemetery record source is provided by the numerous collections of cemetery records which
have been made by the DAR, by the WPA, by state, regional, and local genealogical and historical societies, and
by individuals. Some of these have been published, and
some are in typescript or hand-written form. Many have
been microfilmed. Notable among them is a very large

series of volumes put together by various NY chapters of the DAR:
 DAR of NY, CEMETERY, CHURCH, AND TOWN RECORDS OF NY STATE, Various Chapters, Various Cities, NY, 1926-, over 560 volumes.
This tremendous collection is partially indexed (up to 1978) in the following works:
 MASTER INDEX, NY STATE GENEALOGICAL RECORDS, The DAR, Albany, NY, 1971, and MASTER INDEX, SUPPLEMENT, 1972-8, RECORDS AND CORRECTIONS, The DAR, Albany, NY, 1978. Look under name and county. Many names not indexed, so go through county listings in detail.
The indexes and the numerous volumes to which they refer are available in the NYSL and the NYPL. The indexes, but not the volumes, are also at NYGB, and the indexes and some of the volumes are on microfilm at the FHL (available through FHC). A listing of these records according to the locations (counties) to which they apply is available in the NYSL:
 VITAL RECORDS CARD INDEX, Local History and Genealogy Section, NYSL, Albany, NY. Not indexed by name, but by locality. Many other cemetery records also.
Another important contribution of the DAR is:
 DAR of NY, GRAVES OF REVOLUTIONARY SOLDIERS IN NY, Various Chapters, Various Places, 1922-55, 15 volumes.
These are indexed in a specialized card index at NYSL:
 REVOLUTIONARY WAR SOLDIERS CARD INDEX, Local History and Genealogy Section, NYSL, Albany, NY.

     In addition to the very rich sources mentioned above, there are several other record compilations, listings of records, and indexes. Included are:
 R. J. Wilson, NY STATE CEMETERY RECORDS, The Author, Tonawanda, NY, 1978-, several volumes.
 J. D. and E. D. Stemmons, THE CEMETERY RECORD COMPEN- DIUM, Everton Publishers, Logan, UT, 1979.
 M. J. Brown, HANDY INDEX TO THE HOLDINGS OF THE GENEA- LOGICAL SOCIETY OF UT (FHL), Volume 1, Everton Publish- ers, Logan, UT, 1980.
 Historical Records Survey, GUIDE TO DEPOSITORIES OF MANUSCRIPT COLLECTIONS IN NY STATE, EXCLUSIVE OF NY CITY, WITH SUPPLEMENT, WPA, Albany, NY, 1941-4.
 CARD, PRINTED, MICROFORM, AND COMPUTER CATALOGS, NYSL, NYPL, NYGB, NYHS, FHL(FHC), RL, and LL, check for microfilms and transcripts of epitaphs under surname,

county, city, town, church, and cemetery name, also under heading Epitaphs.

The above records indicate that the main sources of NY cemetery records are NYSL, NYPL, NYGB, NYHS, FHL(FHC), RL, and LL. The LL quite often have records of cemeteries in their own counties, and RL often have those in their regions. The major LL are listed in Chapters 4-5, and Chapter 3 discusses the RL. In these libraries, cemetery records may be located by looking in their catalogs under the surname, county, city, and town, the church, the denomination, the ethnic group, and the cemetery name. Also look under the headings Epitaphs-NY and Cemeteries-NY. Further, you should not forget to inquire if there are special cemetery record indexes or files.

Several other important sources for cemetery records must not be overlooked. These include church records, genealogical periodicals (especially Tree Talks, the NY Genealogical and Biographical Record, the American Genealogist, the New England Historic Genealogical Record, and the DAR Magazine), manuscripts, and newspaper obituaries. The uses of all of these will be treated in later sections of this chapter.

6. Census records

Excellent ancestor information is available in eight types of census reports which have been accumulated for NY: some early census-like lists before 1790 (E), the regular federal censuses (R), NY state censuses (S), agricultural censuses (A), industrial censuses (I), mortality censuses (M), the special 1840 Revolutionary War pensioner census (P), and the special 1890 Union Civil War veteran census (C).

For the colonial period and for the state period before 1790, many lists of NY inhabitants are available. Some of these early lists (E) are colony- or state-wide, most are local (county, city, town), but all are incomplete. They are of various types, the main categories being residents, petitioners, taxpayers, heads of families, militia, free holders, proprietors, and persons taking oaths of allegiance. Major sources of these lists are the following volumes:

__E. B. O'Callaghan and R. Conway, LISTS OF INHABITANTS OF COLONIAL NY, Genealogical Publishing Co., Baltimore, MD, 1979.

__C. M. Meyers, EARLY NY STATE CENSUS RECORDS, 1663-1772, RAM Publishers, Gardena, CA, 1965. Over 7000 names.

__R. V. Jackson, EARLY NY, 1600-1789, Accelerated Indexing Systems, Bountiful, UT, 1980. Many early records indexed.

__E. B. O'Callaghan, THE DOCUMENTARY HISTORY OF THE STATE OF NY, Weed, Parsons, & Co., Albany, NY, 1849-51, 4 volumes. Many lists of names with emphasis on Hudson Valley and Long Island. Partially indexed in volumes by C. M. Meyers.

__E. B. O'Callaghan and B. Fernow, editors, DOCUMENTS RELATIVE TO THE COLONIAL HISTORY OF THE STATE OF NY, AMS Press, New York, NY, 1853-87(1969), 15 volumes. Volume 11 is index to volumes 1-10, volume 15 is general index.

__E. B. O'Callaghan, CALENDAR OF DUTCH (AND ENGLISH) HISTORICAL MANUSCRIPTS IN THE OFFICE OF THE SECRETARY OF STATE, Gregg, Boston, MA, 1865-6(1967-8), 1st volume Dutch(1630-64), 2nd volume English(1664-1776).

A very useful key to several of these volumes and to numerous other special lists for the colony of NY, the state of NY, and the NY counties, cities, and towns is:

__J. D. Stemmons, THE US CENSUS COMPENDIUM, Everton Publishers, Logan, UT, 1973.

Other compilations of names of inhabitants of NY during the early period (1609-1790) will be referred to in other sections of this chapter, particularly those dealing with church records, colonial record compilations, court records, emigration and immigration, ethnic records, genealogical periodicals (most important are the NY Genealogical and Biographical Record, the NY Historical Society Quarterly, and the National Genealogical Society Quarterly), land records, military records (colonial and Revolutionary), naturalization records, and regional compilations.

__Regular census__ records (R), taken by the federal government are available for NY in 1790, 1800, 1810, 1820, 1830, 1840, 1850, 1860, 1870, 1880, 1900, and 1910. A few small portions of the census records for 1890 survive for NY, but not much. The 1840 federal census and all before it listed the head of the household plus a breakdown of the number of persons in the household according to age and sex brackets. Beginning in 1850, the names of all persons were recorded along with age, sex, occupation, real estate, marital, and other information, including the state or country of birth. With the 1880 census and thereafter, the birthplaces of the father and mother of each person are also shown. With the 1900 census and thereafter, the year of immigration is shown for each foreign-born person. Chapters 4 and 5 list the federal census records (R) available for each of the 62 NY counties.

Census data for 1790 are available in both a published transcript and two microfilms, the first and third items being indexed:
__US Bureau of the Census, HEADS OF FAMILIES AT THE FIRST CENSUS OF THE US TAKEN IN 1790 IN NY, Genealogical Publishing Co., Baltimore, MD, 1908(1966).
__US Bureau of the Census, FIRST CENSUS OF THE US, 1790, NY, The National Archives, Washington, DC, Microfilm M637, Roll 6. Unindexed.
__US Bureau of the Census, FIRST CENSUS OF THE US, 1790, NY, The National Archives, Washington, DC, Microfilm T498, Roll 2. Microfilm copy of the printed schedules, indexed.
Microfilms of the remaining original census records (1800-1910) are available as:
__US Bureau of the Census, SECOND CENSUS OF THE US, 1800, NY, The National Archives, Washington, DC, Microfilm M32, Rolls 21-34.
__US Bureau of the Census, THIRD CENSUS OF THE US, 1810, NY, The National Archives, Washington, DC, Microfilm M252, Rolls 26-37.
__US Bureau of the Census, FOURTH CENSUS OF THE US, 1820, NY, The National Archives, Washington, DC, Microfilm M33, Rolls 62-79.
__US Bureau of the Census, FIFTH CENSUS OF THE US, 1830, NY, The National Archives, Washington, DC, Microfilm M19, Rolls 84-117.
__US Bureau of the Census, SIXTH CENSUS OF THE US, 1840, NY, The National Archives, Washington, DC, Microfilm M704, Rolls 263-353.
__US Bureau of the Census, SEVENTH CENSUS OF THE US, 1850, NY, The National Archives, Washington, DC, Microfilm M432, Rolls 471-618.
__US Bureau of the Census, EIGHTH CENSUS OF THE US, 1860,

NY, The National Archives, Washington, DC, Microfilm
M653, Rolls 717-885.

US Bureau of the Census, NINTH CENSUS OF THE US, 1870,
NY, The National Archives, Washington, DC, Microfilm
M593, Rolls 898-1120.

US Bureau of the Census, TENTH CENSUS OF THE US, 1880,
NY, The National Archives, Washington, DC, Microfilm
T9, Rolls 805-949.

US Bureau of the Census, ELEVENTH CENSUS OF THE US,
1890, NY, The National Archives, Washington, DC, Microfilm M407, Roll 3. Contains only Westchester County
(Eastchester) and Suffolk County (Brookhaven Township).

US Bureau of the Census, TWELFTH CENSUS OF THE US,
1900, NY, The National Archives, Washington, DC, Microfilm T623, Rolls 1004-1179.

US Bureau of the Census, THIRTEENTH CENSUS OF THE US,
1910, NY, The National Archives, Washington, DC, Microfilm T624, Rolls 920-1094.

The 1790 census records are indexed in the published volume mentioned above and in the microfilm (T498)
of the printed volume, and indexes have been printed for
the 1800, 1810, 1820, 1830, 1840, 1850, and 1860 census
records. Chief among these indexes are:

R. V. Jackson, NY 1800 CENSUS INDEX, Accelerated Indexing Systems, Bountiful, UT, 1977. About 100,000 entries.

P. W. McMullin, NY IN 1800, AN INDEX TO THE FEDERAL
CENSUS, Everton Publishers, Provo, UT, 1971. About
100,000 names.

B. K. Armstrong, INDEX TO THE 1800 CENSUS OF NY, Genealogical Publishing Co., Baltimore, MD, 1984. About
100,000 names.

R. V. Jackson, NY 1810 CENSUS INDEX, Accelerated Indexing Systems, Bountiful, UT, 1976. About 150,000 entries.

R. V. Jackson, NY 1820 CENSUS INDEX, Accelerated Indexing Systems, Bountiful, UT, 1977. About 230,000 entries.

R. V. Jackson, NY 1830 CENSUS INDEX, Accelerated Indexing Systems, Bountiful, UT, 1977. About 500,000 entries.

R. V. Jackson, NY 1840 CENSUS INDEX, Accelerated Indexing Systems, Bountiful, UT, 1977. About 600,000 entries.

__R. V. Jackson, NY 1850 CENSUS INDEX, Accelerated Index-
ing Systems, Bountiful, UT, 1976-7, 3 volumes. About
960,000 entries.
__R. V. Jackson, NY 1860 CENSUS INDEX, Accelerated Index-
ing Systems, Salt Lake City, UT, 1987, 8 volumes.
There are as yet no state-wide indexes to the 1870 census, even though a few county indexes are now available.

In addition to the above bound indexes, there is a
microfilm index which contains only those families with a
child under 10 in the 1880 census. There is also a
complete microfilm index to the 1900 NY census. These
two census indexes are arranged according to a phonetic
code called Soundex. Librarians and archivists can show
you how to use it. The small surviving fragments of the
1890 census are indexed alphabetically on microfilm.
These indexes are:
__US Bureau of the Census, INDEX (SOUNDEX) TO THE 1880
POPULATION SCHEDULES OF NY, The National Archives,
Washington, DC, Microfilm T765, Rolls 1-187.
__US Bureau of the Census, INDEX TO THE ELEVENTH CENSUS
OF THE US INCLUDING THE [FRAGMENTARY] 1890 POPULATION
SCHEDULES OF NY, The National Archives, Washington, DC,
Microfilm M496, Rolls 1-2. Includes only Suffolk
County (Brookhaven Township) and Westchester County
(Eastchester).
__US Bureau of the Census, INDEX (SOUNDEX) TO THE 1900
POPULATION SCHEDULES OF NY, The National Archives,
Washington, DC, Microfilm T1062, Rolls 1-766.
No index of the 1910 NY census schedules exists.

The indexes listed in the two previous paragraphs
are exceptionally valuable as time-saving devices.
However, few indexes of any sort are perfect, and therefore you need to exercise a little caution in using them.
If you do not find your progenitor in them, do not con-
clude that she or he is not in the state; this may only
mean that your forebear has been accidentally omitted or
that the name has been misspelled, misread, or misprint-
ed. Once you have located a name in the indexes, you can
go directly to the reference in the census microfilms and
read the entry. When indexes are not available (for all
1870 and 1910, and partially for 1880), it is necessary
for you to go through the census listings entry-by-entry.
This can be essentially prohibitive for the entire state,
so it is necessary for you to know the county in order to

limit your search. In the larger NY cities, census
searches in these years (1870/80, 1910) can be greatly
aided by city directory information (see later section).
Addresses obtained from city directories can lead to
proper sections of the census schedules. Both the census
records and the indexes are available in NYSL, NYPL, and
FHL(FHC), and many are available in NYGB, LGL, and RL.
Ones pertaining to specific counties are often in LL.
Both the NA and the 11 NAFB (including the NANYB at
Military Ocean Terminal, Building 22, Bayonne, NJ 07002)
have the microfilms and the printed indexes. Also, the
microfilmed census records and the microfilmed indexes
may be borrowed by you or by your local library through
AGLL (American Genealogical Lending Library, PO Box 244,
Bountiful, UT 84010). There is a charge of a few dollars
per roll.

NY state censuses (S) were taken in 1825, 1835,
1845, 1855, 1865, 1875, 1892, 1905, 1915, and 1925. Not
all of the schedules have survived, but many are available. Some originals are in the counties, some are in
NYSL, and a few are in the NYSA. A number of them are
incomplete in that they omit data for some of the towns
in a county, and sometimes entire counties are missing.
Only the 1915/25 schedules are essentially complete.
Microfilm copies of many of them are available in FHL-
(FHC) and microfilm copies of somewhat fewer may be found
in the NYSL. In short, when searching for these census
records, you should first check FHC(FHL), then NYSL, then
try at the county (city, town) level. Unfortunately,
they are largely unindexed. A detailed listing of the
years and counties for which these state census records
are available is provided in:
__M. Douglas and M. Yates, NY STATE CENSUS RECORDS, 1790-
  1925, NY State Library, Albany, NY, 1981.
The materials on the 62 NY counties in Chapters 4 and 5
of this work also provide the years for which state
census records are available for each county.

The NY state censuses (S) are of exceptional value,
complementing the federal census data. The 1825/35/45
censuses give only the name of the head of the family,
plus the numbers of males and females in the family
according to several categories, plus information on the
family's land, animals, and manufactures. Beginning in
1855, all persons are named along with age, sex, color,

relation to head of family, and NY county or other state or country of birth. In 1892, the amount of data is cut severely, only name, sex, age, color, country of birth, citizenship, and occupation being shown. The 1905 census adds to this the relationship to the head of the family and the number of years in the US.

The 1835/45/55/65/75 censuses also contain special schedules which are of value to genealogists. The special schedules for 1835/45/55 have statistical data (numbers only) on industry, churches, schools, and other items, but no names of persons. The 1855 census lists the number of years the person has been a resident of the town or city. The 1865/75 censuses contain lists of those marrying and those dying in the year preceding the taking of the census. Marriage data include name and age of both husband and wife, date and place of marriage, and type of ceremony. Death data include name, age, sex, color, married or not, date of death, native state or country, and cause of death. The 1865 census also has names of military men who are then or have been in the Civil War. Greater detail on the content of the various state censuses will be found in the book by Douglas and Yates mentioned two paragraphs above.

Agricultural census records (A), also known as farm and ranch censuses, are available for 1850, 1860, 1870, and 1880 for NY. These federally-gathered records list the name of the owner, size of farm or ranch, value of the property, crops, livestock, and other details. If your ancestor was a farmer, it will be worthwhile to seek him in these records. No indexes are available, but you will probably know the county and the area in the county, so your entry-by-entry search should be fairly easy. Microfilm copies of the records can be found in the NYSL.

Industrial census records (I), also known as manufactures censuses, were taken by the federal government in 1820, 1850, 1860, 1870, and 1880 for NY. However, the 1870 records are incomplete with only Essex-through-Yates Counties being represented. The records list manufacturing businesses (in 1850/60/70/80 only those with over $500 of product), owner's name, product, machinery, number of employees, and other details. Indexes accompany the 1820 microfilmed records, but the others are

unindexed. The microfilmed records are available at
NYSL. The 1820 microfilm is also available at the NA.
__US Bureau of the Census, RECORDS OF THE 1820 CENSUS OF
   MANUFACTURES, The National Archives, Washington, DC,
   Microfilm M279, Rolls 1-27.

Mortality census records (M) are available for the
one-year periods 01 June (1849/59/69/79) to 31 May (1850-
/60/70/80), respectively. The federal records give
information on persons who died in the year preceding the
1st of June of each of the census years 1850/60/70/80.
The data contained in the compilations include name,
month of death, age, sex, occupation, place of birth, and
other information. Microfilm copies of the records are
available in NYSL and in FHL(FHC). They are unindexed,
but with a little knowledge of the county and the area in
the county, you should not have too much difficulty in
locating entries.

Revolutionary War pensioners (P) were included in
the data collected in the 1840 regular federal census.
An attempt was made to list all pension holders, however,
there are some omissions and some false entries. The
list has been copied out, indexed, and published:
__US Bureau of the Census, A CENSUS OF PENSIONERS FOR
   REVOLUTIONARY OR MILITARY SERVICES, Genealogical Pub-
   lishing Co., Baltimore, MD, 1841(1965).
This volume is present in NYSL, NYPL, NYGB, NYHS, FHL-
(FHC), in most LGL, in many RL, and in some LL.

Civil War Union veterans (C) of NY were included in
a special federal census taken in 1890, as were widows of
the veterans. These records display the veteran's name,
widow's name (if applicable), rank, company, regiment or
ship, and other pertinent military data.
__US Veterans Administration, SPECIAL SCHEDULES OF THE
   ELEVENTH CENSUS (1890) ENUMERATING UNION VETERANS AND
   WIDOWS OF UNION VETERANS OF THE CIVIL WAR, The National
   Archives, Washington, DC, Microfilm M123, Rolls 45-57.
These special schedules have been indexed in the follow-
ing microfiche:
__B. L. Dilts, 1890 NY CENSUS INDEX OF CIVIL WAR VETERANS
   OR THEIR WIDOWS, Index Publishing, Salt Lake City, UT,
   1984.
The above microforms are available in NYSL, NYPL, FHL-
(FHC), many LGL, and some RL.

The census records of all the above types (E, R, S, A, I, M, P, C) available for each of the 62 NY counties will be shown in the county listings in Chapters 4 and 5. For a county for which all the above censuses are available, the listing will read: Pre-1790E, 1790R, 1800R, 1810R, 1820RI, 1825S, 1830R, 1835S, 1840RP, 1845S, 1850RAIM, 1855S, 1860RAIM, 1865S, 1870RAIM, 1875S, 1880RAIM, 1890C, 1892S, 1900R, 1905S, 1910R, 1915S, 1925S.

7. Church records

NY church records are very important genealogical sources because of the severe lack of official vital record data (birth, marriage, death) before 1880 (1853 for NY City). Church records can carry all sorts of pertinent information including names, dates of birth, christening, intention to marry, marriage, confirmation, dismissal, removal, joining, baptism, war service, death, funeral, and burial. The most important churches in the colonial era are reflections of the two major governing groups: the Dutch Reformed Church and the Anglican (Episcopalian, Church of England). However, as noted in Chapter 1, their tolerant attitudes toward other Protestants permitted numerous other smaller church groups to settle in NY, including Lutherans, Presbyterians, Baptists, Friends, Huguenots, Methodists, Congregationalists, and Jews. In general, freedom of worship was not granted Roman Catholics because of the English-French tensions. When full religious freedom came to be after the Revolution, Roman Catholics joined the immigration. As the frontiers expanded, many persons on the frontiers came to have no church affiliation, even though they remained religious. Then the Methodists and the Baptists began working in these areas and their numbers grew considerably as the result of revivals which swept through central and western NY in the 1820s. As of 1850, the major denominations in NY, listed in the order of the numbers of churches, were Methodist, Baptist, Presbyterian, Episcopal, Dutch Reformed, Congregational, Roman Catholic, Friends, Universalist, Lutheran, Union, Christian, Unitarian, and Jewish. The large influxes of eastern and southern Europeans and Irish in the next several decades changed the order notably. The largest denominations in 1890 were Roman Catholic, Methodist, Presbyterian, Baptist, Episcopalian, Lutheran, Dutch Reformed, Jewish, Congregational, and German Evangelical.

Please bear in mind that in the days of early NY many persons were not church members. It is also well to recognize that of the various denominations mentioned above, the Baptist and Methodist records seem to be the poorest. Sometimes they are simply minutes of congregational meetings, lists of officers, admissions, dismissals, and membership lists. Even so, regardless of denomination, you must not fail to seek church records which relate to your progenitors, since they could be surprisingly informative. Some of the church records of NY have been inventoried, some copied into books, periodicals, and typescripts, some have been microfilmed, some have been deposited in denominational, state, local, or private archives (or libraries), but most remain in the individual churches. The major places where they may be found are in the churches themselves, in denominational archives (listed later), and in LL, RL, NYSL, NYPL, NYHS, FHL(FHC), and in some NY college and university archives.

The single most important overall church record collection for the state of NY is the set of over 560 volumes of DAR transcripts which is available at NYSL and NYPL along with an incomplete name and location index.
_DAR of NY, CEMETERY, CHURCH, AND TOWN RECORDS OF NY STATE, Various Chapters, Various Cities, NY, 1926-, over 560 volumes.
This voluminous collection is partially indexed (up to 1978) in the following works:
_MASTER INDEX, NY STATE GENEALOGICAL RECORDS, The DAR, Albany, NY, 1971, and MASTER INDEX, SUPPLEMENT, 1972-8, RECORDS AND CORRECTIONS, The DAR, Albany, NY, 1978. Look under name and county. Many names not indexed, so go through county listings in detail.
In addition, there are some major listings of records available in numerous NY churches as of about 1940. Most of these listings are still valid, and hence these are valuable volumes:
_Historical Records Survey, INVENTORY OF THE CHURCH ARCHIVES OF NEW YORK CITY, WPA, New York, NY, 1939-41, 9 volumes. Episcopal, Eastern Orthodox, Friends, Lutheran, Methodist, Presbyterian, Reformed, Roman Catholic.

__Historical Records Survey, INVENTORY OF THE CHURCH ARCHIVES OF NY STATE, EPISCOPAL, IN WESTERN NY AND ROCHESTER, WPA, New York, NY, 1939-41, 2 volumes.

__Historical Records Survey, GUIDE TO VITAL STATISTICS RECORDS IN THE CITY OF NY CHURCHES, WPA, New York, NY, 1942, 5 volumes.

__Historical Records Survey, GUIDE TO VITAL STATISTICS RECORDS OF CHURCHES IN NY STATE, EXCLUSIVE OF NY CITY, WPA, Albany, NY, 1942, 2 volumes.

There are also some exceptionally useful listings of church records which have been published, microfilmed, transcribed, or deposited in manuscript collections:

__VITAL RECORDS CARD INDEX, Local History and Genealogy Section, NYSL, Albany, NY. Not a name index, but tells what church records are available for each locality. Look under county, city, town, denomination, church name.

__CATALOGS IN NYPL, NYGB, NYHS, FHL(FHC), LGL, RL, LL. Look under county, city, town, denomination, church name.

__A. H. Eakle and L. R. Gunn, DESCRIPTIVE INVENTORY OF THE NY COLLECTION, University of UT Press, Salt Lake City, UT, 1980.

__J. D. and E. D. Stemmons, THE VITAL RECORD COMPENDIUM, Everton Publishers, Logan, UT, 1979.

__J. Austin, GENEALOGICAL RESEARCH IN NY STATE, AN IN-FORMAL FINDING LIST OF PUBLISHED MATERIALS, Genealogical Conference of NY, Albany, NY, 1983, pages 23-30. Very good for locating periodical articles containing church records.

__E. K. Kirkham, A SURVEY OF AMERICAN CHURCH RECORDS, Everton Publishers, Logan, UT, 1978, pages 203-28.

Another set of volumes which you should not overlook is:

__NY State Historian, ECCLESIASTICAL RECORDS, STATE OF NY, Lyon, Albany, NY, 1901-16, 7 volumes, last volume index.

The above volumes, articles, and indexes list many published and microfilmed church records, and church record inventories, surveys, and sources. Keep them in mind as we now go about describing exactly how to find possible church records on your forebears.

Should you have the good fortune to know or strong-ly suspect your ancestor's church, you can check the above references, and if you find nothing, then write directly. Send an SASE, a check for $5, your progeni-

tor's name, and the pertinent dates. Request a search of
the records or information on the location of the records
if the church no longer has them. If they neither have
them nor know where the records are, dispatch an inquiry
to the NY and/or national denominational repository,
enclose an SASE, and ask them if they know where the
records are. Again, consult all the materials in the
previous paragraph, and also look carefully at all the
denominational materials mentioned later.

If, as is often the case, you know your ancestor's
county but not her/his church, you will need to dig a
little deeper. First, you should examine all the compiled church records of the pertinent county. Many of
these can be located by using the materials in the second
paragraph above. If you know or can guess the denomination, this might narrow your search, but do not too
easily overlook other denominations. Should you still
not find what you are seeking, examine maps of your
progenitor's county which show churches, and observe
those churches near your forebear's property. Suitable
maps for this purpose are listed in a later section of
this chapter, especially those maps available from the US
Geological Survey. Then investigate those nearby churches, seeking their records by using the items listed in
the second paragraph above, and by writing to them.
Letters should be dispatched to LL (listed later) and to
denominational repositories concerning churches in your
forebear's part of the county and the records of these
churches.

Listed in this paragraph and in several to follow
will be the major denominations of NY, their repositor-
ies, and pertinent genealogical and historical volumes.
Baptist repositories and publications include:
__(Archives) American Baptist Historical Society, 1106 S.
  Goodman St., Rochester, NY 14620; Seventh-Day Baptist
  Historical Society, 510 Watchung Ave., Plainfield, NJ
  07006.
__G. H. Howell, REMINISCENCES OF BAPTIST CHURCHES AND
  LEADERS IN NY CITY, 1835-98, 1899.
__NY BAPTIST REGISTER ABSTRACTS, 1825-54, Baptist Histor-
  ical Society Publications, Utica, NY, Volumes 28, 31,
  35.
__J. Peck and J. Lawton, AN HISTORICAL SKETCH OF THE

BAPTIST MISSIONARY CONVENTION OF THE STATE OF NY, Bennett and Bright, Utica, NY, 1837.

__E. C. Starr, A BAPTIST BIBLIOGRAPHY, BEING A REGISTER OF PRINTED MATERIAL BY AND ABOUT BAPTISTS, American Baptist Historical Society, Rochester, NY, 1947-.

__S. Wright, HISTORY OF THE SHAFTSBURY BAPTIST ASSOCIATION, 1781-1853, Johnson, Troy, NY, 1853. Eastern NY churches.

The Congregational archives and a valuable historical work are listed below. It is important for you to recognize that many former Congregational churches are now members of the Unitarian-Universalist Association or the United Church of Christ.

__(Archives) The Congregational Library, 14 Beacon St., Boston, MA 02108.

__W. Willeston, THE HISTORY OF THE CONGREGATIONAL CHURCHES IN THE US, American Congregational Historical Society, New York, NY, 1894.

The importance of the Dutch Reformed Church to the history of NY is reflected in the many volumes available relating to this denomination, especially in colonial times:

__(Archives) Reformed Church in America, 21 Seminary Place, New Brunswick, NJ 08901; Holland Society of NY, 122 East 58th St., New York, NY 1002.

__E. T. Corwin, A MANUAL OF THE REFORMED CHURCH IN AMERICA, 1628-1902, New York, NY, 1902.

__T. G. Evans, RECORDS OF THE REFORMED DUTCH CHURCH IN NEW AMSTERDAM/NEW YORK CITY, BAPTISMS, 1639-1800, NY Genealogical and Biographical Society, New York, NY, 1901-2, 2 volumes.

__FIRST REFORMED DUTCH CHURCH OF ALBANY RECORDS, Genealogical Publishing Co., Baltimore, MD, 1978.

__R. L. Gaseto, GUIDE TO LOCAL CHURCH RECORDS IN THE ARCHIVES OF THE REFORMED CHURCH IN AMERICA, The Archives, New Brunswick, NJ, 1979.

__Holland Society of NY, YEARBOOKS FOR 1891, 1896-9, 1901, 1903-8, 1912-6, 1924-8, The Society, New York, NY.

__A. C. M. Kelly, HUDSON VALLEY BAPTISM AND MARRIAGE RECORDS, The Compiler, Rhinebeck, NY, 1978. Lutheran and Reformed churches.

__MARRIAGES FROM 1639-1801 IN THE REFORMED DUTCH CHURCH, NEW AMSTERDAM/NEW YORK CITY, NY Genealogical and Biographical Society, New York, NY, 1940.

__J. Pearson, CONTRIBUTIONS FOR THE GENEALOGIES OF THE FIRST SETTLERS OF SCHENECTADY, 1662-1800, Genealogical Publishing Co., Baltimore, MD, 1873(1978). First Reformed Church of Schenectady.

__R. C. Sawyer, MARRIAGES AND DEATHS PUBLISHED IN THE CHRISTIAN INTELLIGENCER OF THE REFORMED DUTCH CHURCH, 1830-71, typescript, NYSL, Albany, NY, 1931, 17 volumes.

__A. P. G. J. Van der Linde, NY HISTORICAL MANUSCRIPTS: DUTCH, OLD FIRST DUTCH REFORMED CHURCH OF BROOKLYN RECORDS, 1665-82, Genealogical Publishing Co., Baltimore, MD, 1983.

__D. Versteeg, RECORDS OF THE REFORMED DUTCH CHURCH OF NEW PALTZ, NY, 1683-1816, Holland Society of NY, New York, NY, 1896. Over 10,000 names.

The Episcopal Church maintains no central repository for records, but if you cannot locate records in the parish, sometimes the diocese can be of assistance. Do not forget the Historical Records Survey's inventories of Episcopal records referred to early in this section:

__(Diocesan Offices) Diocese of Albany, 62 South Swan St., Albany, NY, 12210; Diocese of Long Island, 36 Cathedral Ave., Garden City, NY 11530; Diocese of Rochester, 1150 Buffalo Rd., Rochester, NY 14624.

__C. W. Hayes, THE DIOCESE OF WESTERN NY [EPISCOPAL], Scrantom, Wetmore, and Co., Rochester, NY, 1904.

__J. G. Wilson, CENTENNIAL HISTORY OF THE DIOCESE OF NY [EPISCOPAL], 1785-1885, Appleton, New York, NY, 1886.

The Friends (Quaker) archives and a very important volume of records of NY City and Long Island meetings are listed below.

__(Archives) NY Yearly Meeting Archives, Haviland Records Room, 15 Rutherford Pl., New York, NY 10003. Many NY monthly meeting records.

__W. W. Hinshaw, ENCYCLOPEDIA OF AMERICAN QUAKER GENEALOGY, VOLUME 3, MEETINGS ORGANIZED IN NY CITY AND ON LONG ISLAND, 1657 TO THE PRESENT, Genealogical Publishing Co., Baltimore, MD, 1940(1969).

__J. C. Frost, ABSTRACTS OF QUAKER MEETING RECORDS, NYSL, Albany, NY.

Huguenot archives and publications to be used in your research if you had ancestors of this faith include:

__(Archives) Huguenot Historical Association of New Rochelle, North and Paine Aves., New Rochelle, NY

10802; Huguenot Historical Society of New Paltz, Huguenot St., New Paltz, NY 12561.

__R. LeFevre, HISTORY OF NEW PALTZ, NY, AND ITS OLD FAMILIES, 1678-1820, Genealogical Publishing Co., Baltimore, MD, 1909(1973). Old Huguenot settlement.

__M. H. Seacord, BIOGRAPHICAL SKETCHES AND INDEX OF THE HUGUENOT SETTLERS OF NEW ROCHELLE, 1687-1776, Huguenot and Historical Association of New Rochelle, New Rochelle, NY, 1941.

__A. V. Wittmeyer, REGISTERS OF BIRTHS, MARRIAGES, AND DEATHS OF THE EGLISE FRANCAISE [HUGUENOT] OF NY, 1688-1804, Genealogical Publishing Co., Baltimore, MD, 1886(1968).

__C. W. Baird, HISTORY OF THE HUGUENOT EMIGRATION TO AMERICA, Genealogical Publishing Co., Baltimore, MD, 1966.

For Jewish ancestors, consult:

__(Archives) American Jewish Historical Society, 2 Thornton Rd., Waltham, MA 02154; American Jewish Archives, 3101 Clifton Ave., Cincinnati, OH 45220.

__S. Birmingham, OUR CROWD, THE GREAT JEWISH FAMILIES OF NY, Harper and Row, New York, NY, 1967.

__H. B. Grinstein, RISE OF THE JEWISH COMMUNITY OF NY, 1654-1860, Jewish Publication Society, Philadelphia, PA, 1945.

__D. de S. Pool, PORTRAITS ETCHED IN STONE: EARLY JEWISH SETTLERS [NY CITY], 1682-1831, Columbia University Press, New York, NY, 1952.

__M. H. Stern, FIRST AMERICAN JEWISH FAMILIES, 600 GENEALOGIES, 1654-1977, American Jewish Archives, Cincinnati, OH, 1978.

__Jewish Genealogical Society, RESOURCES FOR JEWISH GENEALOGY IN THE NY AREA, The Society, New York, NY, 1985.

The Lutheran archives and books relating to Lutherans which will serve you well are:

__(Archives) Library of the National Lutheran Council, 50 Madison Ave., New York, NY 10010; Lutheran Archives Center, 7301 Germantown Ave., Philadelphia, PA 19119.

__W. C. Berkenmeyer and J. P. Dern, CHRONICLE OF LUTHERAN AFFAIRS IN NY COLONY, 1731-50, Dern, Redwood City, CA, 1971.

__S. Hart and H. J. Kreider, LUTHERAN CHURCH IN NY AND NJ, 1722-60, Monocacy Book Co., Redwood City, CA, 1962.

__A. C. M. Kelly, HUDSON VALLEY BAPTISM AND MARRIAGE
RECORDS, The Compiler, Rhinebeck, NY, 1978. Lutheran
and Reformed churches.

__H. J. Kreider, LUTHERANISM IN COLONIAL NY, The Author,
New York, NY, 1942.

__Palatine Society of the United Evangelical Lutheran
Church of NY and New England, THE PALATINES OF NY
STATE, The Society, Jamestown, NY, 1953.

__G. U. Werner, THE LUTHERANS OF NY, THEIR STORY AND
THEIR PROBLEMS, New York, NY, 1918.

For Methodist research, the following archives and books
may be consulted:

__(Archives) Northern NY Conference Repository, United
Methodist Church, 418 Washington St., Watertown, NY
13601; Southeastern NY Methodist Archives, 23 Route 81,
Killingwood, CT 06417; Western NY Conference Archives,
Williamsville United Methodist Church, 5681 Main St.,
Williamsville, NY 14221; NYPL, 5th Ave. and 42nd St.,
New York, NY 10018; Troy Conference Historical Society,
Green Mountain College, Poultney, VT 05764; Methodist
Materials, Syracuse University Library, Syracuse, NY
13210.

__C. W. Christmas, Jr., THE ONWARD WAY, THE STORY OF THE
NY ANNUAL CONFERENCE OF THE METHODIST CHURCH, The
Conference, New York, NY, 1949.

__F. W. Conable, HISTORY OF THE GENESEE ANNUAL CONFERENCE
OF THE METHODIST EPISCOPAL CHURCH, 1810-72, Nelson and
Phillips, New York, NY, 1876.

__S. Parks, TROY (METHODIST) CONFERENCE MISCELLANY, 1854.

__G. Peck, EARLY METHODISM OF THE OLD GENESEE CONFERENCE
FROM 1788 TO 1828, Carlton and Porter, New York, NY,
1860.

__S. A. Seaman, ANNALS OF NY METHODISM (CENTRAL NY), Hunt
and Eaton, New York, NY, 1892.

Presbyterian archives and published works include:

__(Archives) Presbyterian Historical Society, 425 Lombard
St., Philadelphia, PA 19147; Princeton Theological
Seminary, Speer Library, Mercer St. and Library Pl.,
Princeton, NJ 08540.

__P. H. Fowler, HISTORICAL SKETCH OF PRESBYTERIANISM
WITHIN THE SYNOD OF CENTRAL NY, Curtiss and Childs,
Utica, NY, 1877.

__J. H. Hotchkiss, A HISTORY OF THE PURCHASE AND SETTLE-
MENT OF WESTERN NY AND THE RISE OF THE PRESBYTERIAN
CHURCH, Dodd, New York, NY, 1848.

__T. F. Savage, THE PRESBYTERIAN CHURCH IN NY CITY, New York, NY, 1949.

For Roman Catholic research, these archives can be of value if you cannot locate records at the parish level:
__(Archives) Diocese of Albany, 465 State St., Albany, NY 12206; Diocese of Brooklyn, 75 Greene Ave., Brooklyn, NY 11202; Diocese of Buffalo, 35 Lincoln Parkway, Buffalo, NY 14222; Archdiocese of NY, 1011 First Ave., New York, NY 10022; St. Bernard's Seminary, 2260 Lake Ave., Rochester, NY 14612; Diocese of Syracuse, 240 Onondaga St., Syracuse, NY 13206.
__CATHOLIC ARCHIVES AND MANUSCRIPT COLLECTIONS, The American Archivist, Volume 27, 1964, pages 409-14.
__STUDIES IN AMERICAN (CATHOLIC) CHURCH HISTORY, Catholic University Press, Washington, DC, over 30 volumes.

A volume of value to those who had a member of the colonial clergy as a NY ancestor is:
__F. L. Weis, THE COLONIAL CLERGY OF THE MIDDLE COLONIES, NY, NJ, AND PA, 1628-1776, Genealogical Publishing Co., Baltimore, MD, 1957(1978).

As you search for your forebear's church records, please bear in mind that they might be in a wide variety of places. The original, transcribed, microfilmed, and/or published records may be in the local church, local libraries or archives, or denominational archives, or even in private hands. Inquire at all these repositories, especially LL, RL, FHL(FHC), NYSL, NYPL, NYHS, and NYGB. When seeking church records in a library or archives catalog, you should look under the county name, the church name, and the denomination name. Church records are often found in several other sources, which are discussed in different sections of this chapter: cemetery, city and county histories, colonial, DAR, ethnic, genealogical indexes and compilations, genealogical periodicals, manuscripts, mortuary, newspaper, published genealogies, regional records, and WPA records.

8. City directories

Just before the turn of the 19th century, namely in 1786, NY City began publishing city directories on a regular annual basis. In the early 19th century, several other NY cities began, and others started issuing directories a little later. These volumes usually appeared erratically at first, but then began to come out regular-

ly (annually) later on. They usually list heads of
households and workers plus their home addresses and
their occupations, and sometimes the names and addresses
of their places of employment. Businesses, professions,
institutions, churches, and organizations (sometimes with
officers, rarely with all members) are also usually
listed.

Notable among NY city directories are those of the
following cities. For each of these cities, the earliest
directory is listed. If the date is followed by a dash,
this means that after that date, publication was fairly
regular (annual). If such was not the case, early directories are listed until publication became regular, the
date on which this started being followed by a dash:
Albany(1813-), Auburn(1857-), Binghamton(1857-), Brooklyn
(listings for 1796, 1802, and 1811 included in the NY
City directories, separate Brooklyn directories 1822-),
Buffalo(1828-), Elmira(1857-), Geneva(1857), Morrisania-
(1853), Newburgh(1856-), NY City(1786-), Ogdensburg-
(1857-), Oswego(1852-), Poughkeepsie(1843-), Rochester-
(1827-), Rome(1857-), Schenectady(1841, 1857-), Syracuse-
(1844, 1851-), Troy(1829-), Utica(1817, 1828-), Williams-
burgh(1847-), Yonkers(1858-). There are also NY state
regional directories, which are largely commercially
oriented (1842, 1850, 1859).

Many of the directories mentioned in the previous
paragraph have been microfilmed, quite a few of them
through the 1901 volume. The microfilms and/or the
original directories should be sought in the NYSL, NYPL,
NYHS, FHL(FHC), RL and LL. Other NY cities also issued
directories, usually at starting dates later than the
above ones, but you should not fail to look for them,
especially in RL and LL in the pertinent places.

9. City and county histories

Histories for many NY counties and numerous NY
cities have been published. These volumes usually contain biographical data on leading citizens, details about
early settlers, histories of organizations, businesses,
trades, and churches, and often lists of clergymen,
lawyers, physicians, teachers, governmental officials,
farmers, military men, and other groups. Several works
which list many of these histories are:

__M. J. Kaminkow, US LOCAL HISTORIES IN THE LIBRARY OF CONGRESS, Magna Carta, Baltimore, MD, 1975, 4 volumes.

__P. W. Filby, BIBLIOGRAPHY OF COUNTY HISTORIES IN AMERICA, Genealogical Publishing Co., Baltimore, MD, 1985.

__J. Austin, GENEALOGICAL RESEARCH IN NY STATE, AN INFORMAL FINDING LIST OF PUBLISHED MATERIALS, Genealogical Conference of NY, Albany, NY, 1983, pages 37-43, 47-8.

__H. Nestler, A BIBLIOGRAPHY OF NY STATE COMMUNITIES, COUNTIES, TOWNS, AND VILLAGES, Empire State Historical Publications, Friedman, Port Washington, NY, 1968.

Most of the NY city, county, and community history volumes in these bibliographies can be found in NYSL, NYPL, NYGB, NYHS, and some are available in FHL(FHC). RL and LL are likely to have those relating to their particular areas. In Chapters 4 and 5, you will find listed under the counties recommended county (and some city) histories. In libraries, the easiest way to find local histories is to look in their catalogs under the names of the county, city, town, and community. Towns and communities are often listed under the counties. The state of NY has town, city, and county historians in most of these places. They are continually compiling historical information about their localities and the people in them. Addresses of these historians may be obtained from:

__DIRECTORY OF NY STATE COUNTY AND MUNICIPAL HISTORIANS, County Historians Association of NY State, Comstock, NY, latest edition.

They can often be of considerable assistance to you as you seek information on your progenitor.

10. Colonial records

The colonial period for NY extended from 1609 to 1775, during which time the area was first a colony of the Netherlands (1609-64), then a colony of Great Britain (1664-1775). Many other sections in this chapter describe types of records relating to colonial NY, particularly the sections on census records (early census-like lists), church records, manuscripts, colonial and Revolutionary military records, naturalization records, newspaper records, regional publications, and will and intestate records. This section presents the most important colonial records, and is made up of two sub-sections, one dealing with general reference materials to all the colonies (including NY), and a second dealing with reference materials and records of colonial NY.

Among the most important genealogical materials relating to all the colonies are the following. They should be consulted for your colonial NY ancestor. However, some of the volumes must be used with care since some of the information in them is not from original sources and is therefore often inaccurate.

___F. A. Virkus, THE ABRIDGED COMPENDIUM OF AMERICAN GENEALOGY, Genealogical Publishing Co., Baltimore, MD, 1968(1925-42), 7 volumes. [425,000 names of colonial people]

___G. M. MacKenzie and N. O. Rhoades, COLONIAL FAMILIES OF THE USA, Genealogical Publishing Co., Baltimore, MD, 1966(1907-20), 7 volumes. [125,000 names]

___H. Whittemore, GENEALOGICAL GUIDE TO THE EARLY SETTLERS OF AMERICA, Genealogical Publishing Co., Baltimore, MD, 1967(1898-1906).

___T. P. Hughes and others, AMERICAN ANCESTRY, Genealogical Publishing Co., Baltimore, MD, 1968(1887-9), 12 volumes.

___BURKE'S DISTINGUISHED FAMILIES OF AMERICA, Burke's Peerage, London, England, 1948.

___C. E. Banks, PLANTERS OF THE COMMONWEALTH, Genealogical Publishing Co., Baltimore, MD, 1972.

___G. R. Crowther, III, SURNAME INDEX TO 65 VOLUMES OF COLONIAL AND REVOLUTIONARY PEDIGREES, National Genealogical Society, Washington, DC, 1975.

___W. M. Clemens, AMERICAN MARRIAGE RECORDS BEFORE 1699, Genealogical Publishing Co., Baltimore, MD, 1926(1979). [10,000 entries]

___M. B. Colket, Jr., FOUNDERS OF EARLY AMERICAN FAMILIES, Order of Founders and Patriots of America, Cleveland, OH, 1975.

___H. K. Eilers, NSDAC BICENTENNIAL ANCESTOR INDEX, National Society Daughters of American Colonists, Ft. Worth, TX, 1976.

___National Society of Daughters of Founders and Patriots of America, FOUNDERS AND PATRIOTS OF AMERICA INDEX, The Society, Washington, DC, 1975.

___National Society of the Colonial Dames of America, REGISTER OF ANCESTORS, The Society, Richmond, VA, 1979.

___N. Currer-Briggs, COLONIAL SETTLERS AND ENGLISH ADVENTURERS, Genealogical Publishing Co., Baltimore, MD, 1971. [5000 names]

__P. W. Filby and M. K. Meyer, PASSENGER AND IMMIGRATION LISTS INDEX, Gale Research, Detroit, MI, 1981, 3 volumes, plus annual SUPPLEMENTS. [Over 1.6 million names]

__G. F. T. Sherwood, AMERICAN COLONISTS IN ENGLISH RECORDS, Sherwood, London, England, 1932, 2 volumes.

__P. W. Coldham, ENGLISH ESTATES OF AMERICAN COLONISTS, Genealogical Publishing Co., Baltimore, MD, 1980-1, 3 volumes.

__P. W. Coldham, ENGLISH CONVICTS IN COLONIAL AMERICA, Polyanthos, New Orleans, LA, 1974-6, 2 volumes. [18,000 names]

__J. C. Hotten, THE ORIGINAL LISTS OF PERSONS OF QUALITY, Genealogical Publishing Co., Baltimore, MD, 1874(1980).

__Daughters of the American Revolution, DAR PATRIOT INDEX, The Daughters, Washington, DC, 1966, 1979, 2 volumes.

__National Genealogical Society, INDEX OF REVOLUTIONARY WAR PENSION APPLICATIONS IN THE NATIONAL ARCHIVES, The Society, Washington, DC, 1976.

__F. Rider, THE AMERICAN GENEALOGICAL BIOGRAPHICAL INDEX, Godfrey Memorial Library, Middletown, CT, 1942-52, 48 volumes; THE AMERICAN GENEALOGICAL BIOGRAPHICAL INDEX, NEW SERIES, Godfrey Memorial Library, Middletown, CT, 1952-, in progress, over 140 volumes published.

__W. W. Spooner, HISTORIC FAMILIES OF AMERICA, The Author, New YOrk, NY, 1907-8, 3 volumes. Be careful.

__Daughters of Colonial Wars, BICENTENNIAL ANCESTOR INDEX, The Daughters, Washington, DC, 1976.

__Daughters of Founders and Patriots of America, INDEX TO LINEAGE BOOKS, The Daughters, Somerville, MA, 1943.

__Daughters of American Colonists, BICENTENNIAL ANCESTOR INDEX, 1976-84.

__National Society Colonial Dames 17th Century, 17TH CENTURY COLONIAL ANCESTORS, Genealogical Publishing Co., Baltimore, MD, 1976(1984).

__National Society of Colonial Daughters 17th Century, LINEAGE BOOK, D. Baird, Rotan, TX, 1980.

__National Society Daughters of Colonial Wars, BICENTENNIAL ANCESTOR INDEX, R. Moncure, Clifton, VA, 1984.

__Order of Founders and Patriots of America, REGISTER, The Order, New York, NY, 1927, with SUPPLEMENTS, 1940, 1960, 1981.

__Society of Colonial Wars, INDEX TO ANCESTORS AND ROLL OF MEMBERS, The Society, New York, NY, 1921, with SUPPLEMENTS, 1941 and 1971.

There are also important record collections, published volumes, and typescript and published indexes
relating specifically to colonial NY. Among the most
useful of the original records (especially governmental
records) for looking up your ancestors who came to NY
before 1776 are the following volumes which deal with the
Dutch period (1604-64):

B. Fernow, THE RECORDS OF NEW AMSTERDAM FROM 1653-74,
MINUTES OF THE COURT OF BURGOMASTERS, Genealogical
Publishing Co., Baltimore, MD, 1897(1976), 7 volumes.
Many names.

B. Fernow, MINUTES OF THE ORPHANMASTERS OF NEW AMSTER-
DAM, 1655-63, Harper, New York, NY, 1902-7, 2 volumes.

C. T. Gehring, NY HISTORICAL MANUSCRIPTS: DUTCH, VOL-
UMES GG, HH, & II, LAND PAPERS, Genealogical Publishing
Co., Baltimore, MD, 1980.

J. H. Innes, NEW AMSTERDAM AND ITS PEOPLE, Kennikat
Press, Port Washington, NY, 1902(1969). Inhabitants as
of about 1655.

E. B. O'Callaghan, THE REGISTER OF NEW NETHERLAND,
1626-74, Munsell, Albany, NY, 1865.

E. B. O'Callaghan, THE REGISTER OF SALOMON LACHAIRE,
NOTARY PUBLIC, OF NEW AMSTERDAM, 1661-2, Genealogical
Publishing Co., Baltimore, MD, 1978.

E. B. O'Callaghan, CALENDAR OF DUTCH (AND ENGLISH)
HISTORICAL MANUSCRIPTS IN THE OFFICE OF THE SECRETARY
OF STATE, Gregg, Boston, MA, 1865-6(1967-8), 1st volume
Dutch(1630-64), 2nd volume English(1664-1776).

PROTOCOL OF DIRCK VAN SCHELLOYNE, SECRETARY OF THE
COLONY OF RENSSELAERWYCK, 1660-5, Yearbook of the Dutch
Settlers Society of Albany, Albany, NY, 1940-1.

H. W. Reynolds, DUTCH HOUSES IN THE HUDSON VALLEY
BEFORE 1776, Dover, New York, NY, 1929(1965). Many
names.

A. J. F. Van Laer, NY HISTORICAL MANUSCRIPTS: DUTCH
REGISTERS OF THE PROVINCIAL SECRETARY, 1638-70, AND
COUNCIL MINUTES, 1638-49, Genealogical Publishing Co.,
Baltimore, MD, 1973.

A. J. F. van Laer, SETTLERS OF RENSSELAERWYCK, 1630-
58, Genealogical Publishing Co., Baltimore, MD, 1908-
(1980).

A. J. F. Van Laer, MINUTES OF THE COURT OF FORT ORANGE
AND BEVERWYCK, 1652-60, University of the State of NY,
Albany, NY, 1920-3, 2 volumes.

A. J. F. Van Laer, MINUTES OF THE COURT OF RENNSELAER-

WYCK, 1648-52, University of the State of NY, Albany, NY, 1922.
__ H. E. Veeder, DUTCH SETTLERS SOCIETY OF ALBANY YEAR-BOOKS, The Society, Albany, NY, 1924/5-.

In addition to the above Dutch-period volumes, there are a number of published works which cover both the Dutch (1609-64) and the English (1664-1776) periods of NY colonial history. As was the case above, these volumes are primarily governmental materials, but some others which are not mentioned elsewhere are included:
__ ANCESTRAL REGISTER OF THE NATIONAL SOCIETY OF COLONIAL DAMES IN THE STATE OF NY, The Society, New York, NY, 1979.
__ THE BURGHERS OF NEW AMSTERDAM AND THE FREEMEN OF NEW YORK, 1675-1866, NY Historical Society, New York, NY, 1886. Includes indentures 1694-1708.
__ P. R. Christoph and others, KINGSTON COURT RECORDS AND SECRETARY'S PAPERS, 1661-75, Genealogical Publishing Co., Baltimore, MD, 1976. Dutch manuscript material.
__ COMPLETE INDEX TO COLONIAL LAWS OF NEW NETHERLANDS AND NY, 1638-1775, Bookmark, Knightstown, IN, 1977. Numerous entries.
__ B. Fernow, DOCUMENTS RELATING TO THE HISTORY OF TOWMS ALONG THE HUDSON AND MOHAWK (EXCEPT ALBANY), 1630-84, Weed, Parsons, and Co., Albany, NY, 1881.
__ W. J. Hoffman, SETTLERS FROM THE NETHERLANDS IN AMERICA BEFORE 1700, The Author, New York, NY, no date.
__ R. V. Jackson, EARLY NY, 1600-1789, Accelerated Indexing Systems, Bountiful, UT, 1980. Many early records indexed.
__ W. B. Melius and F. H. Burnap, INDEX TO THE PUBLIC RECORDS OF THE COUNTY OF ALBANY, 1630-1893, Argus Co., Albany, NY, 1902-17, 37 volumes.
__ NY Secretary of State, CALENDAR OF NY COLONIAL MANU-SCRIPTS, ENDORSED LAND PAPERS, 1643-1803, Weed, Parsons, & Co., Albany, NY, 1864.
__ E. B. O'Callaghan and B. Fernow, editors, DOCUMENTS RELATIVE TO THE COLONIAL HISTORY OF THE STATE OF NY, AMS Press, New York, NY, 1853-87(1969), 15 volumes. Volume 11 is index to volumes 1-10, volume 15 is general index.
__ E. B. O'Callaghan, THE DOCUMENTARY HISTORY OF THE STATE OF NY, Weed, Parsons, & Co., Albany, NY, 1849-51, 4 volumes. Many lists of names with emphasis on Hudson

Valley and Long Island. Partially indexed in volumes
by C. M. Meyers.
__E. B. O'Callaghan and R. Conway, LISTS OF INHABITANTS
OF COLONIAL NY, Genealogical Publishing Co., Baltimore,
MD, 1979.
__S. Oppenheim, THE DUTCH RECORDS OF KINGSTON, 1658-84,
NY State Historical Association, Cooperstown, NY, 1912.
__J. Pearson and A. J. F. van Laer, EARLY RECORDS OF THE
CITY AND COUNTY OF ALBANY AND COLONY OF RENSSELAERS-
WYCK, University Microfilms, Ann Arbor, MI, 1869-1919-
(1967), 4 volumes.
__J. Pearson, CONTRIBUTIONS FOR THE GENEALOGIES OF THE
FIRST SETTLERS OF ALBANY, 1630-1800, Genealogical
Publishing Co., Baltimore, MD, 1872(1978).
__REGISTER OF COLONIAL DAMES OF AMERICA OF NY, with
ADDENDA, The Dames, Manchester and New York, NY, 1926
and 1931.
__D. Versteeg, KINGSTON PAPERS, COURT RECORDS AND SECRE-
TARY'S PAPERS, 1661-75, Genealogical Publishing Co.,
Baltimore, MD, 1976.

In this paragraph, colonial record compilations
(largely governmental) for the English period (1664-1775)
of the colonial era of NY will be presented. Among the
most useful ones for locating your ancestor are:
__J. M. Bloch and others, AN ACCOUNT OF HER MAJESTY'S
REVENUE IN THE PROVINCE OF NEW YORK, 1701-9, Gregg,
Boston, MA, 1967.
__P. R. Christoph, NY HISTORICAL MANUSCRIPTS: ENGLISH,
GOVERNORS' ADMINISTRATIVE PAPERS, 1664-73, Genealogical
Publishing Co., Baltimore, MD, 1980.
__THE COLONIAL LAWS OF NY, 1664-1775, AMS Press, New
York, NY, 1894-6, 5 volumes. Indexed.
__J. R. Felldin and C. M. Tucker, POLL LIST OF THE CITY
AND COUNTY OF NY, 1761, Genealogical Publishers,
Tomball, TX, 1977.
__B. Fernow, CALENDAR OF NY COUNCIL MINUTES, 1668-1783,
NYSL, Albany, NY, 1902.
__W. Gandy, THE ASSOCIATION OATH ROLLS OF THE BRITISH
PLANTATIONS, 1696, The Author, London, England, 1922.
__Great Britain Public Record Office, NORTH AMERICAN
RECORDS, COLONIAL OFFICE, ORIGINAL CORRESPONDENCE,
ETC., [NY: 1664-1781], CO5/1037-1132, Kraus-Thomson,
Millwood, NY, 48 microfilm rolls.
__INDENTURES OF APPRENTICES, 1694-1707, 1718-27, NY

Historical Society, New York, NY, 1886 & 1909, volume.
& 42.

__JOURNAL OF THE GENERAL ASSEMBLY OF THE COLONY OF N\,
1691-1775, Gaine, New York, NY, 1861.

__JOURNAL OF THE LEGISLATIVE COUNCIL OF THE COLONY OF NY,
1691-1775, AMS Press, New York, NY, 1861.

__G. E. Kershaw, THE KENNEBECK PROPRIETORS, 1749-75,
Heritage Books, Bowie, MD, 1975.

__MINUTES OF THE COMMON COUNCIL OF THE CITY OF NEW YORK,
1675-1776, 1784-1831, Dodd, Mead, & Co., and Brown
Printing Co., New York, NY, 1905 and 1917, with INDEX
TO THE 1784-1831 PERIOD, 29 volumes. Many names.

__E. B. O'Callaghan, CALENDAR OF NY COLONIAL COMMISSIONS,
1680-1770, NY Historical Society, New York, NY, 1929.

__E. B. O'Callaghan, NEW YORK CITY ORPHANMASTERS, 1663-8,
Genealogical Publishing Co., Baltimore, MD, 1976.

__E. B. O'Callaghan, CALENDAR OF DUTCH (AND ENGLISH)
HISTORICAL MANUSCRIPTS IN THE OFFICE OF THE SECRETARY
OF STATE, Gregg, Boston, MA, 1865-6(1967-8), 1st volume
Dutch(1630-64), 2nd volume English(1664-1776).

__K. Scott, NY CITY APPRENTICES, 1686-1804, National
Genealogical Society Quarterly, Volume 71, Issues 1, 3-
4, 1983-4.

__K. Scott, CALENDAR OF NY COLONIAL COMMISSIONS, 1770-6,
National Society of Colonial Dames, New York, NY, 1972.

__J. A. Stevens, Jr., COLONIAL RECORDS, NY CHAMBER OF
COMMERCE, 1768-84, Burt Franklin, New York, NY, 1867-
(1971).

Most of the published works mentioned in the previous paragraphs are available in NYSL and NYPL, and many in NYGB, NYHS, and FHL(FHC), and some in LGL, RL, and larger LL. As was indicated at the beginning of this section, numerous other sections of this chapter give references to other colonial records. These should not be overlooked. The possibility of finding your colonial ancestor in the above volumes varies widely from book to book, but all should be examined because there is a chance he/she could appear in any of them.

11. Court records

Down through the many years of the existence of the colony and the state of NY, its laws have been administered by a wide array of courts. These courts and/or their agents have handled three major types of legal action: civil actions, criminal actions, and equity actions. <u>Civil</u> actions are cases in which one person (plaintiff) alleges another person (defendant) has done him injury (to his person, property, or reputation). Examples are assault, trespass, damage to property, misrepresentation, defamation, and negligence, and in all monetary redress is sought. <u>Criminal</u> actions are cases in which laws for the protection of society are alleged to have been broken, and the government takes action against the person(s). Examples are murder, robbery, rape, burglary, theft, and fraud. <u>Equity</u> actions are cases in which the rights of two persons are in conflict and legal remedies are inadequate or unjust. What the court does is to attempt to balance the interests of the two parties to maximize the justice to both, and then to issue orders for one or both parties to take specific action (deliver goods, refund money, return an animal, replace a damaged item, rewrite a document). Examples are the probate of an estate, divorce, foreclosure, partnership, receivership, and property partition. In some times, NY had separate courts for these actions; in other times, one judicial body sat sometimes in equity, sometimes as a civil court, and sometimes as a criminal court.

When you look at the history of the NY courts, there is a very important structure to keep in mind. The NY system (as many other state systems) has three levels of courts. The <u>middle</u> level is made up of the courts of original jurisdiction, that is, the courts where all cases of all sorts may originate. The <u>lower</u> level consists of courts beneath them which are set up to handle only certain types of cases or cases of minor proportions. The <u>upper</u> level is made up of a court or courts to which a loser of a case can appeal for reconsideration, the so-called appellate courts. In the early years of the colony, court records were all kept in record books, but as the population increased, the records became more complex in order to manage all the data. The types of records you may expect to encounter are as follows: (1) dockets, which are lists of cases to be considered listed in chronological order, (2) minutes, which are brief descriptions of court actions, (3) orders, which are instructions to police to enforce decrees, (4) judgments, which are decisions of the court, sometimes in detail, (5) case packets or folders or files, which are collections of detailed papers relating to the case, (6) special volumes which list, abstract, or present copies of certain records such as adoptions, jury lists, inquests, naturalizations, wills, administrations, guardianships, and lis pendens (warnings that property is in litigation), (7) loose papers, which may be of many sorts relating to many types of action, (8) indexes to plaintiffs, defendants, makers of wills, administrators, and other name indexes for some of the above records. All these records must be examined, but under no circumstance should the case packets (folders, files) be left unexamined because they are among the richest genealogical sources available.

When the Dutch formally organized a colonial settlement in 1623, they established the Governor and his Council as the first court, a court which dealt with all actions. Appeal from the court was to the Chamber back in Amsterdam. Then in 1647, the Governor set up a Court of Justice to handle all cases with appeal now being to the Governor-Council. In 1653, this court was replaced by a court of city officials in NY, the Court of the Schout, Burgomasters, and Schepens, and similar courts in other parts of the colony, with appeal still being to the Governor-Council. In the English takeover of 1664, justices of the peace were assigned to many towns, each town was given a local court for minor cases, Courts of Sessions were set up for major cases and probate, and the Court of Assizes was established in NY City as the highest court (for appeals and some major cases). In NY City, the Court of Schout, Burgomasters, and Schepens became the Mayor's Court. Then in 1685, a revamped court system was inaugurated. Lower courts (including justices) were established or continued in every town to consider minor matters, a Court of Sessions was given each county, a Court of Oyer and Terminer met in each county once a year, and a Court of Chancery (Equity) served the entire colony. The Court of Assizes was abolished, cases could be appealed to the Governor-Council, and the Governor established a Prerogative Court to handle probate for NY. In 1691, the courts were again reorganized, but this time the general scheme lasted throughout the remainder of the colonial period. Seven types of court were provided for: a Court of Chancery (Equity), Supreme Courts (courts of original jurisdiction), a Court of Common Pleas (County Court) in each county, Courts of Sessions, Justice's Courts (minor matters), a Prerogative Court (probate), and a Court of Vice Admiralty (maritime), with appeals to the Governor-Council and later the Assembly.

In 1777, NY having proclaimed its independence, the courts were left essentially the same, except that the Governor-Council as an appeal court was replaced by a Court of Impeachment and Correction of Errors, and the Prerogative Court (probate) was replaced with a Court of Probate. (In the captured area of NY, the British continued to use the Prerogative Court and the Governor-Council.) After the British evacuation, a Surrogate's Court (probate) was set up in each county as of 1787, with the Probate Court becoming an appeal court. Because of heavy case loads, eight circuit courts with judges exercising Supreme Court powers were put in place in 1821. The year 1846 brought a complete overhaul of the court system. The Supreme Court, with its many meetings in all counties, remained the court of original jurisdiction, that is, the court in which _all_ cases could originate. You must not be confused by the NY use of the name Supreme Court. It does not mean the top court or the highest court in NY. It means the basic or fundamental or foundational type of court, that is, the court of original jurisdiction. Justice's Courts handled minor matters, thus relieving the Supreme Courts of small or lesser cases. The Court of Common Pleas became the County Court and it also handled numerous cases to relieve the Supreme Court. The Court of Chancery was abolished and equity matters were assigned to the Supreme Court. The Court of Impeachment and Correction of Errors was limited to impeachment processes and was renamed the Court of Impeachment, and a new Court of Appeals was constituted to be the highest court in NY state. Surrogate's Courts were continued in each county and several other city and town courts were authorized to assist the Supreme Courts, especially in population centers such as NY City. Special meetings of the Supreme Court were established to provide for intermediate appeals, these meetings being called General Terms of the Supreme Court. Later on, these were renamed Appellate Divisions of the Supreme Court.

Now, let us summarize the court system after 1846. The basic structure was made up of the _middle_ level

courts, all of them together being called the Supreme
Court. The _upper_ level courts were the General Terms
(Appellate Divisions) of the Supreme Court and then the
Court of Appeals. All other courts in the state are
lower level courts in that they are limited to special
types of cases or to local areas: NY Court of Claims,
County Courts, Surrogate's Courts, City Courts, Municipal
Courts, Police Courts, Courts of Justices of the Peace.
Because of its exceptionally large population, NY has an
elaborate system of Supreme Courts and lower courts. In
other sections of this chapter, many types of court
records will be dealt with, including divorce, land,
naturalization, tax, will, and probate. Therefore, this
section will focus on civil, criminal, and equity court
records other than these. In brief, you should thoroughly examine the records of every court which existed
during your forebear's years. Please remember that the
case packets (folders, files) can be especially reward-
ing.

A number of the records of early courts have ap-
peared in published form with indexes. Among them are:
__A. J. F. Van Laer, MINUTES OF THE COURT OF FORT ORANGE
AND BEVERWYCK, 1652-60, University of the State of NY,
Albany, NY, 1920-3, 2 volumes.
__A. J. F. Van Laer, MINUTES OF THE COURT OF RENNSELAER-
WYCK, 1648-52, University of the State of NY, Albany,
NY, 1922.
__B. Fernow, THE RECORDS OF NEW AMSTERDAM FROM 1653-74,
MINUTES OF THE COURT OF BURGOMASTERS, Genealogical
Publishing Co., Baltimore, MD, 1897(1976), 7 volumes.
Many names.
__B. Fernow, MINUTES OF THE ORPHANMASTERS OF NEW AMSTER-
DAM, 1655-63, Harper, New York, NY, 1902-7, 2 volumes.
__P. R. Christoph and others, KINGSTON COURT RECORDS AND
SECRETARY'S PAPERS, 1661-75, Genealogical Publishing
Co., Baltimore, MD, 1976. Dutch manuscript material.
__P. R. Christoph and F. Christoph, NY HISTORICAL MANU-
SCRIPTS: ENGLISH, RECORDS OF THE COURT OF ASSIZES FOR
THE COLONY OF NY, 1665-82, Genealogical Publishing Co.,
Baltimore, MD, 1983.
__J. Munsell, ANNALS OF ALBANY, Volume 4, Albany, NY.
Contains Court of Assizes records.
__A. J. F. van Laer, MINUTES OF THE COURT OF ALBANY,
RENSSELAERWYCK, AND SCHENECTADY, 1668-73, 1675-85, The

University of the State of NY, Albany, NY, 1926-32, 3 volumes.

___ AMERICAN LEGAL RECORDS, Volume 2, NY City Mayor's Court, 1674-1784.

___ K. Scott, NY HISTORICAL MANUSCRIPTS: MINUTES OF THE MAYOR'S COURT OF NY CITY, 1674-5, Genealogical Publishing Co., Baltimore, MD, 1983.

___ P. M. Hamlin and C. E. Baker, SUPREME COURT OF JUDICATURE OF THE PROVINCE OF NY, 1691-1704, University Press of VA, Charlottesville, VA.

___ K. Scott, NY CITY COURT RECORDS, 1684-1797, GENEALOGICAL DATA FROM THE COURT OF QUARTER SESSIONS, National Genealogical Society, Washington, DC, 1982-3.

___ K. Scott, RECORDS OF THE CHANCERY COURT, PROVINCE AND STATE OF NY GUARDIANSHIPS, 1691-1815, Holland Society of NY, New York, NY, 1971.

These volumes, which you should examine carefully if your progenitors fall in the proper time frames, are available in NYSL, NYPL, NYGB, and NYHS. Some are to be found in FHL(FHC), LGL, and RL.

There are also some valuable court records in NYSA, some of which have been microfilmed and are therefore available in NYSL and FHL(FHC), as well as some in the Office of the NY County Clerk.

___ RECORDS OF THE NY COURT OF PROBATES AND ITS COLONIAL PREDECESSORS, 1664-1823, NYSA, Albany, NY. Inventories and accounts 1666-1823, wills 1671-1815, administrations 1700-1823.

___ RECORDS OF THE NY COURT OF CHANCERY (EQUITY), 1684-1847, NYSA, Albany, NY. Decrees, files, indexes (6 volumes, only to some of the records), minutes, orders, papers, registers, wills (out-of-state, 1830-47), others.

___ RECORDS OF THE NY COURT OF CHANCERY (EQUITY), 2ND THROUGH 8TH CIRCUITS, 1823-47, NYSA, Albany, NY. Excludes 1st Circuit which is NY City and surrounding areas. Decrees, files, indexes (7 volumes, only to some records), minutes, naturalizations, orders.

___ RECORDS OF THE NY COURT OF CHANCERY (EQUITY), 1ST CIRCUIT, 1823-47, NY County Clerk, NY City, NY. 1st Circuit is NY City and surrounding areas. Decrees, files, indexes, minutes, orders.

___ RECORDS OF THE NY COURT FOR TRIAL OF IMPEACHMENTS AND CORRECTION OF ERRORS, 1777-1847, NYSA, Albany, NY.

Predecessor to Court of Appeals. Index (1 volume, 1784-1847), files, minutes, judgments, decrees.

__RECORDS OF THE NY SUPREME COURT OF JUDICATURE, OFFICES OF ALBANY, GENEVA, AND UTICA, 1797-1847, NYSA, Albany, NY. Bail pieces, calendars, declarations, dockets, financial records, indexes (3 volumes to dockets of judgments 1829-35, 1 volume to Albany minute books 1797-1847), insolvencies, minutes, motion papers, naturalizations, orders, partitions, pleadings, recognizance rolls, rule books, writs, others. Covers all except southeastern NY state.

__RECORDS OF THE NY SUPREME COURT OF JUDICATURE, OFFICE OF NEW YORK CITY, 1797-1847, NY County Clerk, NY City, NY. Records similar to above. Covers southeastern NY state.

__MICROFILM OF NY STATE CHANCERY COURT MINUTES AND ORDERS, 1701-70, 1783-1847, 22 Rolls, FHL(FHC), Salt Lake City, UT.

There is an exceptionally useful set of volumes which index plaintiffs in NY appeal cases and in many cases of notable legal interest, including cases in most of the above-listed courts. No NY researcher should overlook this resource in an ancestor quest:

__1906 DECENNIAL EDITION OF THE AMERICAN DIGEST: A COMPLETE TABLE OF AMERICAN CASES FROM 1658 TO 1906, West Publishing Co., St. Paul, MN, 1911, Volumes 21-25. Alphabetical by surname.

Included in this massive index are NY cases from the US Supreme Court, US Court of Appeals, US Federal Court, US District Courts, NY Court for Trial Impeachments and Correction of Errors (1796-1848), NY Supreme Court of Judicature (1796-1896), NY Court of Chancery (1814-48), Superior Court of the City of NY (1828-93), NY Court of Vice Chancellor (1831-50), Court of Common Pleas of NY City (1850-88), NY Court of Appeals (1847-1901), and several large city inferior courts. The cases of these NY courts and numerous others are also indexed in the following volumes, which contain both plaintiff and defendant listings:

__ABBOTT NY DIGEST 2D, West Publishing Co., St. Paul, MN, 1960. Use both the Defendant-Plaintiff Table (3 volumes) and the Plaintiff-Defendant Table (4 volumes).

You must under no circumstances fail to look all your NY progenitors up in these two very large indexes (1906 Decennial and Abbott). They, along with the hundreds of

volumes to which they refer, will be found in large law
libraries. These can be most readily located in Colleges
of Law at universities.

Records of civil and criminal courts in the NY
counties and towns which are of interest to you should
also be sought. You should look for the records of several different local courts including the Circuit Court,
Court of Common Pleas, County Court, Court of General
Sessions, Justice of the Peace Courts, lis pendens records, notarial records, Court of Oyer and Terminer, and
Supreme Court (local actions). Most of these records
remain in the counties in the court house (CH), local
historical archives, or local historical societies. Some
have been microfilmed by the FHL and can be located by
examining the microform catalog at the nearest FHC.
Those available as of 1980 are listed in:
__A. H. Eakle and L. R. Gunn, DESCRIPTIVE INVENTORY OF
  THE NY COLLECTION (IN FHL), University of UT Press,
  Salt Lake City, UT, 1980.

12. DAR records

The NY Chapters of the Daughters of the American
Revolution have done genealogists an exceptionally valuable service by compiling and partially indexing over 950
volumes of transcribed NY Bible, cemetery, church, fami-
ly, genealogical, lineage, and Revolutionary grave re-
cords. The many volumes are included in five different
series:
__DAR of NY, BIBLE RECORDS OF NY STATE, Various Chapters,
  Various Cities, NY, 1924-, over 230 volumes.
__DAR of NY, CEMETERY, CHURCH, AND TOWN RECORDS OF NY
  STATE, Various Chapters, Various Cities, NY, 1926-,
  over 560 volumes.
__DAR of NY, FAMILY HISTORIES, Various Chapters, Various
  Places, 1979-, over 5 volumes.
__DAR of NY, GENEALOGICAL DATA: NEW PROJECT, SERIES A,
  Lineage Papers Submitted by NY Applicants for DAR
  Membership, 1960-, over 140 volumes.
__DAR of NY, GRAVES OF REVOLUTIONARY SOLDIERS IN NY,
  Various Chapters, Various Places, 1922-55, 15 volumes.
Complete sets of these volumes are available in NYSL,
NYPL, and the DAR Library in Washington, DC. The first
two series up to 1978 are partially indexed in a master

index located in these same repositories and also at NYGB:

__MASTER INDEX, NY STATE DAR GENEALOGICAL RECORDS, 1971, with SUPPLEMENT, RECORDS AND CORRECTIONS, 1972-8, The DAR, Albany, NY. Look under name and county. Many names are unindexed, therefore go through the county listings in detail.

The first and third series are indexed in:

__SURNAMES CARD INDEX, Local History and Genealogy Section, NYSL, Albany, NY.

And the second, fourth, and fifth series are indexed respectively in these:

__VITAL RECORDS CARD INDEX, Local History and Genealogy Section, NYSL, Albany, NY. Look under county.

__GENEALOGICAL DATA, NEW PROJECT CARD INDEX, Local History and Genealogy Section, NYSL, Albany, NY.

__REVOLUTIONARY WAR SOLDIERS GRAVE CARD INDEX, Local History and Genealogical Section, NYSL, Albany, NY.

In addition to the above transcripts, there are some large compilations put together by the National DAR listing Revolutionary War ancestors and detailing lineages from present-day DAR members back to them. These may be accessed by looking in the following volumes, the references of which will lead you to the pertinent ancestors and/or lineages.

__DAR, PATRIOT INDEX, The Daughters, Washington, DC, 1969-79, 2 volumes.

__DAR, INDEX TO THE ROLLS OF HONOR (ANCESTOR INDEX) IN THE LINEAGE BOOKS OF THE NATIONAL SOCIETY OF THE DAR, Genealogical Publishing Co., Baltimore, MD, 1916-40 (1980). Indexes 166 volumes of lineages 1890-1921.

13. Death records

During the period of Dutch control (1609-64), the New Netherland government did not keep official civil death records, leaving this task to the Dutch Reformed Church. When the English took the colony over (1664), they had a law requiring ministers of parishes and clerks of towns to record deaths, but the colony never systematically enforced the regulation, and only a few records were kept. Early records of deaths were included in the town minutes for a number of NY towns, especially those on Long Island, where this New England custom was practiced. This town record keeping did not spread, but

declined. The situation of practically no death recording continued until 1847 when a law requiring death
registration in towns was passed. Fair conformity to the
law was seen during 1847-49/50, but the system largely
failed thereafter. Many of the fragmentary records
mentioned above will be found in town and county records,
many have been published in NY genealogical periodicals
(Tree Talks, NY Genealogical and Biographical Record),
some have been microfilmed by the FHL, and a few are at
NYSL and NYSA. Listings of a number of those available
will be found in:

__J. D. and E. D. Stemmons, THE VITAL RECORD COMPENDIUM,
Everton Publishers, Logan, UT, 1979.

__A. H. Eakle and L. R. Gunn, DESCRIPTIVE INVENTORY OF
THE NY COLLECTION, University of UT Press, Salt Lake
City, UT, 1980.

__Historical Records Survey, GUIDE TO PUBLIC VITAL STA-
TISTICS IN NY STATE, INCLUDING NY CITY, WPA, Albany,
NY, 1942, 3rd volume.

Just about the turn of the 19th century, NY City
began keeping death records (1798-1804, 1812-), and other
larger cities joined in about or after the midpoint of
the 19th century: Brooklyn (1847-), Albany (1870-),
Syracuse (1873-), Utica (1873-), Rochester (1875-),
Yonkers (1875-), Buffalo (1878-). Then in 1880 a state
law mandating registration was passed, and compliance
gradually increased to 50% by about 1900 and 90% by about
1915, when a more stringent law came into effect. The
records are available as follows. For NY County (1798-
1804, 1812-), Kings County (some 1847-54, 1857-), Queens
County (some 1847-9, 1880-), Richmond County (some 1847-,
1880), Bronx County (1914-), Albany (1870-1914), Syracuse
(1873-80), Utica (1873-80), Rochester (1875-80), Yonkers
(1875-1914), and Buffalo (1878-1914), records should be
sought in the county or city offices for the dates indicated. For Albany (1915-), Yonkers (1915-), Buffalo
(1915-), and all the rest of the state (1880-) except the
5 counties of NY City, write or visit:

__NY State Department of Health, Bureau of Vital Records,
Tower Building, Empire State Plaza, Albany, NY 12237.
Records indexed.

Public access to death records prior to 1938 is available, but those after are restricted.

Since NY is so short on official death records before 1880 (1812 for NY City), other types of records often have to be consulted. Among the better ones are Bible, biography, cemetery, census (especially the 1865/-75 state censuses and the mortality censuses), church, estate, genealogical periodicals, manuscripts, marriage, military, mortuary, naturalization, newspaper, published genealogy, and will. All of these are treated in other sections of this chapter. Numerous non-official sources of this sort are listed in the two books by Stemmons and Eakle cited in the first paragraph of this section. When you are seeking death date and place information in archives and libraries, be certain to explore all the above mentioned sources, and do not fail to look under the county listings and the following heading in library catalogs: Registers of births, etc. (Etc. includes deaths.)

14. Divorce records

Prior to 1787 the only way to obtain a divorce in the colony or state of NY was to petition either the governor or the legislature. Only a few divorces were granted under these arrangements. In 1787, the Court of Chancery was authorized to grant divorces, but only on the ground of adultery. In 1847, when a court reorganization plan went into effect, the Court of Chancery was abolished and its divorce jurisdiction was turned over to the Supreme Court. Divorce records, therefore, need to be sought in these places, and particular attention should be paid to the judgment papers, since they often give the date and place of the marriage, and the names and birthdates of the children. Another useful source of divorce information is in local newspapers, which sometimes published notices of these actions.

15. Emigration and immigration

Since NY was one of the thirteen original colonies, many early settlers came in (immigrated) and many of them or their descendants moved out (emigrated) chiefly to the west (into what is now OH and IN, and beyond). There are a number of good volumes available which list immigrants to the areas that became the US. You should consult these volumes because they include both people who came directly to NY and people who came to some other colony or state and then to NY. The first set of volumes is an index to thousands of ship passenger lists in over 1300 sources and contains well over 1.5 million listings. These references have been abstracted from many published lists. Each listing gives the full name of the immigrant, the names of accompanying relatives, ages, the date and port of arrival, and the source of the information. The volumes in the set are:

___P. W. Filby and M. K. Meyer, PASSENGER AND IMMIGRATION LISTS INDEX, Gale Research Co., Detroit, MI, 1981, with ANNUAL SUPPLEMENTS thereafter.

Do not fail to look for every possible immigrant ancestor of yours in this very large index. Also of importance for locating passengers or passenger lists are:

___H. Lancour, R. J. Wolfe, and P. W. Filby, BIBLIOGRAPHY OF SHIP PASSENGER LISTS, 1538-1900, Gale Research Co., Detroit, MI, 1981.

___US National Archives and Records Service, GUIDE TO GENEALOGICAL RESEARCH IN THE NATIONAL ARCHIVES, The Service, Washington, DC, 1982, pages 41-57.

___A. Eakle and J. Cerny, THE SOURCE, Ancestry Publishing Co., Salt Lake City, UT, 1984, pages 453-516.

___P. W. Coldham, BONDED PASSENGERS TO AMERICA, 1615-1775, Genealogical Publishing Co., Baltimore, MD, 1981-3, 9 volumes.

___P. W. Coldham, THE COMPLETE BOOK OF (ENGLISH) EMIGRANTS, Genealogical Publishing Co., Baltimore, MD, 1987.

___R. J. Dickson, ULSTER IMMIGRATION TO COLONIAL AMERICA, 1718-75, Ulster-Scot Historical Foundation, Belfast, Ireland, 1976.

___J. C. Hotten, THE ORIGINAL LISTS OF PERSONS OF QUALITY, EMIGRANTS, AND OTHERS WHO WENT FROM GREAT BRITAIN TO THE AMERICAN PLANTATIONS, 1600-1700, Genealogical Publishing Co., Baltimore, MD 1874(1980).

___D. L. Kent, BARBADOS AND AMERICA, The Author, Arlington, VA, 1980.

___J. and M. Kaminkow, A LIST OF EMIGRANTS FROM ENGLAND TO AMERICA, 1718-59, Magna Carta Book Co., Baltimore, MD, 1964.

___US Department of State, PASSENGER ARRIVALS, 1819-20, IN THE US, Genealogical Publishing Co., Baltimore, MD, 1967.

___US Department of State, PASSENGERS WHO ARRIVED IN THE US, 1821-3, Magna Carta Book Co., Baltimore, MD, 1969.

__T. Schenk, R. Froelke, and I. Bork, THE WUERTTEMBERG EMIGRATION INDEX, Ancestry, Salt Lake City, UT, 1986, 3 volumes.

__D. Dobson, DIRECTORY OF SCOTTISH SETTLERS IN NORTH AMERICA, Genealogical Publishing Co., Baltimore, MD, 1984-6, 6 volumes.

__R. P. Swierenga, DUTCH EMIGRATION RECORDS, 1847-77, A COMPUTER LIST, Kent State University, Kent, OH, 1976.

Having explored the above records, especially the books by Filby and Meyer, you can then look into some works (microfilms and published volumes) dealing particularly with _immigration_ to NY. As the Filby and Meyer volumes were the most important materials in the above paragraph, the most important reference sources in this and the next paragraphs are the NY passenger arrival lists which the National Archives (NA) has microfilmed. These lists generally show for each passenger: name, age, sex, occupation, and country of origin, in addition to the name of the ship, date of arrival, port of arrival, and port of embarkation. For the state of NY, these microfilms are:

__US Customs Service, PASSENGER LISTS OF VESSELS ARRIVING AT NEW YORK, NY, 1820-97, The National Archives, Washington, DC, Microfilm M237, Rolls 1-675.

__US Customs Service, COPIES OF LISTS OF PASSENGERS ARRIVING AT MISCELLANEOUS PORTS OF THE ATLANTIC AND GULF COASTS AND AT PORTS ON THE GREAT LAKES, 1820-73, The National Archives, Washington, DC, Microfilm M575, Rolls 6 and 16. Includes Oswegatchie, NY (1821-3), Sag Harbor, NY (1829-34), and Rochester (1866).

__US Immigration and Naturalization Service, PASSENGER AND CREW LISTS OF VESSELS ARRIVING AT NEW YORK, NY, 1897-1942, The National Archives, Washington, DC, Microfilm T715, Rolls 1-6674.

These voluminous records are partially indexed in the following microfilms:

__US WPA, INDEX TO THE PASSENGER LISTS OF VESSELS ARRIVING AT NEW YORK, NY, 1820-46, The National Archives, Washington, DC, Microfilm M261, Rolls 1-103.

__A SUPPLEMENTAL INDEX TO PASSENGER LISTS OF VESSELS ARRIVING AT ATLANTIC AND GULF PORTS (EXCLUDING NY CITY), 1820-74, The National Archives, Washington, DC, Microfilm M334, Rolls 1-188.

__INDEX TO PASSENGER LIST OF VESSELS ARRIVING AT NEW

YORK, NY, 1897-1902, The National Archives, Washington, DC, Microfilm T519, Rolls 1-115.

__INDEX (SOUNDEX) TO PASSENGER LISTS OF VESSELS ARRIVING AT NEW YORK, NY, 1902-43, The National Archives, Washington, DC, Microfilm T621, Rolls 1-755.

As yet, indexes have not been provided for the important years 1847-96, but this work is in progress (Balch Institute, Temple University). For these years, it is necessary to know the approximate date of arrival and/or the ship name, since the records are too numerous to search without some such limiting factors. Sometimes your search can be limited by discovering the names of ships arriving from a certain country (say Germany) during a given time (say 1848-50). Information of this sort is obtainable from another National Archives microfilm:

__Officials of the Port of NY City, REGISTER OF VESSELS ARRIVING AT THE PORT OF NY FROM FOREIGN PORTS, 1789-1919, The National Archives, Washington, DC, Microfilm M1066, Rolls 1-27.

All of the above microfilms are available at the NA and many of them at NAFB. Many are also located in NYSL, NYPL, FHL(FHC), and through AGLL (American Genealogical Lending Library, PO Box 244, Bountiful, UT 84010).

In addition to the microfilms mentioned above, there are a lot of books which deal with special groups of immigrants to NY which may be of assistance to you. These include:

__H. G. Bayer, THE BELGIANS, FIRST SETTLERS IN NY AND IN THE MIDDLE STATES, Devin-Adair Co., New York, NY, 1925.

__THE BURGHERS OF NEW AMSTERDAM AND THE FREEMEN OF NEW YORK, 1675-1866, NY Historical Society, New York, NY, 1886. Includes indentures 1694-1708.

__M. Cassady, NY PASSENGER ARRIVALS, 1849-68, Nimmo, Papillion, NE, 1983. Mostly Germans.

__J. O. Evjen, SCANDINAVIAN IMMIGRANTS IN NY, 1630-74, AND GERMAN IMMIGRANTS IN NY, 1630-74, Genealogical Publishing Co., Baltimore, MD, 1916(1972). Use with caution.

__I. A. Glazier and M. H. Tepper, THE FAMINE IMMIGRANTS, LISTS OF IRISH ARRIVING AT THE PORT OF NY, 1846-61, Genealogical Publishing Co., Baltimore, MD, 1983-.

__M. Haiman, POLES IN NY IN THE 17TH AND 18TH CENTURIES, R. and E. Research Associates, San Francisco, CA, 1938(1970).

__INDENTURES OF APPRENTICES, 1694-1707, 1718-27, NY Historical Society, New York, NY, 1886 & 1909, volumes 18 & 42.

__W. A. Knittle, EARLY 18TH CENTURY PALATINE EMIGRATION, Genealogical Publishing Co., Baltimore, MD, 1937(1979). About 12,000 names.

__R. LeFevre, HISTORY OF NEW PALTZ AND ITS OLD FAMILIES, 1678-1820, Genealogical Publishing Co., Baltimore, MD, 1909(1973). Huguenots.

__N. W. Olsson, SWEDISH PASSENGER ARRIVALS IN NY, Swedish Pioneer Historical Society, Chicago, Il, 1967.

__Palatine Society of the United Evangelical Lutheran Church of NY and New England, THE PALATINES OF NY STATE, The Society, Jamestown, NY, 1953.

__RESIDENT ALIENS ENTITLED TO HOLD LAND IN NY STATE, 1790-1825, NY Genealogical Society Quarterly, Volume 67, pages 42ff.

__A. N. Rygg, NORWEGIANS IN NY, 1825-1925, Norwegian News Co., Brooklyn, NY, 1941.

__K. Scott and R. Conway, NY ALIEN RESIDENTS, 1825-48, Genealogical Publishing Co., Baltimore, MD, 1978.

__M. H. Seacord, BIOGRAPHICAL SKETCHES AND INDEX OF THE HUGUENOT SETTLERS OF NEW ROCHELLE, 1687-1776, Huguenot and Historical Association of New Rochelle, New Rochelle, NY, 1941.

__J. E. Stillwell, HISTORICAL AND GENEALOGICAL MISCELLANY: DATA RELATING TO THE SETTLEMENT OF NY AND NJ, Genealogical Publishing Co., Baltimore, MD, 1903-32 (1970), 5 volumes, volumes 1-2 treat Staten Island.

__U. Simmendinger, TRUE AND AUTHENTIC REGISTER OF PERSONS WHO IN 1709 JOURNEYED FROM GERMANY TO AMERICA, Genealogical Publishing Co., Baltimore, MD, 1934(1984). Mohawk Valley Palatine settlers of 1717.

__G. J. Zimmerman and G. Wolfert, GERMAN IMMIGRANTS BOUND FROM BREMEN TO NY, 1847-62, Genealogical Publishing Co., Baltimore, MD, 1985-6, 2 volumes.

These books will be found in NYSL, NYPL, NYGB, and NYHS. Many of them are located in FHL(FHC), LGL, and RL.

Not only did people immigrate to NY, they emigrated from it, the large majority of them going west. There are some volumes on this, and it is possible that they might help you in your search for a migratory NY progenitor.

__A. C. Milner, ORPHAN TRAINS, Genealogical Helper,

Volume 35, Number 6, 1981. NY Orphan Aid Society sent 100,000 children west, 1853-1929.
__E. Myers, OR DONATION CLAIMS, NY CLAIMANTS, Genealogical Forum of Portland, Portland, OR, 1979-, several volumes.
__L. D. Stillwell, MIGRATION FROM VT, VT Historical Society, Montpelier, VT, 1948.
__US Bureau of the Census, A CENTURY OF POPULATION GROWTH, 1790-1900, The Bureau, Washington, DC, 1909. See the tables showing the numbers of people in each of the other states who were born in NY.
__E. Myers, MIGRATION PATTERNS AS SHOWN BY A STUDY OF THE FEDERAL CENSUS OF 1850, Central NY Genealogical Society, Syracuse, NY, 1977.
__J. D. B. DeBow, compiler, THE SEVENTH CENSUS OF THE US, 1850, EMBRACING A STATISTICAL VIEW OF EACH OF THE STATES AND TERRITORIES, US Bureau of the Census, Washington, DC, 1853. Contains information on NY natives who have moved to other states.
The last three references illustrate the value of census records, particularly those of 1850 and after, in tracing the emigration patterns out of NY to other states. (The census records are equally valuable in discerning migration patterns into NY from other states.)

Numerous other immigration and emigration listings, especially ones published in periodicals, are referenced in the following works:
__O. K. Miller, MIGRATION, EMIGRATION, IMMIGRATION, Everton Publishers, Logan, UT, 1974, 1981, 2 volumes.
__J. D. Austin, GENEALOGICAL RESEARCH IN NY STATE, AN INFORMAL FINDING LIST OF PUBLISHED MATERIALS, Genealogical Conference of NY, Albany, NY, 1983.
If you do not locate your immigrant ancestor in the major references listed in the previous paragraphs, use these two reference works to locate many smaller sources. Finally, do not forget to look into the catalogs of NYSL, NYPL, NYGB, NYHS, and other LGL under the heading NY-EMIGRATION AND IMMIGRATION. Also be sure and seek emigration and immigration materials under the county listings.

16. Ethnic records

From its Dutch beginning, the colony of New Amsterdam, the colony of NY, and then the state of NY, have all had populations made up of many ethnic groups. During the earliest period of Dutch governance (1609-64), peoples of these origins were present: Walloons (Belgian), Norwegians, Danes, Germans, Scots, Scotch-Irish, English, and Jewish. During the British period (1664-1776), large numbers of English and Welsh came in, many black slaves were imported, and in 1708-9 sizable numbers of Germans began to immigrate. Scotch-Irish and New Englanders in increasing numbers came, especially to the frontier areas. Following the Revolution, successful efforts were made to attract Scotch-Irish, English, and Germans, and they were joined by Portuguese, Spanish, and French political refugees. Irish laborers were brought over in the 1820s and 1830s to build canals, and the potato famines of the 1840s and 1850s brought many more. The European revolutions of 1830-50 caused the influx of Italians, Hungarians, and many Germans during and after this period. In the post-Civil War period, NY immigrants were predominantly from Italy, Greece, and the Slavic counties of eastern Europe (Poland, Lithuania, Romania, Russia).

The various ethnic groups tended to each be largely affiliated with a particular religious persuasion. These were as follows: Dutch (Dutch Reformed), Norwegians (Lutheran), Danes (Lutheran), Germans from western and north-central Germany (Lutheran), Germans from southern Germany (Catholic), English (Episcopalian or Quaker), New Englanders (Congregational or Baptist), Scots (Presbyterian), Scotch-Irish (Presbyterian), French (Huguenot or Catholic), Italians (Catholic), Portuguese (Catholic), Spanish (Catholic), Irish (Catholic), Hungarians (Catholic), Greeks (Orthodox), Slavic (Catholic or Orthodox). There are some exceptions to these, and you also need to recall that people in frontier areas tended to become Methodist or Baptist. Since there is such a tight tie between ethnic groups and their church affiliations, many pertinent ethnic references will be found in the church records section of this chapter. Other ethnic volumes are listed in the colonial records section and the emigration and immigration section.

Treatment for blacks here is warranted since no references pertinent to special black genealogical materials have been made previously. Among the useful volumes which will go into detail on this subject are:

__A. Eicholz and J. M Rose, FREE BLACK HEADS OF HOUSE-HOLDS IN THE NY STATE FEDERAL CENSUS, 1790-1830, Gale Research, Detroit, MI, 1981.

__A. Eicholz and J. M. Rose, SLAVE BIRTHS IN NY COUNTY AND NY STATE MANUMISSIONS, NY Genealogical and Biographical Record, Volume 11, pages 1ff., Volumes 108-111, passim.

__J. M. Rose and A. Eicholz, BLACK GENESIS, Gale Research, Detroit, MI, 1976.

__A. Jackel, SOURCE MATERIALS FOR BLACK HISTORY, NYSL, Albany, NY, 1972.

__National Black Bibliographic and Research Center, BLACK SOLDIERS IN THE US, 1777-1977, AN EXTENSIVE BIBLIOGRAPHY, The Center, Newark, DE, 1978.

__C. L. Blockson, BLACK AMERICAN RECORDS AND RESEARCH, in J. C. Smith, ETHNIC GENEALOGY: A RESEARCH GUIDE, Greenwood Press, Westport, CT, 1983.

__A. Eakle and J. Cerny, THE SOURCE, A GUIDEBOOK OF AMERICAN GENEALOGY, Ancestry, Salt Lake City, UT, 1984, pages 578-95.

__C. L. Blockson and R. Fry, BLACK GENEALOGY, Prentice-Hall, Englewood Cliffs, NJ, 1977.

With reference to _American Indian_ (native American) genealogy in NY state, it needs to be remembered that most Indians had left NY for Canada or the west by 1800. The several thousand that remained dwelt largely on reservations, the chief ones which continued to exist being Allegany (Cattaraugus County), Cattaraugus (Cattaraugus, Erie, and Chautauqua Counties), Onondaga (Onondaga County), Oneida (Oneida and Madison Counties), Poosepatrick (Suffolk County), St. Regis (Franklin County), Shinnecock (Suffolk County), Tonawanda (Erie, Genesee, Orleans, and Niagara Counties), and Tuscarora (Niagara County). Some useful records relating to Indians are pointed out in:

__E. K. Kirkham, OUR NATIVE AMERICANS AND THEIR RECORDS OF GENEALOGICAL VALUE, Everton Publishers, Logan, UT, 1980-4, 2 volumes.

__J. McEvers, INDIAN GENEALOGY, Polyanthos, New Orleans, LA, 1980.

__National Archives and Records Service, GUIDE TO RECORDS IN THE NATIONAL ARCHIVES RELATING TO AMERICAN INDIANS, The Archives, Washington, DC, 1984.

17. Gazetteers, atlases, and maps

Detailed information regarding NY geography is exceptionally useful to the genealogical searcher, especially with regard to land records. These records usually mention locations in terms requiring an understanding of local geographical features. Several sorts of geographical aids are valuable in this regard: gazetteers, atlases, and maps. Gazetteers are volumes which list geographical features (towns, villages, crossroads, settlements, districts, rivers, streams, creeks, hills, mountains, valleys, coves, lakes, ponds), locate them, and sometimes give a few details concerning them. An atlas is a collection of maps in book form. Among the better gazetteer-type materials for NY are:

__ H. G. Spafford, GAZETTEER OF THE STATE OF NY, Packard, Albany, NY, 1813 and 1824.

__ T. F. Gordon, GAZETTEER OF THE STATE OF NY, Collins, Philadelphia, PA, 1836.

__ J. Disturnell, A GAZETTEER OF THE STATE OF NY, Van Benthuysen, Albany, NY, 1842/3.

__ J. H. French, GAZETTEER OF THE STATE OF NY, 1860, with F. Place, II, INDEX TO PERSONAL NAMES, Heart of the Lakes Publishers, Interlaken, NY, 1977, and SUPPLEMENTARY INDEX TO PLACES IN FRENCH'S GAZETTEER, University of the State of NY, Albany, NY, 1966.

__ F. B. Hough, GAZETTEER OF THE STATE OF NY, Albany, NY, 1873.

__ W. M. Beauchamp, ABORIGINAL PLACE NAMES OF NY, Grand River Books, Detroit, MI, 1971.

__ D. R. Cutts, AIDS TO PLACE NAMES, NY STATE TOWNSHIPS AND COUNTIES, Orange County Genealogical Society, Orange, CA, 1973.

__ GAZETTEER, NY STATE, NY State Department of Health, Albany, NY, 1980.

__ B. Blenzer and T. J. Gergel, ENCYCLOPEDIA OF NY, Somerset Publishers, St. Clair Shores, MI, 1982.

The fourth listing above is an extraordinarily valuable volume giving brief county and town histories, early settlers, church data, population statistics, newspapers being published in 1860, geographical features, and industrial activity. Not only are there these gazetteers for the state of NY, but such volumes have been published for many NY counties. These are usually combined gazetteers and business directories which came out in the period 1865-90. The above gazetteers and the county gazetteers may be found in NYSL, NYPL, and NYHS; some are available in other LGL and RL, and those pertaining to counties are usually located in LL in those counties.

Atlases (collections of maps) published before 1906 are available for the state of NY, for practically every county, and for most of the major cities. Some of the county and city atlases show the names of the landowners on the maps, and a few even have a list of all heads of households. Listings of available atlases for NY are:

__Research Publications, NY COUNTY AND REGIONAL HISTORIES AND ATLASES AVAILABLE ON MICROFILM, Research Publications, Woodbridge, CT, 1975.

__C. E. LeGear, US ATLASES, Library of Congress, Washington, DC, 1950-3, 2 volumes.

__ATLAS CARD CATALOG, 11th Floor, NYSL, Albany, NY. Search by town, city, county, state. Many atlases also in Microform Collection at NYSL.

__NYPL, DICTIONARY CATALOG OF THE MAP DIVISION, Hall and Co., Boston, MA, 1971, 10 volumes. Maps and atlases.

Among the very important atlases and other geographical works carrying NY maps are these volumes:

__D. H. Burr, AN ATLAS OF THE STATE OF NY, The Author, New York, NY, 1829. Maps, charts, place names.

__J. W. Barber and H. Howe, HISTORICAL COLLECTIONS OF THE STATE OF NY, Kennikat Press, Port Washington, NY, 1846(1970). Place origins, early NY map.

__J. W. Barber, PICTORIAL HISTORY OF THE STATE OF NY, Phinney, Cooperstown, NY, 1846. Geographical descriptions of places.

__J. R. Bien, ATLAS OF THE STATE OF NY, Bien & Co., New York, NY, 1895.

__HAMMOND'S ATLAS OF NY CITY AND THE METROPOLITAN DISTRICT, Burns, New York, NY, 1915. Detailed maps, street names.

__R. J. Rayback, RICHARDS' ATLAS OF NY STATE, Richards, Phoenix, NY, 1965. Includes land patent map.

__J. L. Andriot, TOWNSHIP ATLAS OF THE US, Andriot Associates, McLean, VA, 1977. NY maps, incorporated places, town boundaries, index.

__Genealogical Department of the CJCLDS, COUNTY FORMATIONS AND MINOR CIVIL DIVISIONS OF NY, The Department, Salt Lake City, UT, 1978. Detailed county maps showing towns and dates of origins.

__W. Thorndale and W. Dollarhide, MAP GUIDE TO THE FEDER-

AL CENSUSES, NY, 1790-1920, Dollarhide Systems, Bell
ingham, WA, 1985. Invaluable when searching censuses.
__I. N. P. Stokes, ICONOGRAPHY OF MANHATTAN ISLAND, 1498-
1909, Arno Press, New York, NY, 1915-28(1967), 6 volumes. Absolutely essential for maps of NY City.

Many maps are available for NY, for its counties,
for portions of the counties, and for cities and towns.
There are several nation-wide books which either list NY
maps and indicate sources of them or give descriptions of
good map collections:
__National Archives and Records Service, GUIDE TO CARTO-
GRAPHIC RECORDS IN THE NATIONAL ARCHIVES, The Service,
Washington, DC, 1971.
__National Archives and Records Service, GUIDE TO GENEA-
LOGICAL RESEARCH IN THE NATIONAL ARCHIVES, The Service,
Washington, DC, 1982, pages 255-62.
__J. R. Hebert, PANORAMIC MAPS OF ANGLO-AMERICAN CITIES
IN THE LIBRARY OF CONGRESS, The Library, Washington,
DC, 1984. Beautiful pre-1900 maps available for 124 NY
cities and towns.
__R. W. Stephenson, LAND OWNERSHIP MAPS IN THE LIBRARY OF
CONGRESS, The Library, Washington, DC, 1967. Pre-1900
county maps showing land owners, for 58 NY counties.
__Library of Congress, FIRE INSURANCE MAPS IN THE LIBRARY
OF CONGRESS, The Library, Washington, DC, 1981, pages
401-53. Maps of 645 cities and towns 1884-, much
detail.
__M. H. Shelley, WARD MAPS OF US CITIES, Library of
Congress, Washington, DC, 1975. Maps showing ward
divisions to aid you in census searches in Albany,
Brooklyn, Buffalo, NY City, and Rochester.
__NYPL, DICTIONARY CATALOG OF THE MAP DIVISION, Hall and
Co., Boston, MA, 1971, 10 volumes. Maps and atlases.
In addition, there are several sources specifically
devoted to listing NY maps (state, regional, county,
town, city, village):
__Historical Records Survey, INVENTORY OF MAPS LOCATED IN
VARIOUS STATE, COUNTY, MUNICIPAL, AND OTHER PUBLIC
OFFICES IN NY STATE (EXCLUSIVE OF NY CITY), WPA, Al-
bany, NY, 1942.
__D. E. E. Mix, CATALOGUE OF MAPS AND SURVEYS IN THE
OFFICE OF THE SECRETARY OF STATE, STATE ENGINEER AND
SURVEYOR, AND COMPTROLLER, AND THE NYSL, Van Benthuy-
sen, Albany, NY, 1859. NYSL has notes indicating
present locations of the maps. Some in NYSL, some in

NYSA, some in Office of General Services, and some in Department of Taxation and Finance.
__NY State Engineer and Surveyor, CATALOGUE OF MAPS AND FIELD BOOKS IN THE LAND BUREAU OF THE DEPARTMENT OF THE STATE ENGINEER AND SURVEYOR, Lyon, Albany, NY, 1920. Some in NYSL, some in NYSA, some in Department of Transportation.
__MAP CARD CATALOG, 11th Floor, NYSL, Albany, NY. Search by geographic location, town, city, county, state.
__J. B. Koetteritz, CATALOGUE OF MAPS, FIELD NOTES, SURVEYS, AND LAND PAPERS OF PATENTS, GRANTS, AND TRACTS IN COUNTIES IN THE FOREST PRESERVE OF NY, in ANNUAL REPORT OF THE FOREST COMMISSION FOR 1892, Lyon and Co., Albany, NY, 1893, pages 307-501.
__A. H. Wright, A CHECK LIST OF NY STATE COUNTY MAPS PUBLISHED 1779-1945, Cornell University Press, Ithaca, NY, 1965.

Your attention needs to be drawn to several specialized types of maps which can assist you as you attempt to locate your progenitor's land holdings and as you look for streams, roads, bridges, churches, cemeteries, towns, and villages in the vicinity. The first of these are highly detailed maps issued by the US Geological Survey which has mapped the entire state of NY and has produced a series of hundreds of maps, each covering a very small area (a fraction of a county). These maps are available at very reasonable cost. Write the following address and ask for the Index to Topographic Maps of NY and a NY Map Order Form.
__Branch of Distribution, Eastern Region, US Geological Survey, 1200 South Eads St., Arlington, VA 22202.
A second type of map which is very useful are the landowner maps which show the names of persons who own each piece of property. These are available as separate maps and some of them are also often in atlases (see book by Stephenson above). Another type of map is represented by the city and town panorama maps which are careful depictions of cities as they would be viewed from a balloon flying overhead (see book by Hebert above). Detailed city maps were also drawn for fire insurance purposes (see book mentioned above) and they constitute a fourth special type. A fifth category of map is made up of those which have marked the ward boundaries of larger cities. These are useful when you want to search unindexed census records for city dwellers, especially when

they are employed in conjunction with city directories (which give street addresses, and also sometimes contain ward maps or give ward boundaries).

The best collections for genealogically-related maps and atlases of NY are in the NYSL and NYPL. Other good collections are found in NYHS, Cornell University, the NA, and the Library of Congress, as well as in RL and LL in the areas where you are interested. When you seek gazetteers, atlases, and maps in these repositories, please be sure to look both in the main catalogs and the special map catalogs, indexes, listings, and collections. Most of the volumes mentioned in this section are available in NYSL, NYPL, NYGB, and NYHS, and some will be found in FHL(FHC), LGL, RL, and LL.

18. Genealogical indexes and compilations

There are a number of indexes and compilations for the colony and state of NY which list very large numbers of names. These are of considerable utility because they may save you going through many small volumes and detailed records, especially in the early stages of your search for NY ancestors. The nation-wide indexes and compilations of this sort include:

__SURNAME CATALOG and INTERNATIONAL GENEALOGICAL INDEX at FHL, Salt Lake City, UT, also available at every FHC. [See section on FHL and FHC in Chapter 3.] Over 90 million entries.

__FAMILY GROUP RECORDS COLLECTION, FHL, Salt Lake City, UT, access through FHC. [Be sure to search both the Patron and the Archives Sections of the Family Group Records Collection.] Over 9 million entries.

__National Archives, GENERAL INDEX TO COMPILED MILITARY SERVICE RECORDS OF REVOLUTIONARY WAR SOLDIERS, SAILORS, AND MEMBERS OF ARMY STAFF DEPARTMENTS, The Archives, Washington, DC, Microfilm M860, 58 rolls.

__F. Rider, AMERICAN GENEALOGICAL-BIOGRAPHICAL INDEX, Godfrey Memorial Library, Middletown, CT, 1942-, over 180 volumes. Over 12 million entries. Be sure to check both series.

__P. W. Filby and M. K. Meyer, PASSENGER AND IMMIGRATION LISTS INDEX, Gale Research Co., Detroit, MI, 1981-, 3 basic volumes plus annual supplements. Over a million entries.

M. J. Kaminkow, GENEALOGIES IN THE LIBRARY OF CONGRESS, Magna Carta, Baltimore, MD, 1972-7, 3 volumes, plus A COMPLEMENT TO GENEALOGIES IN THE LIBRARY OF CONGRESS, Magna Carta, Baltimore, MD, 1981. Over 50,000 names.

NYPL, DICTIONARY CATALOG OF THE LOCAL HISTORY AND GENEALOGY DIVISION, NYPL, G. K. Hall, Boston, MA, 1974.

Library of Congress, NATIONAL UNION CATALOG OF MANU-SCRIPT COLLECTIONS, The Library, Washington, DC, annual volumes since 1959, index in each volume.

National Society of the DAR, LIBRARY CATALOG, VOLUME 1: FAMILY HISTORIES AND GENEALOGIES, The Society, Washington, DC, 1982.

Newberry Library, GENEALOGICAL INDEX OF THE NEWBERRY LIBRARY, G. K. Hall, Boston, MA, 1960, 4 volumes.

Everton Publishers, COMPUTERIZED ROOTS CELLAR and COMPUTERIZED FAMILY FILE, The Publishers, Logan, UT.

J. Munsell's Sons, INDEX TO AMERICAN GENEALOGIES, 1711-1908, Genealogical Publishing Co., Baltimore, MD, 1967. 60,000 references.

In addition to the above nation-wide indexes and compilations, there are a sizable number of large indexes and compilations dealing exclusively with NY. Among the most notable of these are:

MASTER INDEX, NY STATE GENEALOGICAL RECORDS, The DAR, Albany, NY, 1971, and MASTER INDEX SUPPLEMENT 1972-8, RECORDS AND CORRECTIONS, The DAR, Albany, NY, 1978.

SURNAMES CARD INDEX and VITAL RECORDS CARD INDEX, Local History and Genealogy Section, NYSL, Albany, NY.

INDEXES TO THE FEDERAL NY CENSUS SCHEDULES OF 1790, 1800/10/20/30/40/50/60, 1880, 1900. See census section in this chapter.

CARD, COMPUTER AND PUBLISHED CATALOGS, SPECIAL INDEXES, AND LISTS in NYSL, NYPL, NYGB, and NYHS. See chapter 3.

National Archives, MICROFILM INDEX OF COMPILED SERVICE RECORDS FOR UNION ARMY VOLUNTEERS OF NY, The Archives, Washington, DC, Microfilm M551, 159 rolls.

Holland Society of NY, COMPILED FAMILY GENEALOGIES, MEMBERSHIP FILES, and HISTORICAL AND GENEALOGICAL MANUSCRIPT COLLECTION, The Society, New York, NY. Also on 164 rolls of microfilm at FHL, Salt Lake City, UT, available through FHC.

O. Archer, GENERAL INDEX TO THE DOCUMENTS [GENERAL ASSEMBLY PAPERS] OF THE STATE OF NY, 1777-1865, Weed, Parsons, and Co., Albany, NY, 1866.

__J. Farmer, LIST OF THE GRADUATES AT COLLEGES IN NY AND NJ TO 1834, Perkins & Marvin, Boston, MA, 1838.

__N. O. Ireland and W. Irving, CUTTER INDEX, A CONSOLIDATED INDEX OF CUTTER'S NINE GENEALOGY SERIES, Ireland Indexing Services, Fallbrook, CA, 1973. About 3150 names.

__St. Nicholas Society, ST. NICHOLAS SOCIETY GENEALOGICAL RECORD, The Society, New York, NY, 1905-80, volumes 1-9. Genealogies of members.

__REGISTER OF THE COLONIAL DAMES OF AMERICA OF NY, with ADDENDA, The Dames, Manchester and New York, NY, 1926 and 1931.

__SIX GENERATION ANCESTOR TABLES, Central NY Genealogical Society, Syracuse, NY, 1976-7, 5 volumes. About 5500 surnames.

__S. V. Talcott, GENEALOGICAL NOTES ON NY AND NEW ENGLAND FAMILIES, Genealogical Publishing Co., Baltimore, MD, 1883(1973). 18,000 names. Use with care.

__E. Toedenberg, CATALOG OF THE AMERICAN GENEALOGIES IN THE LIBRARY OF THE LONG ISLAND HISTORICAL SOCIETY, The Society, Brooklyn, NY, 1935.

__H. P. Toler, NEW HARLEM REGISTER, A GENEALOGY OF THE DESCENDANTS OF THE 23 ORIGINAL PATENTEES IN NEW HARLEM, 1630 TO DATE, New Harlem Publishing Co., New York, NY, 1903. 30,000 names. Use with care.

__J. R. Totten, NY Genealogical and Biographical Society, REGISTER OF PEDIGREES, The Society, New York, NY, 1913.

__TREE TALKS, INDEXES TO VOLUMES 1-8, 1970-7, Central NY Genealogical Society, Syracuse, NY, 1978. Almost 100,000 name entries.

__B. A. Falk, Jr., and V. R. Falk, PERSONAL NAME INDEX TO NY TIMES INDEX, 1851-1979, Roxbury, Succasunna, NJ, and Verdi, NV, 1978-85.

__J. D. Worden, MASTER INDEX TO THE NY GENEALOGICAL AND BIOGRAPHICAL RECORD, 1870-1982, The Author, Franklin, OH, 1983. Does not include all names.

Most of the published works mentioned above will be found in NYSL, NYPL, and NYGB, many in NYHS, FHL(FHC), LGL, and RL, and some in LL. The microfilms should be sought in NYSL, NYPL, FHL(FHC), NA, and NAFB.

19. Genealogical periodicals

Several genealogical periodicals and some historical periodicals carrying genealogical data or aids have

been or are being published for NY. These journals and
newsletters contain genealogies, local history data,
genealogical records, family queries and answers, book
reviews, and other pertinent information. If you had a
NY progenitor, you will find it of great value to sub-
scribe to one or more of the state-wide periodicals, as
well as any periodicals published in the region, county,
or city where he/she lived. Periodicals pertinent to NY
research may be divided into four classes: (1) those that
have state-wide coverage, (2) those that are national or
state-wide but apply only to special groups, (3) those
that have regional coverage, and (4) those that cover
individual counties or cities.

Chief among the periodicals which have a state-wide
coverage of NY are:
__THE NY GENEALOGICAL AND BIOGRAPHICAL RECORD, NY Genea-
logical and Biographical Society, New York, NY, 1870-,
volume 1-, with J. D. Worden, MASTER INDEX, 1870-1982,
The Author, Franklin, OH, 1983, with F. E. Youngs,
SUBJECT INDEX, Volumes 1-38, The Author, New York, NY,
with G. A. Barber, SUBJECT INDEX, Volumes 39-94, The
Author, New York, NY, and with G. A. Barber, NY GENEA-
LOGICAL AND BIOGRAPHICAL RECORD SURNAME INDEX TO VOL-
UMES 1-40, The Author, New York, NY, 4 typescript
volumes.
__J. W. Foley, EARLY SETTLERS OF NY STATE, THEIR ANCES-
TORS AND DESCENDANTS, T. J. Foley, Akron, NY, 1934-42,
9 volumes, with INDEX TO NAMES, 1950. Mainly western
and central NY.
__YESTERYEARS MAGAZINE, M. O. Goodelle, editor, 3 Seymour
St., Auburn, NY 13021, since 1957-.
There are also a couple of national genealogical journals
which often carry NY articles:
__THE NEW ENGLAND HISTORICAL AND GENEALOGICAL REGISTER,
New England Historic Genealogical Society, 101 Newbury
St., Boston, MA 02116, with INDEX OF PERSONS, VOLUMES
1-50, and INDEX TO GENEALOGIES AND PEDIGREES, VOLUMES
1-50, and M. W. Parsons, ABRIDGED INDEX, VOLUMES 51-
112, The Author, Marlborough, MA, 1959.
__NATIONAL GENEALOGICAL SOCIETY QUARTERLY, The Society,
4527 17th St., North, Arlington, VA 22207-2363, with
TOPICAL INDEX, VOLUMES 1-50, The Society, Washington,
DC, 1964. Index contains many, but not all, names.

Included in the major periodicals which carry genealogical data of _special_ _groups_ in the state of NY and some which are national in scope are:

__DOROT, THE JOURNAL OF THE JEWISH GENEALOGICAL SOCIETY, The Society, PO Box 6398, New York, NY 10128.

__DE HAELVE MAEN, Holland Society of NY, 122 East 58th St., New York, NY 10022.

__HOLLAND SOCIETY OF NY YEARBOOKS, The Society, 122 East 58th St., New York, NY 10022, with L. Duermyer, INDEX TO PUBLICATIONS, The Society, New York, NY, 1977.

__TOLEDOT, THE JOURNAL OF JEWISH GENEALOGY, 808 West End Ave., Suite 1006, Flushing, NY 10025.

Among the very useful _regional_ periodicals of NY are the ones listed below:

__H. E. Veeder, DUTCH SETTLERS SOCIETY OF ALBANY YEARBOOKS, The Society, Albany, NY, 1924/5-.

__JOURNAL OF LONG ISLAND HISTORY.

__LIFELINES, Northern NY American-Canadian Genealogical Society, PO Box 1256, Plattsburgh, NY 12901.

__LONG ISLAND HISTORICAL SOCIETY QUARTERLY, 1939-42, The Society, 128 Pierrepont St., Brooklyn, NY 11201.

__MID-HUDSON GENEALOGICAL JOURNAL, 1112 Pond Dr., West, Columbia, SC 29169.

__THE MOHAWK (Schenectady and Montgomery Counties), 60 Cedar Hts., Rhinebeck, NY 12572.

__NIAGARA FRONTIER GENEALOGICAL MAGAZINE, Buffalo and Erie County Historical Society, 25 Nottingham Ct., Buffalo, NY 14216.

__OLDE ULSTER, AN HISTORICAL AND GENEALOGICAL MAGAZINE, 1905-14.

__QUARTERLY OF THE ST. LAWRENCE HISTORICAL SOCIETY, Canton, NY.

__ST. LAWRENCE VALLEY GENEALOGICAL SOCIETY NEWSLETTER, The Society, PO Box 86, Potsdam, NY 13676-0086.

__TREE TALKS, Central NY Genealogical Society, PO Box 104, Colvin Station, Syracuse, NY 13205.

__WESTERN NY GENEALOGICAL SOCIETY JOURNAL, The Society, PO Box 338, Hamburg, NY 14075.

The journal TREE TALKS (TT) is especially important for central NY because they have published _many_ records for counties in this area. Included are vital records generated 1847-50, 1850 census mortality data, justice of the peace marriages, estate records, naturalizations, military lists, church records, and municipal records.

Some of the local periodicals which publish valuable ancestor data are given here. Several of these also cover adjacent areas:
_THE CAPITAL (Albany and Rensselaer Counties), 60 Cedar Hts., Rhinebeck, NY 12572.
_THE COLUMBIA, 60 Cedar Hts., Rhinebeck, NY 12572.
_THE DUTCHESS, Dutchess County Genealogical Society, PO Box 708, Poughkeepsie, NY 12603.
_FRANKLIN HISTORICAL REVIEW, Franklin County Historical Society, 51 Milwaukee St., Malone, NY 12953.
_HEAR YE, HEAR YE, Rochester Genealogical Society, PO Box 92533, Rochester, NY 14692.
_NIAGARA COUNTY GENEALOGICAL SOCIETY NEWS, The Society, 2650 Hess Rd., Appleton, NY 14008.
_NASSAU GENEALOGICAL WORKSHOP NEWSLETTER, The Workshop, 245 Main St., Port Washington, NY 11050.
_NYANDO ROOTS, Nyando Roots Genealogical Society, PO Box 175, Massena, NY 13662.
_ORANGE COUNTY GENEALOGICAL SOCIETY QUARTERLY, The Society, Old Court House, 101 Main St., Goshen, NY 10924.
_THE SARATOGA, RD 1, Box 129, Rhinebeck, NY 12572.
_SUFFOLK COUNTY HISTORICAL SOCIETY REGISTER AND CLARION, The Society, 300 West Main St., Riverhead, NY 11901.
_ULSTER GENIE, Ulster County Genealogical Society, PO Box 333, Hurley, NY 11443.
_WESTCHESTER COUNTY GENEALOGICAL SOCIETY NEWSLETTER, The Society, PO Box 518, White Plains, NY 10603.
Good collections of NY genealogically-oriented periodicals will be found in NYSL, NYPL, NYGB, and NYHS, and those relating to specific localities can be located in appropriate RL and LL.

Not only do articles pertaining to NY genealogy appear in the above publications, they are also printed in other genealogical journals. Fortunately, indexes to articles in major genealogical periodicals are available:
_For periodicals published 1858-1952, consult D. L. Jacobus, INDEX TO GENEALOGICAL PERIODICALS, Genealogical Publishing Co., Baltimore, MD, 1973.
_For periodicals published 1957-62, consult the annual volumes by I. Waldenmaier, ANNUAL INDEX TO GENEALOGICAL PERIODICALS AND FAMILY HISTORIES, The Author, Washington, DC, 1957-62.
_For periodicals published 1962-9 and 1974-87, consult the annual volumes by various editors, E. S. Rogers, G.

E. Russell, L. C. Towle, and C. M. Mayhew, GENEALOGICAL
PERIODICAL ANNUAL INDEX, various publishers, most
recently Heritage Books, Bowie, MD, 1962-9, 1974-87.
These index volumes should be sought in NYSL, NYPL, NYGB,
and FHL(available through FHC), most LGL, some RL, and a
few LL. In them, you ought to consult all general NY
listings, then all listings under the counties which
concern you, as well as listings under family names, if
included (only in the earlier index volumes).

20. Genealogical and historical societies

In the state of NY various societies for the study
of genealogy, the discovery of hereditary lineages, the
accumulation of ancestor data, and the publication of the
materials have been organized. In addition to these
genealogical societies, there are many historical societies which devote at least some time and effort to genealogical data collection and publication. Of course,
there are some historical societies which have little or
no genealogical interest. You should further recognize
that some societies which once made notable genealogical
and historical contributions no longer exist, and that
smaller societies tend to come and go. The NY societies
which have a genealogical focus (large or small) are of
several types: (1) societies with a national scope which
are based in NY, (2) state-wide societies, both general
and with special interests, (3) regional societies, and
(4) local societies (county, city, borough, town, village).

The major societies with a national scope which are
based in NY are:
__American-Italian Historical Association, 209 Flagg Pl.,
Staten Island, NY 10304.
__Adoptees Liberty Movement Association, PO Box 154, New
York, NY 10033.
__Colonial Dames of America, 421 East 61st St., New York,
NY 10021.
__Franco-American Genealogical Society, RFD 2, Voorhees-
ville, NY 12186.
__Holland Society, 122 East 58th St., New York, NY 10022.
__Huguenot Historical Society, 14 Forest Glen Rd., New
Paltz, NY 12561.
__Huguenot Society of America, 122 East 58th St., New
York, NY 10022.

__Jewish Genealogical Society, PO Box 6398, New York, NY 10128.

__Russian Historical and Genealogical Society, 971 First Ave., New York, NY 10022.

__Swiss-American Historical Society, PO Box 395, Church Street Station, New York, NY 10005.

Chief among the societies which have state-wide coverage of NY, both general and special interest societies, are:

__Empire State Society, Sons of the American Revolution, 13 Garden Ave., Massapequa, NY 11758.

__Genealogical Conference of NY, Interlaken, NY 14847-0299.

__National Society of Colonial Dames of NY, 215 East 71st St., New York, NY 10021.

__NY Genealogical and Biographical Society, 122 East 58th St., New York, NY 10022.

__NY Historical Society, 170 Central Park West, New York, NY 10024.

__NY State Historical Association, Fenimore House, Lake Rd., Cooperstown, NY 13326.

__Palatines to America, NY Chapter, Rt. 92, Box L72, Selkirk, NY 12158.

__Sons of the Revolution in the State of NY, 54 Pearl St., New York, NY 10004.

   In addition to the above organizations which have state-wide (or nation-wide) coverage, there are some important regional societies which concentrate on genealogical matters or which have some genealogical interests:

__Adirondack Genealogical-Historical Society, 100 Main St., Saranac Lake, NY 12983.

__Capital District Genealogical Society, PO Box 2175, Empire State Plaza Station, Albany, NY 12220.

__Cayuga-Owasco Lakes Historical Society, PO Box 247, Moravia, NY 13118.

__Central NY Genealogical Society, PO Box 104, Colvin Station, Syracuse, NY 13205.

__Finger Lakes Genealogical Society, PO Box 47, Seneca Falls, NY 13148.

__Minisink Valley Historical Society, Port Jervis, NY 12771.

__Northeastern NY Genealogical Society, Rt. 2, Box 3B, Appleton, NY 14008.

__Northern NY American Canadian Genealogical Society, PO Box 1256, Plattsburgh, NY 12901-1256.

__St. Lawrence Valley Genealogical Society, PO Box 86,
Potsdam, NY 13676-0086.
__Western NY Genealogical Society, PO Box 338, Hamburg,
NY 14075.

There are also many local genealogical and historical societies in NY which can be of immense help to you
in your quest for your NY ancestor(s). Many of the
resident members of these societies are generally very
knowledgeable about the background, the early families,
and the available records of their local areas. By
consulting them, you can often save valuable time as they
guide you in your work. The local societies also can
often tell you if anyone else is working on or has worked
on your family lines. The most important of these local
societies are named under the county listings in Chapters
4-5, where their addresses will be given to permit you to
contact them. A detailed listing of many of these and
some others is:
__American Association of State and Local History, DIREC-
TORY OF HISTORICAL AGENCIES IN THE US AND CANADA, The
Association, Nashville, TN, latest edition.
It is advisable for all NY genealogical searchers to join
the NY Genealogical and Biographical Society, as well as
any regional society and/or county organization which is
in your progenitor's area. All correspondence with such
societies should always be accompanied by a long SASE.

Every county, city, town, and village in NY state
has an appointed historian, there being over 1600 of them
in office at the present time. These people are usually
well-informed concerning the histories and available
records in their areas. Some of them have genealogical
interests and some do not. Some have time to help you,
others are far too busy to do so. All correspondence
with them should be very brief, accompanied by a long
SASE, and should inquire what fees are charged in case
they have time to give you assistance. These historians
are listed in:
__P. J. Vogel, DIRECTORY OF NY STATE COUNTY AND MUNICIPAL
HISTORIANS, County Historians Association of NY State
and the NY State Education Department, Albany, NY,
latest edition.

21. Land records

One of the most important types of NY genealogical
records is the type which deals with land. This is
because throughout much of its history, especially early,
NY was heavily involved in agriculture. As with all the
original colonies, NY had an abundance of land which it
distributed to those who would develop it. There are
basically _five_ types of land records in NY. (1) The
first kind involves transactions in which the government
of NY (colonial or state) originally transferred land to
private groups or individuals. These transactions made
use of documents of several sorts and generated several
types of records. Among them were applications for
grants, patents (or grants), surveys, maps, warrants of
survey, and survey field books, the most important being
the first two. (2) The _second_ type of land records
involves the transfer of NY land as military land grants
to NY Revolutionary War veterans. These records involve
documents very similar to those previously mentioned,
except the applications are generally called petitions.
(3) The _third_ kind of land records involves compliance
with a NY state law requiring aliens to file a deposition
of intention to become citizens before they could acquire
land. These depositions were filed with the Secretary of
State during 1825-1913. (4) The _fourth_ type of land
records relates to the fact that NY made many large
grants to entrepreneurs, both individuals and companies.
These receivers of large grants subdivided the land and
leased the smaller tracts to tenants or sold them, usually on long-term credit. Records of the large landholders
(entrepreneurs, speculators, companies, manors, patroonships) often contain data on persons whose names may not
appear in any other types of land records (colony, state,
or county). Chief among these are tenants who leased
land and persons who defaulted on credit purchases. (5)
The _fifth_ sort of land records involves land transferred
from one private individual or company to another private
individual or company (after the original transfer of
land by NY). The documents in these transactions include
deeds, mortgages, and leases.

The _first_ category of land records (transfers from
the colonial or state government to the first private
owners) dates from the earliest years of the Dutch colonial period. There are several major sets of these re-

cords and many other supplementary ones. The major sets
are:

__NY LAND GRANT APPLICATION FILES (COLONIAL MANUSCRIPTS:
INDORSED LAND PAPERS), 1643-1803, NYSA, Albany, NY.
Indexed in Secretary of State, CALENDAR OF NY COLONIAL
MANUSCRIPTS, INDORSED LAND PAPERS, 1643-1803, Weed,
Parsons, and Co., Albany, NY, 1864.

__NY LAND GRANT APPLICATION FILES, 1803-forward, NY
Office of General Services, Albany, NY.

__LAND PATENTS, 1630-64, in Dutch Colonial Records of the
NY Department of State, NYSA, Albany, NY.

__C. T. Gehring, NY HISTORICAL MANUSCRIPTS: DUTCH, VOL-
UMES GG, HH, & II, LAND PAPERS, 1630-51, 1654-64,
Genealogical Publishing Co., Baltimore, MD, 1980.

__TRANSLATIONS OF DUTCH PATENTS AND DEEDS, 1630-74, 4
volumes, in Land Records of the NY Department of State,
NYSA, Albany, NY. Also at FHL(FHC).

__NY LAND PATENTS, 1664-1954, NYSA, Albany, NY, indexed
in MICROFILMED CUMULATIVE NY LAND PATENT INDEX, 1664-
1954, NYSA, Albany, NY. Patents 1666-1912 and index
also at FHL(FHC).

__NY SURVEYOR GENERAL MAPS, 1775-1900, indexed in D. E.
E. Mix, CATALOGUE OF MAPS AND SURVEYS IN THE OFFICE OF
THE SECRETARY OF STATE, STATE ENGINEER AND SURVEYOR,
AND COMPTROLLER, AND THE NYSL, Van Benthuysen, Albany,
NY, 1859. Reprint edition of 1982 gives present loca-
tions of the materials.

__J. B. Koetteritz, CATALOGUE OF MAPS, FIELD NOTES,
SURVEYS, AND LAND PAPERS OF PATENTS, GRANTS, AND TRACTS
IN COUNTIES IN THE FOREST PRESERVE OF NY, in ANNUAL
REPORT OF THE FOREST COMMISSION FOR 1892, Lyon and Co.,
Albany, NY, 1893, pages 307-501.

__NY State Engineer and Surveyor, CATALOGUE OF MAPS AND
FIELD BOOKS IN THE LAND BUREAU OF THE DEPARTMENT OF THE
STATE ENGINEER AND SURVEYOR, Lyon, Albany, NY, 1920.
Records now in the State Department of Transportation.

All of the above records should be examined carefully in your quest for an ancestor who applied for
government land. If you fail to find the name you are
seeking and you have a suspicion that your forebear received land, there are some further records of value in
the NYSA. The ones which you might want to explore
include:

__ACCOUNT BOOKS FOR BONDS AND MORTGAGES FOR THE SALE OF

LANDS, 1797-1910, 41 volumes, in Land Records of the NY Department of Audit and Control, NYSA, Albany, NY.
__DEEDS TO LAND SOLD FOR NON-PAYMENT OF TAXES, 1833-94, in Land Records of the NY Department of Audit and Control, NYSA, Albany, NY.
__BRITISH COLONIAL WARRANTS OF SURVEY, 1721-76, in British Colonial Records of the NY Department of State, NYSA, Albany, NY.
__SURVEYOR GENERALS' REPORTS, 1795-1829, in Legislative Records of the NY Department of State, NYSA, Albany, NY.
__LAND PATENTS, TRANSCRIPTIONS PURSUANT TO AN ACT OF 1786, 1664-1786, 12 volumes, Land Records of the NY Department of State, NYSA, Albany, NY.
__ABSTRACTS OF LAND PATENTS, 1695-1886, 6 volumes, Land Records of the NY Department of State, NYSA, Albany, NY.
__FIELD BOOKS OF THE SURVEYOR GENERAL'S OFFICE, 1762-1881, 54 volumes, with INDEX TO FIELD BOOKS AND MAPS, 1701-1848, Land Records of the NY Department of State, NYSA, Albany, NY. Also at FHL(FHC).
__ABSTRACTS OF LAND GRANTS, 1666-1775, Colonial Treasurer Records of the NY Department of Taxation and Finance, NYSA, Albany, NY.
__LAND SURVEY FIELD NOTES and LAND SURVEY MAPS, Records of the State Engineer and Surveyor in the NY Department of Transportation, NYSA, Albany, NY.
As you can see from the above references, not many of the records are indexed, so information from those in the preceding paragraph may be needed to avoid an extensive search. Other records bearing upon early land grants (patents) are listed in:
__NYSA, GUIDE TO RECORDS IN THE NYSA, The Archives, Albany, NY, 1981, especially pages 59, 124-8, 131, 136-7, and 143.
__NYSA, PUBLIC RECORDS RELATING TO LAND IN NY STATE, The Archives, Albany, NY, 1979.

As mentioned in Chapter 1 and above, NY made many grants of large tracts to individual entrepreneurs, speculators, companies, and corporations. Most of these, along with the patentees (receivers), the dates, the locations, and the numbers of acres, are listed in:
__J. H. French, GAZETTEER OF THE STATE OF NY, Friedman, Port Washington, NY, 1860, pages 49-53.

In addition, the county descriptions in this gazetteer
contain information on numerous smaller grants, tracts,
purchases, and early settlers. An excellent account of
the Phelps and Gorham purchase of all of western NY and
its disposition (Morris, Holland Land Company) is given
on pages 321-3. Among the better sets of maps showing
the detailed boundaries of the larger grants and patents
is the set included in:
___J. R. Bien, ATLAS OF THE STATE OF NY, Bien & Co., New
York, NY, 1895, Map 3.
Another useful publication containing helpful maps of
this sort is:
___E. B. O'Callaghan, THE DOCUMENTARY HISTORY OF THE STATE
OF NY, Weed, Parsons, & Co., Albany, NY, 1849-51, 4
volumes.
Before VT became a state, NH, MA, and NY made grants in
the area. Those made by NY are listed in:
___VT Secretary of State, NY LAND PATENTS IN VT, 1688-
1786, VT State Papers, Montpelier, VT, 1947.

The second category of land records is that which
refers to the transfer of NY land by the state to its
Revolutionary War veterans. You will recall that after
the war NY first set aside land in the northeastern
section of the state (now Clinton, Essex, and Franklin
Counties), but only a few veterans wanted it. Then in
1788-9, land in the new Military Tract (now in Cayuga,
Cortland, Onondaga, Seneca, Oswego, Schuyler, Tompkins,
and Wayne Counties) was offered. Many veterans received
land, but most sold it, only some moving onto the land.
The first place you should look for your progenitor to
see if he received bounty land is this book:
___THE BALLOTING BOOK, AND OTHER DOCUMENTS RELATING TO
MILITARY BOUNTY LANDS IN THE STATE OF NY, Heart of the
Lakes Publishers, Interlaken, NY, 1825(1978).
If you have no success, further searches may be made in a
series of articles relating to Revolutionary bounty lands
which has been published in the periodical Tree Talks:
___ARTICLES ON NY REVOLUTIONARY WAR BOUNTY LAND RECIP-
IENTS, Tree Talks, volumes 4-12, 17.
Further research may be carried out using the original
records in NYSA:
___INDEX TO ABSTRACTS OF LAND PATENTS FOR LANDS IN THE
MILITARY TRACT, 1764-97, Land Records of the NY Depart-
ment of State, NYSA, Albany, NY.

__PETITIONS FOR BOUNTY LANDS FOR REVOLUTIONARY SERVICE, 1778-1830, Legislative Records of the NY Department of State, NYSA, Albany, NY.

__PATENTS FOR LANDS IN THE MILITARY TRACT, Land Records of the NY Department of State, NYSA, Albany, NY.

__ABSTRACTS OF LAND PATENTS FOR LANDS IN THE MILITARY TRACT, 1764-97, 8 volumes, NYSA, Albany, NY.

There is another series of records dealing with land transactions during and after the Revolutionary War. The newly-formed state of NY confiscated the lands of Loyalists and then sold them to Patriot purchasers. Among these records are the following books and articles:

__ABSTRACTS OF SALES BY THE COMMISSIONERS OF FORFEITURE IN THE SOUTHERN DISTRICT OF NY STATE, NY Genealogical and Biographical Record, volume 59, pages 108 ff.

__FORFEITED LOYALIST LANDS IN THE WESTERN DISTRICT OF NY, ALBANY AND TRYON COUNTIES, NY History, volume 35, pages 239 ff.

__R. A. East and J. Judd, THE LOYALIST AMERICANS, A FOCUS ON GREATER NY, Sleepy Hollow Restorations, Tarrytown, NY, 1975.

__H. B. Yoshpe, DISPOSITION OF LOYALIST ESTATES IN THE SOUTHERN DISTRICT OF THE STATE OF NY, Columbia University Press, New York, 1939.

There are also materials of value in the NYSA:

__REPORTS, PETITIONS, AND CORRESPONDENCE RELATING TO FORFEITED ESTATES, Legislative Records of the NY Department of State, NYSA, Albany, NY.

The third category of NY land records is made up of unique materials called alien depositions of intent to become citizens. These depositions were filed by NY aliens with the NY Secretary of State. Only if such documents had been filed could an alien then purchase property. The depositions date from 1825 to 1913. Those for the period 1825-48 have been published as:

__K. Scott and R. Conway, NY ALIEN RESIDENTS, 1825-48, Genealogical Publishing Co., Baltimore, MD, 1978.

The originals of these 1825-48 records plus those beyond 1848 are in the NYSA:

__INDEX TO ALIEN DEPOSITIONS, 1825-1913, Alien Registration Records of the NY Department of State, NYSA, Albany, NY.

__ALIEN DEPOSITIONS OF INTENT TO BECOME CITIZENS, 1825-

1913, Alien Registration Records of the NY Department of State, NYSA, Albany, NY.

__ABSTRACTS OF ALIEN DEPOSITIONS, 1825-1913, Alien Registration Records of the NY Department of State, NYSA, Albany, NY.

The depositions after 1848 contain only the alien's name and his county, but those before that (the published ones) give more data.

The _fourth_ category of NY records is made up of private records of the large land purchasers who subdivided their land and then leased it or sold it on long-term time payments. Their records show the lessees and the persons who made the payments on time. The land was generally not transferred to the persons until all payments had been made. Sometimes the large purchaser's records also appear in the NY county land records, but often they do not or are incompletely included. Among published records of this type are:

__O. Turner, HISTORY OF THE PIONEER SETTLEMENT OF PHELP'S AND GORHAM'S PURCHASE AND MORRIS RESERVE, Heart of the Lakes Publishers, Interlaken, NY, 1854(1976).

__O. Turner, PIONEER HISTORY OF THE HOLLAND PURCHASE OF WESTERN NEW YORK, Heart of the Lakes Publishers, Interlaken, NY, 1850(1976).

__A. H. Wright, OLD NORTHAMPTON OF WESTERN NY AND NORTHAMPTON RECORDS, Rochester Historical Society, Rochester, NY, 1944. All of NY west of the Genesee River was known as Northampton Town of Ontario County 1797-1802.

__Buffalo Historical Society, PUBLICATIONS OF THE BUFFALO HISTORICAL SOCIETY, The Society, Buffalo, NY, volumes for years 1910, 1924, 1937, and 1941.

__T. Witmer, DEED TABLES IN THE COUNTY OF ERIE AS SOLD BY THE HOLLAND LAND COMPANY, Clapp, Matthews, and Co., Buffalo, NY, 1859.

__G. E. Kershaw, THE KENNEBECK PROPRIETORS, 1749-75, Heritage Books, Bowie, MD, 1975.

__H. Melick, THE MANOR OF FORDHAM AND ITS FOUNDER, Fordham University Press, Bronx, NY, 1950. Many early families and land records.

__J. Pearson and A. J. F. van Laer, EARLY RECORDS OF THE CITY AND COUNTY OF ALBANY AND COLONY OF RENSSELAERWYCK, University Microfilms, Ann Arbor, MI, 1869-1919(1967), 4 volumes. Land records 1678-1704, mortgages 1658-60.

__C. Buck and W. McDermott, EIGHTEENTH CENTURY DOCUMENTS

OF THE NINE PARTNERS PATENT, Dutchess County Historical
Society, Poughkeepsie, NY, 1890.
___COSBY MANOR RENT BOOK, Tree Talks, volume 20, page 131.
___DUANESBURGH LEASES, 1785, NY Genealogical and Biograph-
ical Record, volume 71, page 150.
___S. B. Kim, THE MANOR OF CORTLANDT AND ITS TENANTS,
1697-1776, Microfilm, 1966.
___LITTLE PARTNERS RENT BOOK, The Dutchess, December,
1973, page 26.
___RENT ROLL OF PHILIPS' ESTATE, 1776-84, NY Genealogical
and Biographical Record, volume 108, page 74.
___A. J. F. van Laer, SETTLERS OF RENSSELAERWYCK, 1630-58,
Genealogical Publishing Co., Baltimore, MD, 1908(1980).
___PURCHASERS UNDER LAND CONTRACTS IN 1835 (WESTERN NY),
Western NY Genealogical Society Journal, volumes 3-4.

There are also some microfilm copies of important
records of large land purchasers:
___MICROFILMS OF ALBION AND BATAVIA HOLLAND LAND OFFICE
RECORDS, over 20 rolls, FHL, Salt Lake City, UT (avail-
able through FHC). Deeds, registers, ledgers, payment
records, mortgages, land accounts.
___MICROFILM OF HOLLAND LAND COMPANY 1806 STATEMENTS OF
SETTLERS, Microfilm No. 1912, Cornell University Libra-
ry, Ithaca, NY.
___MICROFILMS OF PULTENEY ESTATE RECORDS, 9 rolls, FHL,
Salt Lake City, UT (available through FHC). Land
sales, deeds.
In addition, there are some major collections of land
records of these large purchasers in repositories:
___HOLLAND LAND COMPANY TITLE DOCUMENTS (1786-1910), FIELD
NOTES (1798-9), MAPS (around 1802), Land Records of the
NY Department of State, NYSA, Albany, NY.
___HOLLAND LAND COMPANY RECORDS, State Engineer and Sur-
veyor Land Records of the NY Department of Transporta-
tion, NYSA, Albany, NY.
___HOLLAND LAND COMPANY PAPERS, Buffalo and Erie County
Historical Society, Buffalo, NY.
___HOLLAND LAND COMPANY RECORDS, 1790-1840, NYSL, Albany,
NY.
___OSGOOD PAPERS OF THE HOLLAND PURCHASE, 1781-1848,
Ontario Historical Society, Canandaigua, NY.
___HOLLAND PURCHASE PUBLICATIONS AND MANUSCRIPTS, Holland
Purchase Historical Society, Batavia, NY.
___HOLLAND LAND COMPANY RECORDS, 1802-63, 39 volumes and 8

rolls of microfilm, Cornell University Library, Ithaca, NY.

__LEDYARD PAPERS (1793-1916) and RIDER PAPERS (1828-1945) on THE HOLLAND PURCHASE, Cornell University Library, Ithaca, NY.

__LORENZO COLLECTION, HOLLAND LAND PAPERS, 1793-1897, Syracuse University Library, Syracuse, NY.

__PAPERS OF PHELPS AND GORHAM, 1784-1818, Ontario Historical Society, Canandaigua, NY.

__HURLBURT PAPERS, PULTENEY ESTATE, 1790-1830, NYSL, Albany, NY.

__PULTENEY PAPERS (Proceedings of the NY State Historical Association, volume 20, page 83), Steuben County Department of History and Archives, Bath, NY.

You will notice that the above references pertain largely to the Holland, Phelps and Gorham, and Pulteney lands. As you are well aware from Chapter 1 and from the long list of large NY land grants in French's Gazetteer, many other entrepreneurs and companies received large tracts of land and then leased or sold parcels of it to individuals. The records of a number of these are located in various libraries, archives, museums, and societies in NY. They may be easily located by searching the indexes to:

__US Library of Congress, THE NATIONAL UNION CATALOG OF MANUSCRIPT COLLECTIONS, The Library, Washington, DC, 1959-. Annual volumes. Both annual and cumulative indexes. Search the indexes under county, city, and town names, under name of land company, under land, under land agents, under land grants, under land settlement, under land transactions, under land-NY, under NY-land.

The _fifth_ category of land records is that which refers to transfers of land from one private owner to another. Included among these are conveyances, deeds, mortgages, and leases. It is important to remember that many New Yorkers were tenants and that many others bought land on time. There are not as many recorded deeds before 1830 as one might expect, partly because recording was not required before 1810, and compliance was slow after 1810. In NY state, mortgages were very important because they were instruments used to record title claims of many settlers and to protect their interests. Numerous deeds and mortgages were given out by land companies, but many were not recorded in the counties. In most cases, the land companies did not issue a deed until full payment had been received, and this was often a long time after the initial settlement on the land. In a sizable number of cases, people received a deed to their land, did not record it, and then years later recorded it or simply made notice of it when the property was subsequently sold. Another important aspect of NY land records is that when a new county was created the deed and other land records for the area being split off were copied, and the copies were given to the new county.

Deeds, mortgages, and leases in NY will be found basically in three places: (1) some early ones at the state level, (2) some early ones in towns on Long Island and along the CT and MA borders, and (3) the greatest proportion at the county level where they were recorded by the County Clerks from 1683 onward. Among the state records are the following important ones:

__PROVINCIAL RECORDS OF CONVEYANCES in NY HISTORICAL MANUSCRIPTS, DUTCH, REGISTER OF THE PROVINCIAL SECRETARY, 1638-60, 3 volumes, Genealogical Publishing Co., Baltimore, MD, 1974.
__CONVEYANCES, 1652-3, in C. T. Gehring, NY HISTORICAL MANUSCRIPTS: DUTCH, VOLUMES GG, HH, & II, LAND PAPERS, 1630-51, 1654-64, Genealogical Publishing Co., Baltimore, MD, 1980. In volume II.
__TRANSLATIONS OF DUTCH PATENTS AND DEEDS, 1630-74, 4 volumes, Land Records of the NY Department of State, NYSA, Albany, NY.
__ABSTRACTS AND INDEXES OF DEEDS, 1674-1855, 7 volumes, Land Records of the NY Department of State, NYSA, Albany, NY.
__INDEX TO DEEDS AND MORTGAGES, 1641-1842, Land Records of the NY Department of State, NYSA, Albany, NY.
There are several other series of deed, mortgage, lease, release, and foreclosure records in the NYSA. These are referenced in the GUIDE TO RECORDS IN THE NYSA mentioned at the end of the third paragraph of this section.

County land records (deeds, mortgages, leases) need to be sought in the county court houses (CH) and other county repositories (county archives, historical societies, historians' offices). Many have also been microfilmed by FHL (for 57 counties) and therefore are available through FHC, and some have been put out in printed form, these being found in NYSL, NYPL, NYGB, LGL, and RL.

Since NY City and the Albany area were very important to early NY (and continue to be), the land records there are of particular value. They are indexed in these books:

__INDEXES OF CONVEYANCES RECORDED IN THE OFFICE OF THE REGISTER OF THE CITY AND COUNTY OF NY, MacSpedon and Baker, New York, NY, 1858-64, 51 volumes.

__C. F. Grim, AN ESSAY TOWARDS AN IMPROVED REGISTER OF DEEDS, CITY AND COUNTY OF NY TO 1799, Gould, Banks, and Co., New York, NY, 1832. Indexes NY City deeds on record in both Albany and NY City.

__W. B. Melius and F. H. Burnap, INDEX TO THE PUBLIC RECORDS OF THE COUNTY OF ALBANY, 1630-1893, Argus Co., Albany, NY, 1902-17, 37 volumes.

__J. Pearson and A. J. F. van Laer, EARLY RECORDS OF THE CITY AND COUNTY OF ALBANY AND COLONY OF RENSSELAERS-WYCK, University Microfilms, Ann Arbor, MI, 1869-1919 (1967), 4 volumes.

22. Manuscripts

One of the most useful and yet one of the most unused sources of genealogical data are the various manuscript collections relating to NY. These collections will be found in state, regional, county, and private libraries, archives, museums, societies, and repositories in numerous places in NY, including universities, colleges, and church agencies. Manuscript collections consist of all sorts of records of religious, educational, patriotic, business, social, civil, professional, governmental, and political organizations; documents, letters, memoirs, notes, and papers of early settlers, ministers, politicians, business men, educators, physicians, dentists, lawyers, judges, land speculators, and farmers; records of churches, cemeteries, mortuaries, schools, corporations, and industries; works of artists, musicians, writers, sculptors, photographers, architects, and historians; and records, papers, letters, and reminiscences of participants in various wars, as well as records of military organizations and campaigns.

The major NY sources of manuscripts of genealogical importance are:

__In Albany (Albany County): NYSL, NYSA.

__In Batavia (Genesee County): Holland Land Office Museum

__In Bronxville (Westchester County): Lutheran Church, MO Synod, Atlantic District Archives

__In Brooklyn (Kings County): Brooklyn Historical Society
__In Buffalo (Erie County): Buffalo and Erie County Historical Society
__In Canandaigua: Ontario County Historical Society
__In Canton: St. Lawrence County Historical Association
__In Cooperstown (Otsego County): NY State Historical Association
__In East Meadow: Nassau County Museum Reference Library
__In Fonda: Montgomery County Department of History and Archives
__In Ithaca (Tompkins County): Cornell University Library
__In Jamaica: Queens Borough (County) Public Library
__In New Paltz (Ulster County): Huguenot Historical Society
__In NY City (NY County): NYPL, NYGB, NYHS, NY City Municipal Archives, Holland Society, Museum of the City of NY Library, Leo Baeck Jewish Institute, Protestant Episcopal Church-Diocese of NY Archives Library, Religious Society of Friends-Haviland Records Room
__In Plattsburgh (Clinton County): Fernberg Library of the State University of NY
__In Port Jervis (Orange County): Minisink Valley Historical Society
__In Poughkeepsie: Adriance Memorial Library (Dutchess County Historical Society)
__In Rochester (Monroe County): Rochester Public Library, American Baptist Historical Society
__On Staten Island (Richmond County): Lutheran Church in America-NY Archives
__In Syracuse: Onondaga County Public Library, Syracuse University Library
__In Ticonderoga (Essex County): Ticonderoga Historical Society
__In Tuckahoe: Westchester County Historical Society
__In Utica: Oneida (County) Historical Society

   The holdings of several manuscript depositories in NY are described in special publications. These give considerable detail regarding the manuscript materials in their collections.
__US National Historical Publications and Records Commission, DIRECTORY OF ARCHIVES AND MANUSCRIPT REPOSITORIES IN THE US, The Commission, Washington, DC, 1978, pages 404-80.
__P. M. Hamer, A GUIDE TO ARCHIVES AND MANUSCRIPTS IN THE

US, Yale University Press, New Haven, CT, 1961, pages 373-455.

__Historical Records Survey, GUIDE TO DEPOSITORIES OF MANUSCRIPT COLLECTIONS IN NY STATE (EXCLUSIIVE OF NY CITY), with SUPPLEMENT, WPA, New York, NY, 1941-4.

__Historical Records Survey, GUIDE TO MANUSCRIPT DEPOSI-TORIES IN NY CITY, WPA, New York, NY, 1941.

__Historical Records Survey, GUIDE TO THE TEN MAJOR REPOSITORIES OF MANUSCRIPT COLLECTIONS IN NY STATE (EXCLUSIVE OF NY CITY), WPA, New York, NY, 1941.

__NY State Historical Association, SUPPLEMENT TO THE GUIDE TO DEPOSITORIES OF MANUSCRIPT COLLECTIONS IN NY STATE, The Association, Cooperstown, NY, 1944.

__New York State Archives, GUIDE TO RECORDS IN THE NY STATE ARCHIVES, NY State Education Department, Albany, NY, 1981.

__NY State Library, ANNOTATED LIST OF THE PRINCIPAL MANUSCRIPTS IN THE NY STATE LIBRARY, The Library, Albany, NY, 1899.

__NY State Library, MANUSCRIPTS AND SPECIAL COLLECTIONS, A GUIDE TO COLLECTIONS AND SERVICES, The Library, Albany, NY, latest edition.

__NY Public Library, DICTIONARY CATALOG OF THE MANUSCRIPT DIVISION, Hall and Co., Boston, MA, 1967, 2 volumes.

__A. J. Breton, A GUIDE TO THE MANUSCRIPT COLLECTIONS OF THE NY HISTORICAL SOCIETY, Greenwood Press, Westport, CT, 1972, 2 volumes.

__G. G. Cole, HISTORICAL MATERIALS RELATING TO NORTHERN NY, North Country Reference and Research Resources Council, Canton, NY, 1976.

__Long Island Archives Conference, LONG ISLAND UNION CATALOG OF MANUSCRIPT COLLECTIONS, The Conference, Long Island, NY, 1974.

__Columbia University Library, MANUSCRIPT COLLECTIONS IN THE COLUMBIA UNIVERSITY LIBRARY, The Library, New York, NY, 1959.

__Oneida Historical Society, CATALOG OF THE MANUSCRIPT HOLDINGS AT THE ONEIDA HISTORICAL SOCIETY, The Society, Utica, NY, 1952.

__Montgomery County Department of History and Archives, CATALOGUE OF HISTORICAL AND GENEALOGICAL MATERIAL, The Department, Fonda, NY, 1982.

__Buffalo Historical Society, ROUGH LIST OF THE MANU-SCRIPTS IN THE LIBRARY OF THE BUFFALO HISTORICAL SOCIE-TY, in Publications of the Buffalo Historical Society, volume 14, pages 423 ff.

__C. J. Gehring, A GUIDE TO DUTCH MANUSCRIPTS RELATING TO NEW NETHERLANDS IN US REPOSITORIES, University of the State of NY, Albany, NY, 1978.

__Saratoga County Historical Society, CATALOG OF THE MANUSCRIPT COLLECTION, The Society, Ballston Spa, NY, 1979.

__W. C. Pieters, INVENTORY OF THE ARCHIVES OF THE HOLLAND LAND COMPANY, Municipal Printing Office, Amsterdam, Netherlands, 1976.

__E. B. Greene and R. B. Morris, GUIDE TO THE PRINCIPAL SOURCES FOR EARLY AMERICAN HISTORY 1600-1800 IN NY CITY, Columbia University Press, New York, NY, 1953.

__H. J. Carman and A. Thompson, A GUIDE TO THE PRINCIPAL SOURCES FOR AMERICAN CIVILIZATION 1800-1900 IN THE CITY OF NY, MANUSCRIPTS, Columbia University Press, New York, NY, 1970.

There is an exceptionally valuable series of guides being issued by the NY Historical Resources Center at Cornell University. The Center is compiling detailed information on records of all sorts in the NY counties along with the exact locations of them. There is at least one volume for most counties, more than that in a number of instances. It is extremely important that you examine these for every county in which you had an ancestor.

__NY Historical Resources Center, GUIDES TO HISTORICAL RESOURCES IN NY COUNTY REPOSITORIES, Cornell University Press, Ithaca, NY, 1978-. Available now for most counties.

Finally, we need to call to your attention an indispensible series of volumes which you must not fail to look into. These books were published by the Library of Congress in order to put into print the manuscript holdings of archives and repositories all over the US. There is an annual volume from 1959 to the present. And best of all, this tremendous finding aid is thoroughly indexed:

__US Library of Congress, THE NATIONAL UNION CATALOG OF MANUSCRIPT COLLECTIONS, The Library, Washington, DC, issued annually 1959-. Cumulative indexes 1959-62, 1963-6, 1967-9, 1970-4, 1975-9, 1980-4. Volumes indexed separately thereafter.

Be certain to look in all these indexes for your family surnames, then under the counties of interest to you, then under pertinent cities and towns, then under NY, then under various subjects (for example, cavalry, churches, Civil War, colonial period, coroners, courts, customs, Dutch, estates, family papers, French and Indian War, genealogy, history, immigration, Indian Wars, infantry, Jews, juries, justices of the peace, land, leases, licenses, local history, maps, military affairs, militia, mortgages, newspapers, pardon and parole, personal accounts, pioneer life, ports of entry, prisons, Revolutionary War, slavery, surveys, tax records, travel, trials, vital records, War of 1812, wills). Do not overlook the many listings under the general heading genealogy and don't forget to look under New York City. These efforts will introduce you quickly and easily to the vast world of NY manuscript materials.

The reference books mentioned in the previous paragraphs are available in NYSL, NYPL, NYGB, and NYHS. Many of them may be found at FHL(FHC), LGL, and RL. If you find in these volumes materials which you suspect relate to your progenitor, write to the appropriate repository asking for details. Don't forget to send a long SASE and to request names of researchers if you cannot go in person. In NYSL, NYSA, NYPL, NYGB, NYHS, and most other NY manuscript repositories there are special indexes, catalogs, and other finding aids to facilitate your search. In some cases, there are several of these, so you need to be careful to examine all.

23. Marriage records

During the Dutch period of New Amsterdam (1609-64), the recording of marriages was left to the state church, the Dutch Reformed Church. When the English took over in 1664, the official church became the Anglican Church or the Church of England. The accepted procedure for marriage involved the posting of banns (announcements) at the church on three Sundays prior to the wedding. For those who chose not to do this, the procurement of a marriage license and/or posting of a marriage bond with the civil authorities was required, although there was apparently much laxity in enforcement, especially on the frontier. In some counties which had been settled early by New Englanders, the town minutes often contained marriage records, as was the New England custom, but this practice gradually declined. Following the Revolutionary War and the demise of a state church, very few marriage records were kept by governmental authorities. Many of

the fragmentary surviving marriage records before 1784
have been listed and/or abstracted in the following
volumes:
__K. Scott, MARRIAGE BONDS OF COLONIAL NY, 1753-84,
Trumbull Publishing Co., New York, NY, 1972. 4000
items.
__NAMES OF PERSONS FOR WHOM MARRIAGE LICENSES WERE ISSUED
BY THE SECRETARY OF THE PROVINCE OF NY PREVIOUS TO
1784, Genealogical Publishing Co., Baltimore, MD,
1860(1968). 25,000 names.
__MARRIAGES FROM 1639-1801 IN THE REFORMED DUTCH CHURCH,
NEW AMSTERDAM/NEW YORK CITY, NY Genealogical and Biographical Society, New York, NY, 1940.
In 1847, a law was passed requiring marriage registra-
tion. Fair conformity to the law was seen during 1847-
49/50, but the system largely failed thereafter. The
extant 1847-49/50 records (and a few beyond) will be
found in towns and counties, many have been published in
NY genealogical journals (Tree Talks, NY Genealogical and
Biographical Record), some have been microfilmed by the
FHL(FHC), and a few are at NYSL and NYSA. Listings of a
number of those available will be found in:
__J. D. and E. D. Stemmons, THE VITAL RECORD COMPENDIUM,
Everton Publishers, Logan, UT, 1979.
__A. H. Eakle and L. R. Gunn, DESCRIPTIVE INVENTORY TO
THE NY COLLECTION (AT FHL), University of UT Press,
Salt Lake City, UT, 1980.
__Historical Records Survey, GUIDE TO PUBLIC VITAL STA-
TISTICS IN NY STATE, INCLUDING NY CITY, WPA, Albany,
NY, 1942, volume 2.

About the middle of the 19th century, NY City began
keeping marriage records (1847-8, 1853-), and other large
cities joined in later: Brooklyn (1866-), Albany (1870-),
Syracuse (1873-), Utica (1873-), Rochester (1875-),
Yonkers (1875-), Buffalo (1878-). Then in 1880 a state
law mandating registration was passed, and compliance
gradually increased to 50% by about 1900 and 90% by 1915,
when a more stringent law came into effect. The records
are available as follows. For NY County (1847-8, 1853-),
Queens County (some 1847-9, 1880-), Richmond County (some
1848-9, 1880-), Kings County (some 1847-52, 1866-), Bronx
County (1914-), Albany (1870-1907), Yonkers (1875-1907),
and Buffalo (1878-1907), records should be sought in the
county or city offices for the dates indicated. For
Albany (1908-), Yonkers (1908-), Buffalo (1908-), and all

the rest of the state (1880-), except the 5 counties of
NY City, write or visit:
__NY State Department of Health, Bureau of Vital Records,
Tower Building, Empire State Plaza, Albany, NY 12237.
Records indexed.
Public access to marriage records prior to 1938 is avail-
able, but those after are restricted.

Since NY is so short on official marriage records
prior to 1880 (1853 for NY City), other types of records
have to be consulted. Among the better ones are Bible,
cemetery, census (especially the 1865/75 NY state censuses), church, manuscript, military, pension, mortuary,
newspaper, published genealogies, tax lists, and will-
probate records. The most fruitful of these are usually
the church and newspaper records. All of them are treated in other sections of this chapter. Numerous non-
official sources of this sort are listed in the two books
by Stemmons and by Eakle cited in the first paragraph of
this section. When you are seeking marriage date and
place information in archives and libraries, be certain
to explore all the above-mentioned sources, and don't
fail to look under the county listings and the following
heading in library catalogs: Registers of births, etc.

24. Military records: colonial

Before going into detail on sources of military
records (sections 24-27), you need to understand the
types of records which are available and what they contain. There are five basic types which are of value to
genealogists: (a) service, (b) pension, (c) bounty land,
(d) claims, and (e) military unit history. Service
records contain a number of the following: name, rank,
military unit, personal description, plus dates and
places of enlistment, mustering in, payrolls, wounding,
capture, death, imprisonment, hospital stay, release,
oath of allegiance, desertion, promotion, battles, heroic
action, re-enlistment, leave of absence, mustering out,
and discharge. Pension records (applications and payment
documents) contain a number of the following: name, age,
rank, military unit, personal description, name of wife,
names and ages of children, residences during pension
period, plus dates and places of enlistment, service,
wartime experiences, birth, marriage, pension payments,
and death. Bounty land records (applications and awards

of land) contain a number of the following: name. age, rank, military unit, plus dates and places of enlistment, service, wartime experience, and birth. <u>Claims</u> of military participants for back pay and of civilians for supplies or service contain some of the following: name, details of the claim, date of the claim, witnesses to the claim, documents supporting the claim, action on the claim, amount awarded. <u>Military unit history</u> records trace the detailed events of the experiences of a given military unit throughout a war, often referring to officers, enlisted men, battles, campaigns, and deaths, plus dates and places of organization, mustering in, reorganization, mustering out, and other pertinent events. Now with this background, you are ready to learn where these records may be found.

Colonial NY maintained a militia for defense and for other emergencies. The major wars during colonial times centered around the struggle between Great Britain and France for control of North America. The chief conflicts were known as King William's War (1689-97), Queen Anne's War (1702-13), the War of Jenkin's Ear (1739), King George's War (1740-8), and the French and Indian War (1754-63). After many years of French attacks on the expanding British frontier and many counterattacks by the British and the colonists, with Indians fighting on both sides, the French and Indian War ended in a British victory. The French and their Spanish allies ceded to Britain all of Canada and essentially all lands resting east of the MS River including FL.

NY military men participated in these wars, and a fair number of records exist, but they are not very detailed. The records related to these wars which contain names of participants and describe the NY activities include:
__DUTCH COLONIAL SOLDIERS, listed in Dutch colonial records cited in section on colonial records in this chapter.
__NY State Historian, MUSTER ROLLS, 1664-1775, in 2ND AND 3RD ANNUAL REPORTS OF THE STATE HISTORIAN, Wynkoop, Hallenbeck, Crawford Co., Albany, NY, 1897-8, 2 volumes. See Appendix H in 1st volume and Appendix M in 2nd, also index at end of 2nd volume.
__E. B. O'Callaghan, CALENDAR OF NY COLONIAL COMMISSIONS, 1680-1770, NY Historical Society, New York, NY, 1929.

__C. M. Meyers, EARLY MILITARY RECORDS OF NY, 1689-1738,
RAM Publishers, Saugus, CA, 1967.
__NY Historical Society, MUSTER ROLLS OF NY PROVINCIAL
TROOPS, 1755-64, The Society, New York, NY, 1891.
__K. Scott, CALENDAR OF NY COLONIAL COMMISSIONS, 1770-6,
National Society of Colonial Dames, New York, NY, 1972.
__LAWS OF THE COLONY OF NY, Chapter 347, passed 02 Decem-
ber 1717, compensations for military service and sup-
plies, with awards sometimes going to widows or rela-
tives.

The colony of NY issued land patents north and east of
the Hudson Valley to colonial war veterans. These were
recorded in the Colonial Secretary's Office. Many are
included, along with later patents, in:
__NY Secretary of State, LIST OF NAMES OF PERSONS TO WHOM
MILITARY PATENTS HAVE BEEN ISSUED, Child and Swaine,
Albany, NY, 1793.

Another source of information on NY colonial soldiers is
provided by the data gathered by members of colonial
ancestral societies which relate to the wars:
__General Society of Colonial Wars, AN INDEX TO ANCESTORS
AND ROLL OF MEMBERS, The Society, New York, NY, 1922.
__National Society of Colonial Wars, MEMBERSHIP LIST AND
INDEX OF ANCESTORS, The Society, Somerville, MA, 1941/-
50, 2 volumes.

25. Military records: Revolutionary War

NY was involved in almost every major northern
campaign of the Revolutionary War, largely because of its
two strategic areas: northeastern NY which connected to
Canada, and NY City which the British captured early and
used as an operational base. Albany was the goal of two
British attacks from Canada, mainly because the Hudson
River Valley was crucial to control of the northern
colonies. The Valley was thus the site of many important
battles, and it was here that the British lost the war in
the north. During the war, the central and western
frontiers of NY were the arenas for intense Indian fighting. It needs to be emphasized also that NY had a large
population of Loyalists, as well as many people who
either declared neutrality, disinterest, or who went with
whoever was winning in their area. The state of NY sent
over 17,700 men to the Continental Army (united colonies)
and almost 4000 militia men fought. In NY there were
basically three types of military service: 1st, the NY

Line was made up of nine regiments who served in the Continental Army under General Washington, 2nd, the NY state militia served predominantly in NY, but could be called upon to leave the state for short periods of time, and 3rd, the NY levies were drafted from the militia and the citizenry to serve outside the state. The age bracket for military service in NY state was 16 to 50 (later 60).

The first step you should take in searching for your NY ancestor who may have served in this war or supported it is to employ the following large indexes and look for him in them:

__The National Archives, GENERAL INDEX TO COMPILED SERVICE RECORDS OF REVOLUTIONARY WAR SOLDIERS, SAILORS, ARMY STAFF, The Archives, Washington, DC, Microfilm Publication M860, 58 rolls. [Mostly Continental forces plus militia who supported them. Copies in NYSL, NYPL, FHL(FHC), NA, NAFB, may be borrowed through your LL or directly from AGLL, PO Box 244, Bountiful, UT 84010, or Census Microfilm Rental Program, PO Box 2940, Hyattsville, MD 20784.]

__The National Archives, INDEX TO COMPILED SERVICE RECORDS OF NAVAL PERSONNEL DURING THE REVOLUTIONARY WAR, The Archives, Washington, DC, Microfilm Publication M879, 1 roll. [Includes Marines. Sources same as above.]

__The National Genealogical Society, INDEX TO REVOLUTIONARY WAR PENSION [AND SOME BOUNTY LAND] APPLICATIONS IN THE NATIONAL ARCHIVES, The Society, Washington, DC, 1976.

__F. Rider, AMERICAN GENEALOGICAL INDEX, Godfrey Memorial Library, Middletown, CT, 1942-52, 48 volumes, and F. Rider, AMERICAN GENEALOGICAL-BIOGRAPHICAL INDEX, Godfrey Memorial Library, Middletown, CT, 1952-87, over 160 volumes, more to come. [Continental, state, and militia service.]

__US Pay Department, War Department, REGISTERS OF CERTIFICATES ISSUED BY JOHN PIERCE TO OFFICERS AND SOLDIERS OF THE CONTINENTAL ARMY, Genealogical Publishing Co., Baltimore, MD, 1983.

__National Society of the DAR, DAR PATRIOT INDEX, The Society, Washington, DC, 1966/79, 2 volumes. [Continental, state, militia, public service, military aid.]

The four reference works immediately above will be found

in NYSL, NYPL, NYGB, NYHS, FHL(FHC), LGL, and in many RL and some LL.

If you discover from these sources that your ancestor served in the Continental forces or units which aided them, you may proceed to obtain his service records from the NA or read them from these microfilms:

__The National Archives, COMPILED SERVICE RECORDS OF SOLDIERS WHO SERVED IN THE AMERICAN ARMY DURING THE REVOLUTIONARY WAR, The Archives, Washington, DC, Microfilm Publication M881, 1097 rolls.

__The National Archives, COMPILED SERVICE RECORDS OF AMERICAN NAVAL, QUARTERMASTER, AND COMMISSARY PERSONNEL WHO SERVED DURING THE REVOLUTIONARY WAR, The Archives, Washington, DC, Microfilm Publication M880, 4 rolls.

__The National Archives, REVOLUTIONARY WAR ROLLS, 1775-83, The Archives, Washington, DC, Microfilm Publication M246, 138 rolls.

And the pension and bounty land records are found in:

__The National Archives, REVOLUTIONARY WAR PENSION AND BOUNTY LAND WARRANT APPLICATION FILES, The Archives, Washington, DC, Microfilm Publication M804, 2670 rolls.

These microfilm sets are available at NA, NAFB, FHL(FHC), and some can be borrowed from your LL, or AGLL, PO Box 244, Bountiful, UT 84010, or CMRF, PO Box 2940, Hyattsville, MD 20784. Alternately, you can write the NA (8th and PA Ave., Washington, DC 20408) for 3 copies of NATF-80 which you can use to request service, pension, and bounty land records by mail. A third alternative is to hire a searcher in Washington, DC to go to the NA for you. Lists of such searchers will be found in:

__J. N. Chambers, editor, THE GENEALOGICAL HELPER, Everton Publishers, Logan, UT, latest September-October issue.

The second step you should take, especially if you failed to find your progenitor in the first step, is to look into published state sources. Even if you did find your ancestor in the first step, you should not neglect this second possible source of data. Foremost among these state sources are:

__J. A. Roberts, NY Comptroller's Office, NY IN THE REVOLUTION AS COLONY AND STATE, with E. C. Knight, SUPPLEMENT, NY State Comptrollers Office, Quayle, Albany, NY, 1904, 2 volumes. Names of soldiers, Ameri-

can and British prisoners, refugees, claimants for
damages, estates confiscated, and Loyalists.

___E. B. O'Callaghan and B. Fernow, editors, DOCUMENTS
RELATIVE TO THE COLONIAL HISTORY OF THE STATE OF NY,
AMS Press, New York, NY, 1853-87(1969), 15 volumes.
Volume 11 is index to volumes 1-10, volume 15 is gene-
ral index.

___CALENDAR OF HISTORICAL MANUSCRIPTS RELATIVE TO THE WAR
OF THE REVOLUTION IN THE OFFICE OF THE SECRETARY OF
STATE, Weed, Parsons, and Co., Albany, NY, 1868, 2
volumes.

___A. Comstock, REVOLUTIONARY WAR VETERANS (PENSIONS)
BEARING ON NY FAMILIES, Yesteryears, Volumes 19-20,
Numbers 73-80, 1975-7.

___DAR of NY, GENEALOGICAL DATA: NEW PROJECT, Lineage
Papers Submitted by NY Applicants for DAR Membership,
1960-, 6 volumes, indexed in New Project Genealogical
Data Card Index, NYSL, Albany, NY.

___DAR of NY, GRAVES OF REVOLUTIONARY SOLDIERS IN NY,
Various Chapters, Various Places, 1922-55, 15 volumes,
indexed in Revolutionary Soldiers Card Index, NYSL,
Albany, NY.

___F. G. Mather, THE REFUGEES OF 1776 FROM LONG ISLAND TO
CT, Genealogical Publishing Co., Baltimore, MD, 1913-
(1972). About 20,000 names.

___Society of Old Brooklynites, A CHRISTMAS REMINDER: 8000
PERSONS CONFINED ON BOARD BRITISH PRISON SHIPS DURING
THE REVOLUTION, The Society, Brooklyn, NY, 1888.

A number of other references for the Revolution in NY are
listed in a valuable reference work:

___S. Bielinski, A GUIDE TO THE REVOLUTIONARY WAR MANU-
SCRIPTS IN THE NYSL, State Bicentennial Commission,
Albany, NY, 1976.

All the above volumes are available in NYSL, most in
NYPL, NYGB, and NYHS, and some in FHL(FHC), LGL, RL, and
LL. As you continue your search in NY state records,
please do not fail to search for state Revolutionary War
bounty land applications and awards. These were discussed in a section on land records which appeared above
in this chapter.

The large number of Loyalists in NY, their activities, and the actions against them gave rise to many
records, both within and outside of NY state. Chief
among these are:

__W. Kelby, ORDERLY BOOK OF THREE BATTALIONS OF LOYALISTS IN NY CITY, NY Historical Society, New York, NY, 1917, 3 volumes.

__J. Johnson, ORDERLY BOOK OF JOHNSON DURING THE ORISKANY CAMPAIGH, 1776-7, Munsell's Sons, Albany, NY, 1882.

__J. A. Roberts, NY Comptroller's Office, NY IN THE REVOLUTION AS COLONY AND STATE, with E. C. Knight, SUPPLEMENT, Quayle, Albany, NY, 1904, 2 volumes.

__V. H. Paltsits, MINUTES OF THE COMMISSIONERS FOR DETECTING AND DEFEATING CONSPIRACIES IN THE STATE OF NY, 1778-81, Lyon Co., Albany, NY, 1909-10, 3 volumes. Loyalists.

__M. B. Penrose, MOHAWK VALLEY IN THE REVOLUTION, COMMITTEE OF SAFETY PAPERS AND GENEALOGICAL COMPENDIUM, The Author, Franklin Park, NJ, 1978.

__A. C. Flick, MINUTES OF THE ALBANY COMMITTEE OF CORRESPONDENCE, 1775-8, University of the State of NY, Albany, NY, 1923, 2 volumes. Loyalists.

__A. C. Flick, LOYALISM IN NY DURING THE AMERICAN REVOLUTION, AMS Press, New York, NY, 1901(1970). Many names.

__TRANSCRIPTS OF MANUSCRIPT BOOKS AND PAPERS OF THE COMMISSION OF ENQUIRY INTO LOSSES AND SERVICES OF AMERICAN LOYALISTS, NYPL, New York, NY, 60 manuscript volumes.

__H. B. Yoshpe, DISPOSITION OF LOYALIST ESTATES IN THE SOUTHERN DISTRICT OF THE STATE OF NY, Columbia University Press, New York, 1939.

For further Loyalist records, see:

__NYSL, LOYALIST RECORDS IN THE NYSL, Leaflet, NYSL, Albany, NY, latest edition.

__G. Palmer, BIBLIOGRAPHY OF LOYALIST SOURCE MATERIAL IN THE US, CANADA, AND GREAT BRITAIN, Mecker, Westport, CT, 1982.

For considerably more detail about genealogical data which can be gleaned from Revolutionary War records, you may consult a book especially dedicated to this:

__Geo. K. Schweitzer, REVOLUTIONARY WAR GENEALOGY, available from the author at the address shown on the title page of this volume.

This volume goes into detail on local, state, and national records, discusses both militia and Continental Army service, deals in detail with service, pension, bounty land, and claims records, and treats the subject of regimental histories, battle accounts, medical records, courts-martial, foreign participants, Loyalist data, maps, museums, historic sites, patriotic organizations, and many other related topics. Two other very useful detailed source books listing Revolutionary War records are:

__J. C. and L. L. Neagles, LOCATING YOUR REVOLUTIONARY WAR ANCESTOR, Everton Publishers, Logan, UT, 1983.

__M. Deputy and others, REGISTER OF FEDERAL US MILITARY RECORDS, VOLUME 1, 1775-1860, Heritage Books, Bowie, MD, 1986, pages 1-137.

26. Military records: War of 1812

During the period between the Revolutionary War and the Civil War (1784-1861), the US was involved in two major foreign wars: The War of 1812 (1812-5) and the Mexican War (1846-8). In addition, there were several minor conflicts in which NY soldiers participated, the most notable of which was the Patriot War (1838). Since so few were engaged in the other minor conflicts, we will only refer you to three main reference works where you will find the pertinent records discussed. However, we will treat the major wars in some detail because sizable numbers of New Yorkers were involved. The basic sources which will lead you to military service, pension, and bounty land records of New Yorkers who gave military service in minor conflicts during 1784-1861 are:

__The National Archives, GUIDE TO GENEALOGICAL RESEARCH IN THE NA, The Archives, Washington, DC, 1982, Chapters 4-9.

__The National Archives, MILITARY SERVICE RECORDS, The Archives, Washington, DC, 1985.

__M. Deputy and others, REGISTER OF FEDERAL US MILITARY RECORDS, VOLUME 1, 1775-1860, Heritage Books, Bowie, MD, 1986.

Particular attention needs to be paid to the NA microfilm indexes to volunteer service during 1784-1811 (Microfilm M694) and in Indian Wars 1815-58 (M629), as well as pensions for Indian War service (T318) and for regular army service 1784-1861 (T316).

A number of NY men were involved in the War of 1812. They served both in national and state organizations, and therefore several types of national records (service, bounty land, pension), as well as state records need to be sought. Only relatively few national pensions were given before 1871, by which time not too many veterans

were still living. To obtain <u>national</u> records (only for
men who served in national units) you may write the NA
and request copies of NATF-80, which may be used to order
military service, bounty land, and pension information.
Or you may choose to visit the NA or to employ a searcher
in Washington to do the work for you. Alternately, some
of the indexes and records are available on loan from
AGLL, PO Box 244, Bountiful, UT 84010, and also through
your local library. Among the microfilm indexes and
alphabetical files which you need to search or have
searched for you are:

__The National Archives, INDEX TO COMPILED SERVICE RE-
CORDS OF VOLUNTEER SOLDIERS WHO SERVED DURING THE WAR
OF 1812, The Archives, Washington, DC, Microfilm Publication M602, 234 rolls. [Leads to service records,
which are available at the NA.]

__The National Archives, INDEX TO WAR OF 1812 PENSION
(AND SOME BOUNTY LAND) APPLICATIONS, The Archives,
Washington, DC, Microfilm Publication M313, 102 rolls.
[Leads to applications, which are available at the NA.]

__The National Archives, WAR OF 1812 MILITARY BOUNTY LAND
WARRANTS, 1815-58, The Archives, Microfilm Publication
M848, 14 rolls, 4 indexes in first roll. [Leads to
bounty land warrant applications, which are alphabetically filed in NA.]

__The National Archives, POST-REVOLUTIONARY WAR BOUNTY
LAND WARRANT APPLICATION FILE, The Archives, Washington, DC, arranged alphabetically.

Copies of the three microfilm publications mentioned
above are available at NA, some NAFB, some LGL, and at
FHL (and through FHC). Microfilm publications M602,
M313, and M848 are available on interlibrary loan from
AGLL (address above). Among published national sources
for War of 1812 data are:

__F. I. Ordway, Jr., REGISTER OF THE GENERAL SOCIETY OF
THE WAR OF 1812, The Society, Washington, DC, 1972.

__E. S. Galvin, 1812 ANCESTOR INDEX, National Society of
the US Daughters of 1812, Washington, DC, 1970.

__C. S. Peterson, KNOWN MILITARY DEAD DURING THE WAR OF
1812, The Author, Baltimore, MD, 1955.

Among the <u>state</u> source volumes, records, and microfilms which you should search for NY War of 1812 military
service records are:

__NY Adjutant General's Office, INDEX OF AWARDS ON CLAIMS
OF SOLDIERS OF THE WAR OF 1812, Genealogical Publishing

Co., Baltimore, MD, 1860(1969). Claims made after 1859
by militiamen. Over 17,000 entries.
__E. V. Becker, NY STATE SOLDIER RECORDS, WAR OF 1812,
The Author, Amsterdam, NY, 1960, 2 volumes.
__CLAIMS, APPLICATIONS, AND AWARDS FOR SERVICE IN THE WAR
OF 1812, NYSA, Albany, NY.
__H. Hastings, NY COUNCIL OF APPOINTMENT MILITARY MIN-
UTES, 1783-1821, Lyon Co., Albany, NY, 1901-2, 4 vol-
umes, last one index. Officers of the militia.
__WAR OF 1812 PAYROLL CARD FILES, NYSA, Albany, NY.
__E. Cruickshank, DOCUMENTARY HISTORY OF THE CAMPAIGN ON
THE NIAGARA FRONTIER, 1812-4, New York, NY, 7 volumes,
1899-1905.
__INDEX TO AMERICAN PRISONERS OF THE WAR OF 1812, News-
letter of the National Society, US Daughters of the War
of 1812, Volume 13, Number 4, 1938.
__PRISONERS' MEMOIRS OR DARTMOOR PRISON [AMERICAN PRISON-
ERS 1813-5], Charles Andrews, New York, NY, 1852, pages
138-51.
__MISCELLANEOUS WAR OF 1812 MANUSCRIPTS: SERVICE RECORDS,
OFFICERS, PAYROLLS, MUSTER ROLLS, AND ORDERLY BOOKS,
NYHS, New York, NY.
__REGISTER OF BOUNTY LAND ISSUED IN IL FOR SERVICE IN THE
WAR OF 1812, NYSA, Albany, NY.
__K. Scott, BRITISH ALIENS IN THE US (INCLUDING NY)
DURING THE WAR OF 1812, Genealogical Publishing Co.,
Baltimore, MD, 1979.
For considerably more detail about genealogical informa-
tion which can be derived from the above War of 1812
records plus the many more that are available, you may
consult a detailed book especially dedicated to this:
__Geo. K. Schweitzer, WAR OF 1812 GENEALOGY, available
from the author at the address given on the title page
of this book.

    In 1837-8, many French citizens of Lower Canada
(later Quebec) entered into a series of rebellious upris-
ings (the Patriot War) against the British. NY soldiers
were called into military service to protect the US
border from both sides. Records of those who served are
indexed in:
__The National Archives, INDEX TO THE COMPILED SERVICE
RECORDS OF VOLUNTEER SOLDIERS FROM THE STATE OF NY
DURING THE PATRIOT WAR OF 1838, The Archives, Washington, DC, Microfilm Publication M631, 1 roll. Leads to
service records which are available at the NA.

The Mexican War was fought 1846-8. As before, NATF-80 should be obtained and used, or you should visit the NA, or you should hire a researcher as indicated in previously-given instructions (see Revolutionary War section). Again, military service, pension, and bounty land records should all be asked for. The NA indexes which lead to the records and some alphabetical national records include:

__The National Archives, INDEX TO THE COMPILED SERVICE RECORDS OF VOLUNTEER SOLDIERS DURING THE MEXICAN WAR, The Archives, Washington, DC, Microfilm Publication M616, 41 rolls.

__The National Archives, INDEX TO MEXICAN WAR PENSION FILES, The Archives, Washington, DC, Microfilm Publication T317, 14 rolls.

__The National Archives, POST-REVOLUTIONARY WAR BOUNTY LAND APPLICATION FILE, The Archives, Washington, DC, arranged alphabetically.

Three useful publications, one a complete roster of officers in the Mexican War, another a list of the dead, a third an index to pension applications, are:

__W. H. Roberts, MEXICAN WAR (OFFICER) VETERANS, 1846-8, Washington, DC, 1887.

__C. S. Peterson, KNOWN MILITARY DEAD DURING THE MEXICAN WAR, The Author, Baltimore, MD, 1957.

__B. S. Wolfe, INDEX TO MEXICAN WAR PENSION APPLICATIONS, Ye Olde Genealogie Shoppe, Indianapolis, IN.

Among state sources available for the Mexican War are the following:

__NY VOLUNTEERS IN CA, STEVENSON'S REGIMENT, Rio Grande Press, Glorieta, NM, 1970.

__REPORTS OF THE SPECIAL COMMITTEE --- OF THE NY REGIMENT OF VOLUNTEERS --- ON THEIR RETURN FROM MEXICO, Common Council, New York, NY, 1850. Rolls of 11 companies of the 1st Regiment of NY Volunteers.

27. Military records: Civil War

Records which are available for NY participants in the Civil War (1861-5) include national service records for soldiers, sailors, and marines, national pension records for the same participants, national claims records, numerous state records (service, bounty, claims, pension), and some county and town records. No bounty land awards were made for service in this war. A major index lists NY military _service_ records which are in the NA:

__The National Archives, INDEX TO COMPILED SERVICE RE-
CORDS OF VOLUNTEER UNION SOLDIERS WHO SERVED IN ORGANI-
ZATIONS FROM THE STATE OF NY, The Archives, Washington,
DC, Microfilm Publication M551, 159 rolls.

This index leads to the compiled service records which
are in files in the NA. The index to Union veteran
national _pension_ applications is:

__The National Archives, GENERAL INDEX TO PENSION FILES,
1861-1934, The Archives, Washington, DC, Microfilm
Publication T288, 544 rolls.

The pension file index points to pension records which
are filed in the NA. The first index may be consulted in
NYSL, NYPL, NA, NAFB, and FHL(FHC). The second is available at NA, NAFB, and FHL(FHC), and can also be borrowed
by your local library or by you from AGLL. Or you may
choose to have the indexes examined and to obtain the
service and pension records on your NY Civil War veteran
by employing NATF-80 in a mail request, or by going to
the NA personally, or by hiring a researcher to do the
work at NA for you. Instructions for these three possi-
bilities were given in the Revolutionary War section.
Details of many other Civil War records which are in the
NA will be found in:

__National Archives Staff, GUIDE TO GENEALOGICAL RESEARCH
IN THE NATIONAL ARCHIVES, The Archives, Washington, DC,
1982, Chapters 4-10, 16.

The most important published materials on Civil War
personnel of NY are:

__NY Adjutant General's Office, A RECORD OF COMMISSIONED
OFFICERS, NON-COMMISSIONED OFFICERS, AND PRIVATES OF
THE REGIMENTS OF NY IN SUPPRESSING THE REBELLION,
Comstock & Cassidy, Albany, NY, 1864-8, 8 volumes.
Index in NYSL, Albany, NY.

__NY State Adjutant General's Office, REGISTERS OF NY
REGIMENTS IN THE WAR OF THE REBELLION, Lyon Co., Albany, NY, 1894-1906, 43 volumes. Military summaries
for each regiment and for each soldier.

__F. Phisterer, NY IN THE WAR OF THE REBELLION, 1861-5,
Lyon Co., Albany, NY, 1912. Summary of each regiment's
history. Only officers listed.

The first two volumes list NY soldiers in the Civil War
under their regiments (infantry 1-194, cavalry 1-26,
artillery 1-16, others). You need first to discover your

ancestor's regiment by using the microfilm index (M551) noted in the previous paragraph. There are other important Civil War records in the NYSA:
__ABSTRACTS OF CIVIL WAR MUSTER ROLLS, copied out 1870-85, NYSA, Albany, NY. Name, enlistment date and place, age, date mustered in and out, rank, company, remarks.
__TOWN CLERKS' REGISTERS OF OFFICERS, SOLDIERS, AND SEAMEN COMPOSING THE QUOTAS OF TROOPS FURNISHED TO THE US DURING THE CIVIL WAR, 1865-7, NYSA, Albany, NY. Name, residence, birthdate and place, rank, regiment and company, dates of enlistment and muster, bounty paid, marital status, previous occupation, parents' names, dates of promotions, discharge, or death. Alphabetical by county, then by name of city, town, or village.
__RETURNS OF OFFICERS AND ENLISTED MEN WHO HAVE BEEN AND ARE NOW IN THE MILITARY OR NAVAL SERVICE, 1865, 6 volumes, NYSA, Albany, NY. Information similar to that just above, but usually much more.
The NYSA has further records relating to Civil War deaths, commissions, medical personnel, petitions, bounties, claims, and regimental histories. These are described in detail in the NYSA pamphlet:
__NYSA, CIVIL WAR RECORDS IN THE NYSA, The Archives, Albany, NY.
Please do not forget that the 1865 NY state census carries special schedules relating to Civil War service. The content of these includes a brief version of the items contained in the 6 volumes of RETURNS listed above: name, residence, age, place of birth, occupation, alien status, regiment, dates of entering and leaving the service, rank, promotions, wounds, and sometimes other data. The military schedules follow the general population schedule for each town or village. In the cases of cities, they appear after each ward.

For a detailed in-depth discussion of Civil War records as sources of genealogical information, consult:
__Geo. K. Schweitzer, CIVIL WAR GENEALOGY, order from the author at the address given on the title page of this book.
This book treats local, state, and national records, service and pension records, regimental and naval histories, enlistment rosters, hospital records, court-martial reports, burial registers, national cemeteries, gravestone allotments, amnesties, pardons, state mili-

tias, discharge papers, officer biographies, prisons, prisoners, battle sites, maps, relics, weapons, museums, monuments, memorials, deserters, black soldiers, Indian soldiers, and many other topics.

There is in the NA an index to service records of the Spanish-American War (1898-9) which has been microfilmed:
__The National Archives, GENERAL INDEX TO COMPILED SERVICE RECORDS OF VOLUNTEER SOLDIERS WHO SERVED DURING THE WAR WITH SPAIN, The Archives, Washington, DC, Microfilm Publication M871, 126 rolls, leads to service records in the NA.
The pension records for this war are indexed in:
__The National Archives, GENERAL INDEX TO PENSION FILES, 1861-1934, The Archives, Washington, DC, Microfilm Publication T288, 544 rolls, leads to pension records in the NA.
Both these indexes should be sought in NYSL, NYPL, NA, NAFB, FHL(FHC), and from AGLL. Again properly submitted NATF-80s (see section 26 for instructions) will bring you both military service and pension records (there were no bounty land records). Or you may choose to hire a searcher or go to the NA yourself. State of NY sources which you may find of value include:
__R. H. Saldana, INDEX TO THE NY SPANISH-AMERICAN WAR VETERANS, Saldana and Co., Salt Lake City, UT, 1987. Name, age, date enlisted, rank, regiment, dates mustered in and out, promotions.
__NY State Adjutant General's Office, NY IN THE SPANISH AMERICAN WAR, Lyon Co., Albany, NY, 1900, 3 volumes, with C. W. Herrick, INDEX, Lyon Co., Albany, NY, 1914. Summary for each regiment and for each man.
__SPANISH-AMERICAN WAR MUSTER ROLLS AND CARD INDEX, NYSA, Albany, NY.

Some national records for World War I and subsequent wars may be obtained from the following address. However, many documents were destroyed by an extensive fire in 1972. Write for Form 160:
__National Personnel Records Center (MPR), 9700 Page Blvd., St. Louis, MO 63132.
Draft records for World War I are in Record Group 163 (Records of the Selective Service System of World War I) at:

__The National Archives, Atlanta Branch, 1557 St. Joseph
Ave., East Point, GA 30344.
There are also useful NY sources of some data on World
War I and II veterans:
__CARD FILE OF NY STATE SERVICE MEN OF WORLD WAR I, NYSA,
Albany, NY.
__CARD FILE OF NY STATE SERVICE MEN OF WORLD WAR II,
NYSA, Albany, NY.

28. Mortuary records

Very few NY mortuary records have been transcribed
or microfilmed, even though a few are to be found in
manuscript form in archives. This means that you must
write directly to the mortuaries which you know or suspect were involved in burying your ancestor. Sometimes a
death account will name the mortuary; sometimes it is the
only one nearby; sometimes you will have to write several
to ascertain which one might have done the funeral arrangements. And you need to realize that before there
were mortuaries, the furniture or general merchandise
store in some communities handled burials, especially in
the supplying of coffins. You may discover that the
mortuary that was involved is now out of business, and so
you will have to try to discover which of the existing
ones may have inherited the records. Mortuaries for NY
with their addresses are listed in the following volumes:
__C. O. Kates, editor, THE AMERICAN BLUE BOOK OF FUNERAL
DIRECTORS, Kates-Boyleston Publications, New York, NY,
latest issue.
__NATIONAL DIRECTORY OF MORTICIANS, The Directory,
Youngstown, OH, latest issue.
One or both of these reference books will usually be
found in the offices of most mortuaries. In general, the
older mortuaries should be the more likely sources of
records on your progenitor. Please don't forget that
contemporary mortuaries are listed in city directories.
In all correspondence with mortuaries be sure to enclose
an SASE and make your letters very brief and to the
point.

29. Naturalization records

In the colonial period, many of the immigrants to
the territory that later became the US were from the
British Isles and since the colonies were British, they

were citizens. When immigrants of other nationalities began to arrive, they found that English traditions, customs, governmental structures, and language generally prevailed. The immigrant aliens were supposed to take oaths of allegiance and abjuration and/or to become naturalized by presenting themselves in court. In a few cases, naturalizations were by special acts of the colonial assemblies. In 1740, the English Parliament passed a law setting requirements for naturalization: 7 years residence in one colony plus an oath of allegiance to the Crown.

In 1776-7, all those who supported the Revolution were automatically considered to be citizens. During the period 1777-91, immigrants were obligated to take an oath of allegiance. In the year 1778, the Articles of Confederation of the newly established US made all citizens of states citizens of the new nation. The US Congress in 1790 enacted a national naturalization act which required one year's state residence, two year's US residence, and a loyalty oath taken in court. In 1795, a five year's residence came to be required along with a declaration of intent three years before the oath. Then in 1798, these times became 14 and 5 years respectively. Revised statutes of 1802 reverted to the 5 and 3 years of 1795. The declaration and oath could be carried out in any court which kept records (US, NY, county, city, town). Wives and children of naturalized males became citizens automatically. And persons who gave military service to the US and received an honorable discharge also received citizenship.

In 1906, the Bureau of Immigration and Naturalization was set up, and this agency has kept records on all naturalizations since then. Thus, if you suspect your ancestor was naturalized after September 1906, write to the following address for a Form 6641 which you can use to request records:
  Immigration and Naturalization Service, 425 I Street, Washington, DC, 20536.
For naturalization records before October 1906, you need to realize that the process could have taken place in any of several courts, in fact, any court which kept records could have been used.

Important books and articles containing <u>colonial</u>
naturalization records for NY include:

__L. F. Bellinger, OUR EARLY CITIZENS, NAMES OF THOSE
TAKING THE OATH OF ALLEGIANCE FROM 1715-73, in L. D.
MacVethy, THE BOOK OF NAMES, St. Johnsville, NY, 1933.

__THOSE TAKING THE OATH OF ABJURATION, 1715-6, NY Histor-
ical Quarterly, Volume 3, pages 35ff.

__M. S. Gueseppe, NATURALIZATIONS OF FOREIGN PROTESTANTS
IN THE AMERICAN COLONIES PURSUANT TO STATUTE 13 GEORGE
II, Huguenot Society of London, London, England, Volume
24. Naturalizations 1743-72.

__K. Scott and K. Stryker-Rodda, DENIZATIONS, NATURALIZA-
TIONS, AND OATHS OF ALLEGIANCE IN COLONIAL NY, Genealogical Publishing Co., Baltimore, MD, 1975. 18th-19th
centuries.

__R. J. Wolfe, THE COLONIAL NATURALIZATION LAW OF 1740
WITH LIST OF PERSONS NATURALIZED IN NY COLONY, 1740-69,
NY Genealogical and Biographical Register, Volume
94(1963), pages 132-147.

During the post-colonial period up to 1906, naturalization records will be found in many courts: federal,
state, and county. In the counties, the records (declarations, petitions, certificates, oaths, case papers,
depositions) are usually filed with the county clerk.
The most frequently used court before 1906 was the Court
of Common Pleas, but others were often involved. Records
after 1906 are also in the county clerk's office. Many
of these county records have been microfilmed and are
available at FHL and through FHC. They are listed in
Chapters 4 and 5 under the counties. Among published and
collected records for this period are:

__K. Scott, EARLY NY NATURALIZATIONS FROM FEDERAL, STATE,
AND LOCAL COURTS, 1792-1840, Genealogical Publishing
Co., Baltimore, MD, 1981.

__NATURALIZATION ARTICLES, NY Genealogical and Biograph-
ical Record, Volumes 94, 97, and 112, and Tree Talks,
Volumes 3, 4, 6, 9, 11, 12, and 22. [The former include NY federal court naturalizations 1790-1828, and
the latter include records from Allegany, Cayuga,
Cortland, Onondaga, St. Lawrence, Saratoga, Steuben,
and Wayne Counties.]

__NY CITY NATURALIZATIONS, PHOTOCOPIES AND INDEX FROM
FEDERAL, STATE, AND LOCAL COURTS, 1792-1906, Federal
Archives and Records Center, GSA, Building 22 Military
Ocean Terminal, Bayonne, NJ 07002.

__NY LEGISLATIVE NATURALIZATIONS in THE LAWS OF NY, 1777-
__1801, Weed, Parsons, and Co., Albany, NY, 1886-7.
__SUPREME COURT NATURALIZATIONS, FIRST NY JUDICIAL DIS-
__TRICT, 1896-1906, 11 volumes, NYSA, Albany, NY.
__NATURALIZATION RECORDS, 1824-1906, AND DECLARATIONS OF
__INTENTION, 1824-1940, US DISTRICT COURT FOR SOUTHERN NY
[NY CITY], Federal Archives and Records Center, Bay-
onne, NJ. Minutes of this court microfilmed on Nation-
al Archives Microfilm M886, rolls 1-9.
__DECLARATIONS OF INTENTION, 1845-1911, AND MINUTES 1790-
__1841, US CIRCUIT COURT FOR SOUTHERN NY, National Ar-
chives Microfilm M854, rolls 1-3.
__DECLARATIONS OF INTENTION, 1865-1929, AND NATURALIZA-
TION RECORDS 1865-1929, US DISTRICT COURT FOR EASTERN
NY [BROOKLYN], Federal Archives and Records Center,
Bayonne, NJ.

30. Newspapers

The first newspaper published in the colony of NY
was William Bradford's NY Gazette, started in NY City on
08 November 1725. The second newspaper was John P.
Zenger's NY Weekly Journal, a publication also based in
NY City and beginning in 1733. Other important early NY
City newspapers included Parker's NY Weekly Post Boy
(1743) and DeForeest's NY Evening Post (1744). The first
newspaper outside NY City was the Albany Gazette (1771)
and the second was the NY Journal and General Advertiser,
which John Holt moved from NY City to Kingston in 1777,
then had to move to Poughkeepsie when the British burned
Kingston. Samuel London started the NY Packet and American Advertiser in Fishkill. About 18 different newspapers were inaugurated in the colonial period, some expir-
ing quickly, some surviving. The contents of these
papers were largely political commentary and reports plus
advertisements, little space being devoted to local
events of other types. After the Revolution, many newspapers were set up, both in the older cities and in the
newly established population centers to the west. By
1810, they were being published in Bath and Canandaigua,
by 1820 in Batavia, Buffalo, Ogdenburg, Plattsburgh,
Rochester, and Watertown. Most of the early papers were
weekly or bi-weekly. Important early papers were the
Schenectady Mohawk Mercury (1796), the Kingston Ulster
County Gazette (1798), the Buffalo Gazette (1811), the
Albany Argus (1813), the Rochester Gazette (1816), the

Utica Observer (1817), and the Syracuse Onondaga Gazette (1823). In order to discover what newspapers were published in your ancestor's county before 1860, look under the county listings in:
__J. H. French, GAZETTEER OF THE STATE OF NY, Friedman, Port Washington, LI, NY, 1860.

Unfortunately, many of the newspapers listed in the above volume have not survived, but quite a number have, so you should seek them out. As time went on, newspapers became more and more valuable as genealogical reference sources because they increased their coverage of local news, including marriages, anniversaries, deaths, court actions, and obituaries. The best repositories for original and microfilm copies of NY newspapers are the NYSL, NYPL, and NYHS. In addition, local libraries and historical societies, as well as some NY university libraries, have newspaper holdings. To locate them, consult first these four national listings and finding aids which will point the way to many NY newspapers:
__C. S. Brigham, HISTORY AND BIBLIOGRAPHY OF AMERICAN NEWSPAPERS, 1690-1820, American Antiquarian Society, Worcester, MA, 1961, 2 volumes.
__W. Gregory, AMERICAN NEWSPAPERS, 1821-1936, H. W. Wilson, New York, NY, 1937.
__Library of Congress, NEWSPAPERS IN MICROFORM, The Library, Washington, DC, 1973, plus SUPPLEMENTS, to date.
__N. Schreiner-Yantis, NY NEWSPAPERS ON MICROFILM, in GENEALOGICAL AND LOCAL HISTORY BOOKS IN PRINT, The Author, Springfield, VA, 1985, Volume 2, pages 881-923.
Then, you need to pursue some published specialized NY lists of papers (along with their locations in some cases):
__CHECKLIST OF NY CITY NEWSPAPERS, 1725-1811, in I. N. P. Stokes, ICONOGRAPHY OF MANHATTAN ISLAND, 1498-1909, Arno Press, New York, NY, 1915-28(1967), Volume 2, pages 431-52.
__L. H. Fox, NY CITY NEWSPAPERS, 1820-50, A BIBLIOGRAPHY, in Papers of the Bibliographic Society, Volume 21, pages 1-131.
__P. Mercer, BIBLIOGRAPHIES AND LISTS OF NY STATE NEWS-PAPERS, NYSL, Albany, NY, latest edition.
__NYSL, A CHECKLIST OF NEWSPAPERS IN MICROFORM IN THE NYSL, The Library, Albany, NY, latest edition.

__S. Faibisoff and W. Tripp, A BIBLIOGRAPHY OF NEWSPAPERS IN 14 NY COUNTIES, in NY History, Volume 53 and following.

__Southern Tier Library System, NEWSPAPERS AND MICROFILMS IN ALLEGANY, CHEMUNG, SCHUYLER, STEUBEN, AND YATES COUNTIES, The System, Corning, NY, 1981.

__Rochester Public Library, UNION LIST OF SERIALS IN THE LIBRARIES OF ROCHESTER, The Library, Rochester, NY, 1917. Includes newspapers.

__D. Schultes, NEWSPAPERS ON MICROFILM IN THE SYRACUSE UNIVERSITY LIBRARIES, Syracuse University, Syracuse, NY, 1971.

__Chautauqua County Historical Society, A GUIDE TO NEWS-PAPERS IN MICROFORM IN CHAUTAUQUA COUNTY, NY, The Society, Westfield, NY, 1981.

In the major newspaper repositories (NYSL, NYPL, NYHS), you will find these catalogs, which will lead you to newspapers which they hold for your ancestor's county:
__NYSL, NOTEBOOK LIST OF NYSL NEWSPAPERS, NYSL, Albany, NY. Lists originals and microform copies. Search by city and town.

__NYPL, US NEWSPAPER CARD INDEX, at desk, Room 315, NYPL, New York, NY. Newspapers available at Annex.

__NYHS, NEWSPAPER CARD CATALOG, NYHS, New York, NY. Look under NY, then under city and town.

Also be sure to inquire about newspaper holdings of regional and local libraries, archives, historical and genealogical societies, historians' offices, and museums. Many of these organizations will be listed under the counties in Chapters 4 and 5. It is also well for you to recognize that many of the older NY newspaper publishers have files of their previous issues, and a few have even indexed some or all of them. Unfortunately, not too many newspapers are indexed, so you will need to go through them one-by-one. This means that you can avoid arduous searching only if you have a good idea of the approximate dates of the events you are seeking (marriage, anniversary, death, court action). Some useful indexes have been published, and they can be very valuable, especially for NY City, but most are incomplete:
__NY Times, NY TIMES INDEX, 1851–1982, The Times, New York, NY, 1983.

__B. A. and V. R. Falk, PERSONAL NAME INDEX TO THE NY TIMES INDEX, 1851–1974, Roxbury Data Interface, Succasunna, NJ, 1976–81.

__NY Times, NY TIMES OBITUARY INDEX, 1858-1968, The Times, New York, NY, 1970.

__NY Daily Tribune, NY DAILY TRIBUNE INDEX, 1875-1906, The Tribune, New York, NY, 10 volumes.

Don't fail to ask in various newspaper repositories, especially in pertinent LL, about newspaper indexes, since these often exist in card file or manuscript form in these places.

A considerable amount of work has been done in abstracting, indexing, and publishing genealogical information from early NY newspapers. Some of the derived data has been printed in various NY genealogical periodicals, and much of it appears in published volumes and typescripts. Among the more extensive works of this sort are:

__American Antiquarian Society, INDEX OF MARRIAGES AND DEATHS IN THE NY WEEKLY MUSEUM, 1788-1817, The Society, New York, NY, 1952.

__G. A. Barber, DEATHS FROM THE BROOKLYN EAGLE, 1841-71, The Compiler, New York, NY, 1963-4, 15 volumes. Typescript in NYGB and NYHS.

__G. A. Barber, MARRIAGES AND DEATHS IN THE NY EVENING POST, 1801-90, The Compiler, New York, NY, 1933-48, 78 volumes. Typescript in NYGB and NYHS.

__F. Q. Bowman, 10,000 VITAL [NEWSPAPER] RECORDS OF CENTRAL NY, 1813-50, Genealogical Publishing Co., Baltimore, MD, 1985. Newspaper abstracts.

__F. Q. Bowman, 10,000 VITAL [NEWSPAPER] RECORDS OF EASTERN NY, 1777-1834, Genealogical Publishing Co., Baltimore, MD, 1987. Newspaper abstracts.

__F. Q. Bowman, 10,000 VITAL RECORDS OF WESTERN NY, 1809-50, Genealogical Publishing Co., Baltimore, MD, 1985. Newspaper abstracts.

__J. Gavit, AMERICAN DEATHS AND MARRIAGES (NY), 1784-1829, Polyanthos, New Orleans, LA, 1976, 2 reels of microfilm. 40,000 names from 65 newspapers mostly from Hudson and Mohawk Valleys. Available in NYSL.

__F. B. Hough, AMERICAN BIOGRAPHICAL NOTES, SHORT NOTICES OF DECEASED PERSONS, Harbor Hill Books, Harrison, NY, 1975. Includes death notices from upstate NY newspapers.

__A. C. M. Kelly, HUDSON, NY, NEWSPAPERS, DEATHS AND MARRIAGES, 1802-51, The Compiler, Rhinebeck, NY, 2 volumes.

__A. C. M. Kelly, RHINEBECK, NY, NEWSPAPERS, DEATHS AND MARRIAGES, 1849-99, The Compiler, Rhinebeck, NY, 2 volumes.

__J. P. Maher, INDEX TO MARRIAGES AND DEATHS IN THE NY HERALD, 1825-55, Genealogical Publishing Co., Baltimore, MD, 1987.

__MARRIAGE AND DEATH NOTICES FROM BUFFALO NEWSPAPERS, in J. W. Foley, EARLY SETTLERS OF NY STATE, The Author, Akron, NY, 1934-42, 9 volumes, passim, with J. W. Foley, INDEX TO NAMES, The Author, Akron, NY, 1950.

__NY BAPTIST REGISTER ABSTRACTS, 1825-54, Baptist Historical Society, Utica, NY, Volumes 28, 31, 35.

__H. W. Reynolds, NOTICES OF MARRIAGES AND DEATHS IN POUGHKEEPSIE NEWSPAPERS, 1778-1825, Dutchess County Historical Society, Poughkeepsie, NY, 1930.

__J. Rush, MISSING PERSON ITEMS FROM THE NY WEEKLY TRIBUNE, 1843-64, The Compiler, Winter Park, FL, 1979.

__J. Rush, MARRIAGE ITEMS FROM THE NY WEEKLY TRIBUNE, 1843-9, The Compiler, Winter Park, FL, 1979.

__R. C. Sawyer, MARRIAGES AND DEATHS PUBLISHED IN THE CHRISTIAN INTELLIGENCER OF THE REFORMED DUTCH CHURCH, 1830-71, typescript, NYSL, Albany, NY, 1931, 17 volumes.

__K. Scott, DEATHS AND MARRIAGES FROM THE DOUBLE QUARTO EDITION OF THE NEW YORKER, 1836-41, National Genealogical Society, Washington, DC, 1980. 3000 marriages.

__K. Scott, GENEALOGICAL DATA FROM COLONIAL NY NEWSPAPERS, 1726-83, Genealogical Publishing Co., Baltimore, MD, 1977. 10,000 names.

__K. Scott, GENEALOGICAL DATA FROM THE NY MERCURY, 1752-96, NY Genealogical and Biographical Register, 1965-76, Volumes 96-107.

__K. Scott, GENEALOGICAL DATA FROM THE NY WEEKLY POST BOY, 1743-73, National Genealogical Society, Washington, DC, 1970. 5000 names.

__K. Scott, RIVINGTON'S NY NEWSPAPER, EXCERPTS FROM A LOYALIST PRESS, 1773-83, NY Historical Society, New York, NY, 1973.

__K. Scott and K. L. Gibbons, THE NY MAGAZINE: MARRIAGES AND DEATHS, 1790-7, Polyanthos, New Orleans, LA, 1975. Covers US.

__K. Scott, GENEALOGICAL ABSTRACTS FROM THE AMERICAN WEEKLY, 1719-46, Genealogical Publishing Co., Baltimore, MD, 1974.

__M. F. Stevens and R. L. Simpson, INDEX TO THE LONG

ISLANDER, 1839-81, Huntington Historical Society, Huntington, NY, 1974/6.

31. Published indexes for the US

There are many published indexes, microfilm indexes, and card indexes which list exceptionally large numbers of published genealogies or lots of genealogical data at the national level. The most important indexes dealing exclusively with NY have been listed in a previous section, the one entitled genealogical indexes. This section sets out further indexes to genealogies all over the US (and overseas in some instances). These indexes contain many references to genealogies of NY people and therefore you must not fail to look into them. Among the larger ones are:

__INTERNATIONAL GENEALOGICAL INDEX, FHL and FHC, microfilm. [over 90 million entries]
__FAMILY GROUP RECORDS COLLECTION, at FHL, applications to have it searched at FHC. [40 million entries]
__AIS INTEGRATED CENSUS INDEXES, 1790/1800/10, 1820, 1830, 1840, 1850NE, 1850S, 1850MW&W, FHL and FHC. [19 million entries]
__F. Rider, AMERICAN GENEALOGICAL (AND BIOGRAPHICAL) INDEX, Godfrey Memorial Library, Middletown, CT, Series 1(1942-52), 48 volumes, Series 2(1952-), over 160 volumes, more to come. [13 million entries so far]
__P. W. Filby and M. K. Meyer, PASSENGER AND IMMIGRATION LISTS INDEX, Gale Research Co., Detroit, MI, 1981-, 9 volumes, SUPPLEMENT volumes being published. [1.5 million entries so far]
__The Newberry Library, THE GENEALOGICAL INDEX OF THE NEWBERRY LIBRARY, G. K. Hall, Boston, MA, 1960, 4 volumes. [512 thousand entries]
__1906 DECENNIAL EDITION OF THE AMERICAN DIGEST: A COMPLETE TABLE OF AMERICAN CASES, 1658-1906, West Publishing Co., St. Paul, MN, 1911, volumes 21-25. [500 thousand entries]
__COMPUTERIZED GENEALOGICAL LIBRARY, 1864 S. State, Salt Lake City, UT 84115. [400 thousand entries]
__COMPUTERIZED ROOTS CELLAR, COMPUTERIZED FAMILY FILE, and COMPUTERIZED 4-GENERATION PEDIGREE CHART DATA BANK, Genealogical Helper, PO Box 368, Logan, UT 84321. [400 thousand entries in each of the first two, 250 thousand in the third]

_NY Public Library, DICTIONARY CARD CATALOG OF THE LOCAL HISTORY AND GENEALOGY DIVISION OF THE NY PUBLIC LIBRARY, G. K. Hall, Boston, MA, 1974, 20 volumes. [318 thousand entries]

_Library of Congress, LIBRARY OF CONGRESS INDEX TO BIOGRAPHIES, The Library, Washington, DC, 40 rolls of microfilm. [170 thousand entries]

_National Society of the DAR, DAR PATRIOT INDEX, The Society, Washington, DC, 1966/79, 2 volumes. [115 thousand entries]

_FHL LIBRARY CATALOG, SURNAME SECTION, original at FHL, microfilm copies at each FHC. [70 thousand entries]

_J. Munsell's Sons, INDEX TO AMERICAN GENEALOGIES, 1711-1908, Genealogical Publishing Co., Baltimore, MD, 1967. [60 thousand entries]

_M. J. Kaminkow, GENEALOGIES IN THE LIBRARY OF CONGRESS, Magna Carta, Baltimore, MD, 1981, and COMPLEMENT TO GENEALOGIES IN THE LIBRARY OF CONGRESS, Magna Carta, Baltimore, MD, 1981. [Over 50 thousand entries]

The books listed above are generally available at NYSL, NYPL, NYGB, NYHS, and FHL, as well as most LGL, some RL, and a few LL. The FHL materials are at FHC or access to them can be had through FHC. And the computerized data materials may be accessed through the places named.

32. Regional publications

In addition to national, state, and local publications, there are also some regional publications which should not be overlooked by any NY researcher. For the most part, these are volumes which are basically historical in character, but carry much genealogical information. They vary greatly in accuracy and coverage, so it is well to treat the data cautiously. In general, they cover specific regions which are usually made up of a few or many NY counties. In deciding which ones of these books to search for your forebears, you will need to make good use of the geographic and county maps of Chapter 1. The following works are ones which should prove useful to you. The classification into regions is only approximate and there may be overlap with neighboring regions.

Notable works relating to central NY include:

_F. Q. Bowman, 10,000 VITAL RECORDS OF CENTRAL NY, 1813-50, Genealogical Publishing Co., Baltimore, MD, 1985.

__C. E. Carley, GUIDE TO FINGER LAKES REGION HISTORICAL MATERIAL, Finger Lakes Library System, Ithaca, NY, 1976.

__F. H. Chase, SYRACUSE AND ITS ENVIRONS, Lewis Historical Publishing Co., New York, NY, 1924, 3 volumes.

__W. R. Cutter, GENEALOGICAL AND FAMILY HISTORY OF CENTRAL NY, Lewis Historical Publishing Co., New York, NY, 1912, 3 volumes.

__W. F. Galpin, CENTRAL NY, AN INLAND EMPIRE, COMPRISING ONEIDA, MADISON, ONANDAGA, CAYUGA, TOMPKINS, CORTLAND, AND CHENANGO COUNTIES AND THEIR PEOPLE, Lewis Historical Publishing Co., New York, NY, 1941, 4 volumes, volume 4 biographical.

__H. R. Malone, HISTORY OF CENTRAL NY, Historical Publishing Co., Indianapolis, IN, 1932, 3 volumes, volumes 2-3 biographical.

__SIX GENERATION ANCESTOR TABLES, Central NY Genealogical Society, Syracuse, NY, 1976-7, 5 volumes. About 5500 surnames.

__TREE TALKS, INDEXES TO VOLUMES 1-8, 1970-7, Central NY Genealogical Society, Syracuse, NY, 1978. Almost 100,000 name entries.

Published materials giving data on eastern NY are:

__F. Q. Bowman, 10,000 VITAL RECORDS OF EASTERN NY, 1777-1834, Genealogical Publishing Co., Baltimore, MD, 1987.

__N. Greene, THE STORY OF OLD FORT PLAIN AND THE MIDDLE MOHAWK VALLEY, 1690-1912, Clarke Publishing Co., Chicago, IL, 1913.

__N. Greene, HISTORY OF MOHAWK VALLEY, 1614-1925, Clarke Publishing Co., Chicago, IL, 1925, 4 volumes, volumes 3-4 biographical.

__N. Greene, HISTORY OF THE VALLEY OF THE HUDSON, 1609-1930, Clarke Publishing Co., Chicago, IL, 1931, 5 volumes, volumes 3-5 biographical.

__F. B. Hough, AMERICAN BIOGRAPHICAL NOTES, SHORT NOTICES OF DECEASED PERSONS, Harbor Hill Books, Harrison, NY, 1975. Includes death notices from upstate NY newspapers.

__T. P. Hughes, AMERICAN ANCESTRY, Munsell's Sons, Albany, NY, 1887, Volumes 1-2. Albany and Columbia County.

__A. C. M. Kelly, HUDSON VALLEY BAPTISM AND MARRIAGE RECORDS, The Compiler, Rhinebeck, NY, 1978. Lutheran and Reformed churches.

__L. D. McWethy, THE BOOK OF NAMES RELATING TO THE EARLY PALATINES AND THE FIRST SETTLERS IN THE MOHAWK VALLEY, Genealogical Publishing Co., Baltimore, MD, 1933(1981).

__C. Reynolds, HUDSON-MOHAWK GENEALOGICAL AND FAMILY MEMOIRS, Lewis Historical Publishing Co., New York, NY, 1911, 4 volumes. Use with care.

There are also a number of volumes dealing with Long Island:

__T. G. Bergen, GENEALOGIES OF THE STATE OF NY, LONG ISLAND EDITION, Lewis Historical Publishing Co., New York, NY, 1915, 3 volumes.

__T. G. Bergen, REGISTER IN ALPHABETICAL ORDER OF THE EARLY SETTLERS OF KINGS COUNTY, LONG ISLAND FROM ITS SETTLEMENT TO 1700, Polyanthos, New Orleans, LA, 1881-(1973).

__M. P. S. Bunker, LONG ISLAND GENEALOGIES, Genealogical Publishing Co., Baltimore, MD, 1895(1976).

__GENEALOGIES OF LONG ISLAND FAMILIES FROM THE NY GENEAL-OGICAL AND BIOGRAPHICAL RECORD, Genealogical Publishing Co., Baltimore, MD, 1987, 2 volumes.

__LONG ISLAND SOURCE RECORDS FROM THE NY GENEALOGICAL AND BIOGRAPHICAL RECORD, Genealogical Publishing Co., Baltimore, MD, 1987.

__H. I. Hazelton, THE BOROUGHS OF BROOKLYN AND QUEENS, COUNTIES OF NASSAU AND SUFFOLK, LONG ISLAND, NY, 1609-1924, Lewis Historical Publishing Co., New York, NY, 1925, 5 volumes, 4-5 biographical.

__W. S. Pelletreau and J. H. Brown, AMERICAN FAMILIES OF HISTORIC LINEAGE, LONG ISLAND EDITION, North Americana Society, New York, NY, 1913, 2 volumes.

__P. Ross, HISTORY OF LONG ISLAND, Lewis Publishing Co., New York, NY, 1902, 3 volumes. With genealogical notes.

__R. B. Sealock and P. A. Seely, LONG ISLAND BIBLIOG-RAPHY, Edwards Brothers, Ann Arbor, MI, 1940.

__H. F. Seversmith, COLONIAL FAMILIES OF LONG ISLAND, The Author, Washington, DC, 1939-64, 5 volumes. Further volumes on microfilm at NY State Library.

__H. F. Seversmith and K. Stryker-Rodda, LONG ISLAND GENEALOGICAL SOURCE MATERIAL, National Genealogical Society, Washington, DC, 1962.

__M. F. Stevens and R. L. Simpson, INDEX TO THE LONG ISLANDER, 1839-81, Huntington Historical Society, Huntington, NY, 1974/6.

__B. F. Thompson and C. J. Werner, HISTORY OF LONG IS-
LAND, Dodd, New York, NY, 1918, 4 volumes, 4th volume
biography and genealogy.

Now let us take a look at some books dealing with
the northern region of the state:
__G. G. Cole, HISTORICAL MATERIALS RELATING TO NORTHERN
NY, North Country Reference and Research Resources
Council, Canton, NY, 1976.
__W. R. Cutter, GENEALOGICAL AND FAMILY HISTORY OF NORTH-
ERN NY, Lewis Historical Publishing Co., New York, NY,
1910, 3 volumes.
__H. F. Landon, THE [NY] NORTH COUNTRY, Historical Pub-
lishing Co., Indianapolis, IN, 1932, 3 volumes, volumes
2-3 biographical.
The northeastern region of the state is dealt with in:
__F. Q. Bowman, LANDHOLDERS OF NORTHEASTERN NY, 1739-
1802, Genealogical Publishing Co., Baltimore, MD, 1983.
9000 names.
__W. E. Lamb, THE LAKE CHAMPLAIN AND LAKE GEORGE VALLEYS,
American Historical Co., New York, NY, 1940, 3 volumes,
volume 3 biographical.

As you might imagine, there are also numerous NY
City works. Among them are:
__M. Y. Beach, WEALTH AND BIOGRAPHY OF THE WEALTHY CITI-
ZENS OF THE CITY OF NY, Sun Office, New York, NY, 1855.
__ORIGINAL BOOK OF NEW YORK CITY DEEDS, 1672-5, AND
DOCUMENTS OF THE CITY OF NY AND LONG ISLAND, 1642-96,
NY Historical Society, New York, 1914.
__W. S. Pelletreau, HISTORIC HOMES AND INSTITUTIONS AND
GENEALOGICAL AND FAMILY HISTORY OF NY CITY, Lewis
Publishing Co., New York, NY, 1907, 4 volumes.
__J. A. Scoville, THE OLD MERCHANTS OF NY CITY, Greenwood
Press, New York, NY, 1968, 5 volumes.
__J. A. Stevens, Jr., COLONIAL RECORDS, NY CHAMBER OF
COMMERCE, 1768-84, Burt Franklin, New York, NY, 1867-
(1971).
__J. E. Stillwell, HISTORICAL AND GENEALOGICAL MISCEL-
LANY: DATA RELATING TO THE SETTLEMENT OF NY AND NJ,
Genealogical Publishing Co., Baltimore, MD, 1903-32-
(1970), 5 volumes.
__D. T. Valentine, MANUAL OF THE CORPORATION COUNCIL OF
THE CITY OF NY, New York, NY, 1841/2-70, 28 volumes,
with O. Hufeland, HISTORICAL INDEX, New York, NY, 1900.
2325 references.

M. Van Rensselaer, HISTORY OF THE CITY OF NY IN THE 17TH CENTURY, Macmillan, New York, NY, 1909, 2 volumes.

L. H. Weeks, PROMINENT FAMILIES OF NY CITY, The Historical Co., New York, NY, 1898.

Many, many other NY City reference works with varying amounts of genealogical data have been published. These include directories of ministers, attorneys, physicians, teachers, mariners, bank directors and officers, mechanics, carpenters, hatters, butchers, members of numerous societies (German, French, literary, musical, social, benevolent), firemen, merchants, manufacturers, actors, booksellers, cartmen, tradesmen, and hack drivers. A partial listing of these will be found in:

R. F. Bailey, GUIDE TO GENEALOGICAL AND BIOGRAPHICAL SOURCES FOR NY CITY (MANHATTAN), 1783-1898, New York, NY, 1954.

Published works relating to the southern and southeastern regions of the state of NY are:

R. F. Bailey, PRE-REVOLUTIONARY DUTCH HOUSES AND FAMILIES IN NORTHERN NJ AND SOUTHERN NY, Dover, New York, NY, 1936(1968).

W. R. Cutter, GENEALOGICAL AND FAMILY HISTORY OF SOUTHERN NY, Lewis Historical Publishing Co., New York, NY, 1913, 3 volumes.

C. J. Gehring, NY HISTORICAL MANUSCRIPTS, DUTCH, DELAWARE PAPERS, Volumes 18-19, Genealogical Publishing Co., Baltimore, MD, 1981. 17th century records while area was held by Swedes.

C. Reynolds, GENEALOGICAL AND FAMILY HISTORY OF SOUTHERN NY AND HUDSON RIVER VALLEY, Lewis Historical Publishing Co., New York, NY, 1914, 3 volumes. Use with care.

L. S. Zimm, SOUTHEASTERN NY, A HISTORY OF THE COUNTIES OF ULSTER, DUTCHESS, ORANGE, ROCKLAND, AND PUTNAM, Lewis Historical Publishing Co., New York, NY, 1946, 3 volumes, 3rd volume biographical.

Finally, let us look at some of the many volumes published on the western and southwestern areas of NY state:

F. Q. Bowman, 10,000 VITAL RECORDS OF WESTERN NY, 1809-50, Genealogical Publishing Co., Baltimore, MD, 1985.

W. R. Cutter, GENEALOGICAL AND FAMILY HISTORY OF WESTERN NY, Lewis Historical Publishing Co., New York, NY, 1912, 3 volumes.

__L. R. Doty, HISTORY OF THE GENESEE COUNTRY, Clarke Publishing Co., Chicago, IL, 1925, 4 volumes. Allegany, Cattaraugus, Chautauqua, Chemung, Erie, Genesee, Livingston, Monroe, Niagara, Ontario, Orleans, Schuyler, Steuben, Wayne, Wyoming, & Yates Counties. Volumes 3-4 biographical.

__W. J. Doty, THE HISTORIC ANNALS OF SOUTHWESTERN NY, Lewis Historical Publishing Co., New York, NY, 1940, 3 volumes.

__J. W. Foley, EARLY SETTLERS OF NY STATE, THEIR ANCESTORS AND DESCENDANTS, T. J. Foley, Akron, NY, 1934-42, 9 volumes, with INDEX TO NAMES.

__J. H. Hotchkiss, A HISTORY OF THE PURCHASE AND SETTLEMENT OF WESTERN NY AND THE RISE OF THE PRESBYTERIAN CHURCH, Dodd, New York, NY, 1848.

__W. E. Morrison, MORRISON'S ANNALS OF WESTERN NY, Morrison, Orvis, NY, 1975.

__O. Turner, HISTORY OF THE PIONEER SETTLEMENT OF PHELP'S AND GORHAM'S PURCHASE AND MORRIS RESERVE, Heart of the Lakes Publishers, Interlaken, NY, 1854(1976).

__O. Turner, PIONEER HISTORY OF THE HOLLAND PURCHASE OF WESTERN NEW YORK, Heart of the Lakes Publishers, Interlaken, NY, 1850(1976).

__M. R. Wilner, THE NIAGARA FRONTIER, Clarke Publishing Co., Chicago, IL, 1931, 4 volumes.

The above volumes will be found in NYSL, NYPL, and NYHS, most in NYGB, many in FHL (and through FHC), and in LGL, and those pertinent to their locations in RL and LL.

33. Tax lists

During NY state's history, there have been various direct taxes. These have been levied upon individuals (the poll or head tax), on land (the real property tax), on personal belongings (the personal property tax), and on income (the income tax). In addition, there have been some indirect taxes: tariffs, duties, licenses, and permits. During colonial times in NY, there was a land tax called quitrent. This was an annual money payment which generated some records. A series of these records is available in the NYSA:

__ACCOUNTS OF QUITRENTS AND COMMUTATIONS, 1728-79, Colonial Treasurer Records, NYSA, Albany, NY.

In the early years of NY state, taxes came to be collected on a town, village, or city level. Records were generally kept in the offices of these local units, and consisted largely of assessment rolls and tax lists. They generally give names, amount of property, and location of the property. By following tax records for consecutive years, you can sometimes tell when young men came of age, when individuals purchase and sell land, when people leave or enter an area, and when persons die and leave their land to heirs. Beginning in the 1850s or 1860s, records in some areas were turned in to county offices and are therefore available there. In short, NY tax lists should be sought in towns, villages, cities, and counties. The locations of many of these are indicated in the following series of volumes:

NY Historical Resources Center, GUIDES TO HISTORICAL RESOURCES IN NY COUNTY REPOSITORIES, Cornell University Press, Ithaca, NY, 1978-. A guide for each county.

Some of the tax records for 16 NY counties have been microfilmed by the FHL and are available through FHC. These are listed in Chapters 4 and 5 and in the following volume:

A. Eakle and others, DESCRIPTIVE INVENTORY OF THE NY COLLECTION, University of UT Press, Salt Lake City, UT, 1980, pages 195-9. Counties of Albany, Broome (1837/-40/69-70), Chenango (1851-65), Cortland (1830-80), Dutchess (1717-79, 1803-90), Herkimer (1817), Madison (1805/12), Montgomery (1795-6), Onondaga (1827), Ontario (1813-22), Orange (1798, 1803-4), Saratoga (1840), Sullivan (1776), Ulster (1709-38, 1767), Warren (1857-69), Westchester (1763). All records incomplete.

There also exist in many counties voter lists for various years and jury lists for different court sessions. Some of these (as is the case for tax lists) have been destroyed or lost. However, many still exist and may be sought out in the counties, but you need to realize that they generally carry very little genealogical information. About all they do is to place your ancestor in the county at the indicated time(s).

34. Will and intestate records

When a person died leaving property (an estate), it was necessary for NY governmental authorities to see that it was properly distributed according to the law. If a will had been written, it had often been recorded with a governmental official, but whether it had or not, it was

presented for authentication (probate) to the proper
officials. When the process had been carried through,
the administrator(s) named in the will did the actual
work of distributing the estate, usually under the super-
vision of the officials. If no will had been written,
this being called an <u>intestate</u> situation, the authorities
appointed an administrator who carried out the distribution of the estate. Estate records consist of wills,
petitions listing all possible heirs with their addresses, letters of administration, administration bonds,
accounts, inventories, bills, receipts, indexes, and case
files (packets or folders containing detailed papers
relating to the estate). The early records do not contain all these items, but later on, especially after
1823, the records became richer.

Under Dutch rule, the governor was responsible for
managing estate matters. He usually delegated this
activity to his secretary or to notaries who kept appropriate records. When the English took over in 1664, the
governor continued as the responsible officer for estates, and instructed the colony's six Courts of Sessions
and the Court of Assizes to manage them. After 1686, the
governor, his secretary, and/or his council constituted a
Prerogative Court which took over the handling of estates. Then in 1691, each city and county in the colony
got a Court of Common Pleas. Those far away from NY City
handled small estates, but the colony-wide Prerogative
Court continued to handle all large estates and all those
for counties near NY City. In other words, most estates
were handled on a colony-wide level until the Revolutionary War, the major centers for record keeping being
Albany and NY City. In 1778, in the sections of NY that
were under Patriot control, the Prerogative Court was
replaced by a state-wide Court of Probates. In addition,
some special estate agents (called surrogates) were
appointed in northern counties. In 1787, a Surrogate
Court was established in each NY county to take care of
estates and guardianships, and the Court of Probates
became an appeal court for estate matters. It also
handled a few specialized estate cases, but the vast
majority were now taken care of by the county-level
Surrogate Courts. The Court of Probates was abolished in
1823, with the estate appeals function falling to the
Court of Chancery. This court was in turn abolished in
1847, and the Appellate Division of the Supreme Court

took over the appeals. During the early post-Revolutionary years up to 1829, the Supreme Court and the Court of
Common Pleas sometimes managed estates.

Many of the records prior to the 1787 establishment
of the county Surrogate Courts have been transcribed,
abstracted, indexed, and/or published. Among the important volumes which you should search for your forebears'
estate records are:

__ABSTRACTS OF WILLS ON FILE IN THE SURROGATE'S OFFICE OF
NEW YORK COUNTY, 1665-1800, NY Historical Society, New
York, NY, 1892-1909, 17 volumes. 90,000 names. Also
some from Hudson Valley, Long Island, Staten Island,
and NJ.

__G. A. Barber, INDEX OF THE LETTERS OF ADMINISTATION
FILED IN NY COUNTY, 1743-1875, The Author, New York,
NY, 1950-1, 3 volumes.

__B. Fernow, CALENDAR OF NY WILLS ON FILE IN THE OFFICES
OF THE CLERK OF THE COURT OF APPEALS, OF THE COUNTY
CLERK AT ALBANY, AND OF THE SECRETARY OF STATE, 1626-
1836, Genealogical Publishing Co., Baltimore, MD,
1896(1967), 17 volumes. 2000 NY wills, over 15,000
names.

__L. M. Friedman, WILLS OF EARLY NY SETTLERS, Baltimore,
MD, 1915.

__L. Hershkowitz, THE WILLS OF EARLY NEW YORK JEWS, 1704-
99, American Jewish Historical Society, Waltham, MA,
1967. Also some Christians.

__A. C. M. Kelly, INDEX TO WILLS, 1777-1800, ON FILE IN
THE SURROGATE'S OFFICE, CITY OF NY, The Author, Rhinebeck, NY, 1981.

__R. C. Sawyer, INDEX OF WILLS OF NY COUNTY, 1662-1875,
The Author, New York, NY, 1930, 1950-1, 5 volumes.

__K. Scott, GENEALOGICAL DATA FROM ADMINISTRATION PAPERS
OF THE NY STATE COURT OF APPEALS, National Society of
Colonial Dames of NY, New York, NY, 1972. 8000 names
from the 17th, 18th, and 19th centuries.

__K. Scott and J. A. Owre, GENEALOGICAL DATA FROM INVEN-
TORIES OF NY ESTATES, 1666-1825, NY Genealogical and
Biographical Society, New York, NY, 1970. 4700 names.

__K. Scott, GENEALOGICAL DATA FROM NY ADMINISTRATION
BONDS, 1753-99, NY Genealogical and Biographical Society, New York, NY, 1969. 4000 names.

__K. Scott, RECORDS OF THE CHANCERY COURT, PROVINCE AND
STATE OF NY GUARDIANSHIPS, 1691-1815, Holland Society
of NY, New York, NY, 1971.

__EARLY WILLS, MAYOR'S COURT GUARDIANSHIPS, AND EARLY
  INVENTORIES (1666-1775), National Genealogical Society
  Quarterly, Volumes 51, 54-56, passim.
__W. A. D., Eardeley, EARDELEY MANUSCRIPT COLLECTION OF
  NY STATE WILLS, at NYGB and Brooklyn Historical Socie-
  ty.
__W. A. D. Eardeley, INDEX TO WILLS OF NY STATE, The
  Author, 1653-1815, Brooklyn, NY, 1941.
__R. C. Sawyer, INDEX OF NY STATE WILLS, 1662-1850, IN
  THE OFFICE OF THE SURROGATE FOR NY COUNTY, The Author,
  New York, NY, 1932, 2 volumes.
__R. C. Sawyer, INDEX OF WILLS OF NY COUNTY, 1662-1875,
  The Author, New York, NY, 1930, 1950-1, 5 volumes.
__R. C. Sawyer and G. A. Barber, ABSTRACTS OF WILLS FOR
  NY COUNTY, 1801-56, The Authors, New York, NY, 1936-50.

    The original will, probate, estate, inventory,
dower, administrator, and guardianship records from 1787
until now are located in the NY counties, in the Clerk's
Office or in the Surrogate's Office or in a county repository such as that of the county historian or the county
historical society. Records for 48 counties have been
indexed in a valuable series of genealogical periodical
articles:
__ESTATE AND GUARDIANSHIP RECORDS FOR NY COUNTIES, Tree
  Talks, Volumes 1-23, passim, and NY Genealogical and
  Biographical Record, Volumes 11, 47, 55-57, 61, 65,
  passim.
There also exist typescript abstracts and/or indexes of
the records for about 20 NY counties. These should be
sought out in NYSL, NYPL, NYGB, NYHS, and in pertinent RL
and LL. The estate records of practically all NY counties have been microfilmed by the FHL and are therefore
available through the FHC. An extensive listing of them
may be had in:
__A. Eakle and others, DESCRIPTIVE INVENTORY OF THE NY
  COLLECTION, University of UT Press, Salt Lake City, UT,
  1980, pages 69ff.
You will discover from this volume that FHL has also
microfilmed most of the important colony-wide and state-
wide pre-1787 estate records. It is very important when
you investigate estate records to seek out the petition
(gives date and place of death, lists all possible heirs
and their addresses) and the case file or packet (contains detailed papers, usually with family data) in
addition to the will.

35. WPA records

During the late 1930s and early 1940s, the Historical Records Survey of the Works Progress Administration (WPA) did a very large amount of work in surveying and inventorying many NY records. The typescript volumes which they produced are exceptionally valuable for indicating what records existed and where they were about 50 years ago. They, therefore, serve as guides to records which you might want to use in your progenitor search. You need, of course, to remember that these materials are out of date, and thus some of the records have been lost and others are no longer in the places indicated. Among the state and regional typescripts are the following, many of which have been noted previously:

__Historical Records Survey, GUIDE TO DEPOSITORIES OF MANUSCRIPT COLLECTIONS IN NY STATE, EXCLUSIVE OF NY CITY, WITH SUPPLEMENT, WPA, Albany, NY, 1941-4.

__Historical Records Survey, GUIDE TO MANUSCRIPT DEPOSITORIES IN NY CITY, WPA, New York, NY, 1941.

__Historical Records Survey, GUIDE TO THE TEN MAJOR REPOSITORIES OF MANUSCRIPT COLLECTIONS IN NY STATE (EXCLUSIVE OF NY CITY), WPA, New York, NY, 1941.

__Historical Records Survey, GUIDE TO PUBLIC VITAL STATISTICS IN NY STATE, INCLUDING NY CITY, WPA, Albany, NY, 1942, 3 volumes.

__Historical Records Survey, GUIDE TO VITAL STATISTICS RECORDS OF CHURCHES IN NY STATE, EXCLUSIVE OF NY CITY, WPA, Albany, NY, 1942, 2 volumes.

__Historical Records Survey, GUIDE TO VITAL STATISTICS RECORDS IN THE CITY OF NY CHURCHES, WPA, New York, NY, 1942, 5 volumes.

__Historical Records Survey, INVENTORY OF THE COUNTY ARCHIVES, NY CITY: BRONX, KINGS, AND RICHMOND COUNTIES, WPA, New York, NY, 1939-42, 3 volumes. Unpublished volumes on the other boroughs are in the NY Municipal Reference Library, New York, NY.

__Historical Records Survey, INVENTORY OF THE COUNTY ARCHIVES OF NY STATE, ALBANY, BROOME, CATTARAUGUS, CHAUTAUQUA, CHEMUNG, AND ULSTER COUNTIES, WPA, Albany, NY, 1937-40, 6 volumes. Unpublished volumes on the other counties in NYSL.

__Historical Records Survey, INVENTORY OF THE CHURCH ARCHIVES OF NY CITY, WPA, New York, NY, 1939-41, 9 volumes. Episcopal, Eastern Orthodox, Friends, Lutheran, Methodist, Presbyterian, Reformed, Roman Catholic.

__Historic Records Survey. INVENTORY OF THE CHURCH ARCHIVES OF NY STATE, PROTESTANT EPISCOPAL CHURCH: DIOCESES OF WESTERN NY AND OF ROCHESTER, WPA, Albany, NY, 1939/41, 2 volumes.

__Historical Records Survey, INVENTORY OF MAPS LOCATED IN VARIOUS STATE, COUNTY, MUNICIPAL, AND OTHER PUBLIC OFFICES IN NY STATE (EXCLUSIVE OF NY CITY), WPA, Albany, NY, 1942.

Abbreviations

A	Agricultural Census
AGLL	American Genealogical Lending Library, Bountiful, UT
C	Union Civil War Veteran Census
CH	Court House(s) and County Archives
DAR	Daughters of the American Revolution
E	Early Pre-1790 Census-Like Lists
FHC	Family History Center(s), Genealogical Society of UT
FHL	Family History Library, Genealogical Society of UT, Salt Lake City, UT
I	Industrial Censuses
LGL	Large Genealogical Libraries
LL	Local Library(ies) and Other Local Repositories
M	Mortality Censuses
NA	National Archives, Washington, DC
NAFB	National Archives Field Branch(es)
NYSA	New York State Archives, Albany, NY
NYGB	New York Genealogical and Biographical Society, New York, NY
NYHS	New York Historical Society, New York, NY
NYPL	New York City Public Library, New York, NY
NYSL	New York State Library, Albany, NY
P	Pensioner Census, Revolutionary War
R	Regular Federal Censuses
RL	Regional Library(ies)
S	NY State Censuses

Chapter 3

RECORD LOCATIONS

1. Introduction

The purpose of this chapter is to describe for you the major genealogical record repositories for NY records. These repositories are of two major types, libraries and archives. In general, libraries hold materials which have been published in printed, typescript, photocopies, and microfilm (microcard, microfiche) forms. Archives, on the other hand, are repositories for original records, largely in manuscript (handwritten) form, but also often as microfilm copies. Usually, libraries will have some original materials, and archives will have some published materials, but the predominant character of each is as indicated. When visiting and making use of the materials of repositories, there are several rules which almost all of them have. (1) You are required to check all overcoats, brief cases, and packages. (2) You are required to present some identification and to sign a register or fill out a form. (3) There is to be no smoking, no eating, no loud talk, and the use of pencils only. (4) All materials are to be handled with extreme care, with no injury to or defacing of any of them. (5) Materials are usually not to be returned to the stacks or drawers from which they came, but are to be returned to designated carts, tables, or shelves. (6) Upon leaving you should submit all materials for inspection and/or pass through security devices.

As mentioned at the beginning of Chapter 2, the major repositories for NY genealogical materials are the NY State Library (NYSL), the NY State Archives (NYSA) plus some other state agencies, all in Albany, the NY Genealogical and Biographical Society Library (NYGB), the NY Historical Society Library (NYHS), the NY Public Library (NYPL), all three of these in NY City, the Genealogical Society of Utah, Family History Library (FHL) in Salt Lake City and its numerous Family History Center branches (FHC) all over the world, the National Archives (NA) in Washington and its Field Branches (NAFB) in several cities, regional libraries (RL) in various NY cities, local libraries (LL) in many cities and towns of NY, and county court houses (CH) and record repositories

in NY county seats. Libraries and archives have finding
aids to facilitate locating the records which they hold.
These aids are usually alphabetically arranged lists or
indexes according to names or locations or subjects or
authors or titles, or combinations of these, or they may
be by dates. They consist of computer catalogs, card
catalogs, microform catalogs, printed catalogs, typed
catalogs and lists, various indexes, inventories, calendars, and tables of contents. In using these aids,
especially computer, card, and microform catalogs, they
must be searched in as many ways as possible to ensure
that you extract everything from them. These ways are by
name, by location, by subject, by author, by title, and
sometimes by date. Sometimes certain catalogs are arranged by only one or two of these categories, but other-
wise be sure and search them for all that are applicable.
To help you to recall these categories, remember the word
SLANT, with S standing for subject, L for location, A for
author, N for name, and T for title. This is not, however, the order in which they should be searched for the
maximum efficiency. They should be searched N-L-S-A-T.
First, search the catalog for N(name), that is, for the
surnames of all your NY forebears. Second, search the
catalog for L(location), that is, look under all places
where your ancestor lived (NY colony, NY state, region,
county, town, village), but especially the county.
Examine every entry in order to make sure you miss nothing. Third, look under appropriate S(subject) headings,
such as the titles related to the sections in Chapter 1
[Bible, biography, birth, cemetery, census, church denomination, church name, court, Daughters of the American
Revolution, death, divorce, emigration, ethnic group name
(such as Germans, Huguenots, Irish), genealogy, historical records, immigration, marriage, US-history-Revolu-
tionary War, US-history-War of 1812, US-history-Civil
War, naturalization, newspaper, NY (colony), pensions,
tax, will], but never neglecting these [biography, deeds,
epitaphs, family records, genealogy, registers of births
etc., wills]. Then finally, look under A(author) or
T(title) for books mentioned in the sections of Chapter 2
which you need to examine.

When you locate references in finding aids to materials you need to examine, you will usually find that a
numbered or alphabetized or combined code accompanies the
listing. This is the access code which you should copy

down, since it tells you where the material is located.
For books it will usually be a code which refers to shelf
positions. For microfilms, it usually refers to drawers
and reel numbers. For manuscripts, it usually refers to
folders, files, or boxes. In some repositories, the
materials will be out on shelves or in cabinets to which
you have access. In other repositories you will need to
give the librarian or archivist a call slip on which you
have written the title and code for the material so that
it can be retrieved for you. In the microfilm areas of
repositories you will find microform readers which
attendants can help you with, if necessary.

Never leave a library or archives without discussing
your research with a librarian or archivist. These
people are trained specialists who know their collections
and the ways for getting into them. And they can often
suggest innovative approaches to locating data relating
to your progenitors. They also can usually guide you to
other finding aids. When you do discuss your work with
librarians and archivists, please remember that they are
busy people with considerable demand on their time. So
be brief, get to the point, and don't bore them with
irrelevant detail. They will appreciate this, and you
and others will get more and better service from them.

In general, you cannot expect to do much of your
genealogy by corresponding with libraries and archives.
The reason is that the hard-working professionals who run
these repositories have little time to give to answering
mail. This is because of the heavy demands of serving
the institutions which employ them, of maintaining the
collection, and of taking care of patrons who visit them.
Some simply cannot reply to mail requests. Others will
answer one brief question which can be quickly looked up
in a finding aid, but none of them can do even brief
research for you. If you do write them, make your letter
very brief, get right to the point, enclose an SASE, and
be prepared to wait. Repositories will generally not
recommend researchers you can hire, but they will sometimes provide you with a list of researchers. Such a
list will bear no warranty from the repository, and they
in no way have any responsibility toward either you or
the researcher, because they are not in the business of
certifying searchers.

2. The NY State Library (NYSL)

The NY State Library (NYSL) is the major repository
for printed, typescript, photocopied, microform, and
original NY genealogical records in the state of NY. The
NYSL is located on the 7th and 11th floors of the Cultural Education Center, Empire State Plaza, Albany, NY
12230. The hours are 9:00 am–5:00 pm, Monday–Friday,
except holidays, and the telephone number is 1–(518)–474–
5161. Be sure and call before you visit since the hours
could be changed. The Empire State Plaza sits in downtown Albany, and the Cultural Education Center (housing
the NYSL) is at its south end, sitting opposite the State
Capitol, which occupies the north end. There is parking
under the Plaza and on the east side of the Cultural
Education Center. To get to the Plaza, connect with I–
787, take it toward downtown Albany, then get off at the
Empire Plaza Exit, which will take you directly to the
Plaza. Several accommodations are within walking dis-
tance: Albany Hilton Hotel [State and Lodge, Zip 12205,
1–(518)–459–9105], Econolodge Inn Towne [300 Broadway,
Zip 12207, 1–(518)–434–4222], Mansion Hill Inn [115
Philip St., Zip 12202, 1–(518)–465–2083]. Many others
are within a couple of miles. A detailed list may be
obtained from the Albany County Visitors Bureau, 32 South
Pearl St., Albany, NY 12207.

Before visiting the NYSL, you should write them for
their major how-to materials, sending them $5 for the
cost of the large brochure and postage. These publications describe their holdings and tell you how to access
and use them.

__NYSL, GATEWAY TO AMERICA, GENEALOGICAL RESEARCH IN THE
NYSL, The Library, Albany, NY, latest edition.
__NYSL, HOW TO FIND INFORMATION IN THE LOCAL HISTORY AND
GENEALOGY AREA, The Library, Albany, NY, latest
edition.
__NYSL, INFORMATION SHEETS ON ADOPTION, CENSUS, DAR,
MILITARY, NATURALIZATION, VITAL RECORDS, AND OTHER
SUBJECTS, The Library, Albany, NY, latest editions.
__NYSL, MANUSCRIPTS AND SPECIAL COLLECTIONS, A GUIDE TO
COLLECTIONS AND SERVICES, NYSL, Albany, NY, latest
edition.
__NYSL, CARTOGRAPHIC RESOURCES AND SERVICES OF THE NYSL,
NYSL, Albany, NY, latest edition.

Upon going into the NYSL, you will discover that it has three research areas of particular importance to genealogical researchers: the Local History and Genealogy Area, the Microforms Center, both on the 7th Floor, and the Manuscripts and Special Collections Room on the 11th Floor. The Local History and Genealogy Area has printed and typescript genealogical and historical works, and original newspapers, along with many indexes, catalogs, and other finding aids. The Microforms Center has microforms of censuses, census indexes, city directories, newspapers, and periodicals, plus printed indexes and catalogs. The Manuscripts and Special Collections Room has manuscripts, maps, atlases, and some censuses, with indexes and finding aids. The major finding aids in the local History and Genealogy Area are as follows.

__(LHG-1) MICROFICHE CATALOG, search by name, location (NY colony, NY state, region, county, city, town, village), subject, author, title. Look up all your NY surnames and examine every listing under the locations where they lived.

__(LHG-2) AUTOMATED SUBJECT/TITLE COMPUTER CATALOG, search by name, location (NY colony, NY state, county, city, town, village), subject, title.

__(LHG-3) AUTOMATED AUTHOR/TITLE COMPUTER CATALOG, search by author, title.

__(LHG-4) SURNAME CARD INDEX, look up every NY ancestor's name. Catalog lists genealogical data in books, periodicals, pamphlets, manuscripts, compilations, and Bibles.

__(LHG-5) VITAL RECORDS CARD INDEX, look under every NY county of interest to you, then under place within the county. Identifies church and cemetery record lists which you can then examine for your ancestors. Also identifies some census, obituary, tax, and will lists.

__(LHG-6) CITY DIRECTORY CARD INDEX, look under city and county. Also refers to older telephone directories.

__(LHG-7) LOCAL HISTORY ARTICLE CARD INDEX, in 5 parts: (1) Albany, (2) US, (3) NY State, (4) Subjects, (5) Biography. Part (2) is inactive. Lists only articles, not books.

__(LHG-8) NEW PROJECT GENEALOGICAL DATA CARD INDEX, look under surnames of interest to you. Lists names on genealogical forms submitted for DAR membership.

__(LHG-9) REVOLUTIONARY WAR SOLDIERS CARD INDEX, look under name of every ancestor who may have been a Revolutionary War veteran.

__(LHG-10) MASTER INDEX TO NY STATE DAR GENEALOGICAL RECORDS, NY DAR Chapters, Albany, NY, 1971, and SUPPLE-MENT, 1972-8, NY DAR Chapters, Albany, NY, 1978. Look up every NY surname and location of interest to you. Indexes over 600 volumes of Bible, cemetery, census, church, county, naturalization, obituary, and town records collected by the DAR.

You can use these finding aids to locate the numerous books referred to in Chapter 2, and to locate many others which may refer to your forebears. When you find a book or typescript or article you want to see, simply copy down the access numbers on the listing, then go to the shelves and get the work. Some items may need to be requested from a librarian. Do not go to the above finding aids in the order in which they are listed. Later on, after we have discussed many other finding aids in the NYSL, we will tell you the most efficient order in which to use them.

Now, let's look at some of these other finding aids. In the Microfilm Center, the following will be found:

__(MIC-11) A GUIDE TO THE MICROFORM COLLECTIONS IN THE NYSL, The Library, Albany, NY, latest edition. See especially these listings: American Directories, Early American Newspapers, Friends NY Yearly Meeting, Gavit's Deaths and Marriages, Great Britain Colonial NY Records, Great Britain Loyalist Records, Index to Compiled Service Records of NY Volunteer Union Soldiers in the Civil War, Index to Passenger Lists at NY 1820-46, NY County and Regional Histories and Atlases, NYHS Early Orderly Books, NY State Balloting Book 1825, NY State Censuses, Published NY Colonial Records, Shaker Manuscripts 1723-1952, US Censuses, US City Director-ies.

__(MIC-12) FEDERAL NY CENSUS INDEXES, PRINTED FOR 1790-1860, and MICROFILM FOR 1880 AND 1900, Look up all pertinent ancestors' names.

__(MIC-13) GUIDE TO MICROFILM OF NY STATE 1915-25 CEN-SUSES, look up all pertinent ancestors' names in cen-suses.

__(MIC-14) M. Douglas and M. Yates, NY STATE CENSUS RECORDS, FEDERAL AND STATE, 1790-1925, NYSL, Albany, NY, 1981. Search all available censuses for your ancestor(s).

__(MIC-15) Research Publications, CITY DIRECTORIES OF THE

US THROUGH 1901, Research Publications, Woodbridge, CT, 1983. Look for your ancestor's city and county.

__(MIC-16) NOTEBOOK LISTING OF NYSL NEWSPAPERS, NYSL, Albany, NY. Lists both microfilms located in Microform Center and originals in Manuscripts and Special Collections Room. Look under city or town.

__(MIC-17) J. T. Ericson, GENEALOGY AND LOCAL HISTORY GUIDES, Parts 1-9, Microfilming Corp. of America, Sanford, NC, 1982-6. Listing of large collection of microfilms of family genealogies, genealogical compilations, and local histories. Search name, location, author, title.

__(MIC-18) REEL INDEX TO MICROFILMS OF NY COUNTY AND REGIONAL HISTORIES AND ATLASES, Research Publications, Woodbridge, CT, 1977. Search by location.

The NYSL has all the microforms listed in the above finding aids. When you locate censuses, directories, newspapers, genealogies, histories, or atlases in them that you want to see, copy down the accession numbers, and request the microforms at the desk. Then take them to a reader and use them. Return all materials to the desk.

On the 11th floor, the Manuscripts and Special Collections Room will be found. They have a number of major finding aids which will facilitate your locating of pertinent manuscripts, maps, atlases, and censuses. These include:

__(MSC-19) MANUSCRIPT CARD CATALOG, 11th Floor, Manuscripts and Special Collections Room, NYSL. Search by name, location (NY state, NY colony, region, county, city, town), and subject.

__(MSC-20) D. E. E. Mix, CATALOGUE OF MAPS AND SURVEYS IN THE OFFICES OF THE SECRETARY OF STATE, STATE ENGINEER AND SURVEYOR, AND COMPTROLLER, AND THE NYSL, Benthuysen, Albany, NY, 1859, with location notes added to the NYSL copy. Many available in NYSL, some in Office of General Services (Bureau of Land Management, Tower Building, Empire State Plaza, Albany, NY 12230), some in NYSA, some in Office of General Services (Bureau of Land Management, Tower Bldg., Empire State Plaza, Albany, NY 12230), some in NYSA, some in Department of Taxation and Finance (Transfer Tax Unit, Room 403, Bldg. 9, State Office Campus, Albany, NY 12227). Search by location.

___(MSC-21) State Engineer and Surveyor, CATALOGUE OF MAPS AND FIELD BOOKS IN THE LAND BUREAU, Lyon, Albany, NY, 1920. Some in NYSL, some in NYSA, some in Department of Transportation (Room 216, Bldg. 5, State Office Campus, Albany, NY 12227). Search by location.

___(MSC-22) MAP CARD CATALOG, 11th Floor, Manuscripts and Special Collections Room, NYSL. Search by location.

___(MSC-23) ATLAS CARD CATALOG, 11th Floor, Manuscripts and Special Collections Room, NYSL. Search by location.

Now that we have seen the 23 major finding aids in the NYSL, we can recommend to you the best order in which to use them the first time you visit (or have a hired searcher visit). Practically all of the printed and typescript materials, many of the microform materials, and some of the manuscript materials mentioned in Chapter 2 are in NYSL and can be located by using these finding aids. First, you should sign into the NYSL, remember the regulations mentioned in section 1 of this chapter, remember the way to search alphabetical card and computer catalogs as detailed in section 1 of this chapter, then proceed to the Local History and Genealogy Area. Search the following indexes for your ancestral name(s): LHG-1, 2, 4, 8, 9, 10. Second, go to the Microforms Room and look your ancestral names up in the pertinent census indexes, MIC-12, and censuses MIC-13, 14, and in the appropriate city directories, MIC-15 and LHG-6 (examine both), if applicable. Third, look into the following indexes and lists, searching them for the locations (NY state, NY colony, region, county, city, town) where your progenitor(s) lived. Examine every listing under each of the location topics. Then request and search the entries that you think might include your forebear(s): LHG-1, 2, 5, 7, 10. Fourth, check back into Chapter 2 and look up the numerous federal, NY state, and NY regional reference works which are mentioned there and which you have not yet seen. They can be easily located by using LHG-1, 3 to look for them under their authors and/or titles. Fifth, dig deeply into the major catalogs (LHG-1, 2) looking under any subjects that you think might be especially applicable to your ancestor. Important subjects to search were listed in section 1 of this chapter. Finally, use the other finding aids to dredge up any further possible data on your ancestor: MIC-11, 16, 17, 18, MSC-19, 20, 21, 22, 23.

3. The NY State Archives (NYSA) and other state agencies

The NY State Archives (NYSA) is the official repository for original NY colonial and NY state records. It
is located on the 11th Floor, Cultural Education Center,
Empire State Plaza, Albany, NY 12230. It shares the NYSL
Manuscript and Special Collections Room with the NYSL,
but has a separate telephone number 1-(518)-474-1195.
Information on coming to the Plaza and on accommodations
in Albany is the same as that given in the previous
section for the NYSL. Before visiting the NYSA, you
should write them for their major reference materials,
sending them $5 for the cost of the guide book and pos-
tage. These publications describe the holdings of the
NYSA and permit you to decide whether any of them can
help you in your research.
__NYSA, GUIDE TO RECORDS IN THE NYSA, NYSA, Albany, NY,
1981.
__NYSA, LOCAL RECORDS ON MICROFILM IN THE NYSA, Albany,
NY, 1979.
__NYSA, INFORMATION CONCERNING RECORDS OF GENEALOGICAL
INTEREST, NYSA, Albany, NY, 1983, 7 pages.
__NYSA, LIST OF PRE-1847 COURT RECORDS IN THE STATE
ARCHIVES, NYSA, Albany, NY, 1984, 18 pages.
__NYSA, COURT RECORDS AND THE STATE ARCHIVES, NYSA,
Albany, NY, 1985, 2 pages.
__NYSA, CIVIL WAR RECORDS IN THE NYSA, NYSA, Albany, NY,
1983, 5 pages.
Special attention should be paid to the following sec-
tions in the GUIDE TO RECORDS: Paymaster General (page
35), Land and Land Taxation (page 59), Federal WPA Pro-
jects (pages 89-90), Dutch Colonial Records (page 124),
British Colonial Records (page 125), Legislative Records
(page 126), Census Records (page 127), Land Records
(pages 127-8), Alien Registration and Naturalization
Records (page 131), Colonial Treasurer (pages 136-7),
State Engineer and Surveyor (page 143).

The above materials provide the major genealogical
finding aids to the collections of the NSYA. You will
notice from the INFORMATION CONCERNING RECORDS OF GENEA-
LOGICAL INTEREST that many of the NYSA holdings have been
calendared, indexed, and/or abstracted in published
works. These published volumes, as well as other important genealogical records in the NYSA, have been mentioned in Chapter 2 of this book. Using these references

as well as any others you think might be useful to you,
you can make your request to an archivist in the Manuscripts and Special Collections Room, 11th Floor, Cultural Education Center.

A number of other state agencies in Albany hold
specialized series of records. Included are these:
_ NY State Department of Public Health, Vital Records
Section, Genealogy Unit, Tower Bldg., Empire State
Plaza, Albany, NY 12237. Birth, death, and marriage
registrations for all NY state from 1880 forward,
except Albany, Buffalo, and Yonkers records only from
1914 forward, and none for NY City.
_ NY State Office of General Services, Tower Bldg.,
Empire State Plaza, Albany, NY 12230. Land grant
applications from 1803 forward.
_ NY Department of Taxation and Finance, State Office
Campus, Albany, NY 12226. Several thousand maps show-
ing lands sold for tax arrears.
_ NY State Division of Military and Naval Affairs, Public
Security Bldg., State Office Campus, Albany, NY 12226.
Military records, name index to 300 cubic feet of
muster rolls held by NYSA.
_ NY State Department of Transportation, Bldg. 5, State
Office Campus, Albany, NY 12226. Maps and field books
of the Land Bureau of the Department of State Engineer
and Surveyor.

4. The NY Genealogical and Biographical Society Library
(NYGB)

The NY Genealogical and Biographical Society Library
(NYGB) is an exceptionally well-stocked repository of
genealogical, biographical, family history, and local
history materials relating to NY state and city. The
records include many types in printed, typescript, microfilm, and manuscript form. The Society, which has func-
tioned since 1869, has its library at 122 East 58th St.,
New York. NY 10022-1939, between Lexington and Park
Avenues. The times of opening are 9:30-5:00 Monday-
Saturday, except holidays, closed Saturday during June-
September, closed entire month of August, and the telephone number is 1-(212)-755-8532. The main finding aids
and the published materials are available to non-members
for a $3 minimum daily contribution. However, the micro-
forms and manuscripts are available only to members. All

persons with NY ancestors are encouraged to join this
very important society so as to support its excellent
library and its exceptionally useful periodical. The
library is located near the southern end of Central Park,
and therefore it is recommended that you stay at a hotel
in that general area. Parking is a bad problem in Manhattan and especially so in this area, so leave your car
at your hotel and take subway train 4, 6, N, or R to the
59th St. stop, the nearest one to NYGB.

Before you visit the NYGB, send them a long SASE and
ask for two very helpful leaflets:
__NYGB, FLOOR PLAN OF THE LIBRARY, NYGB, New York, NY.
__NYGB, HOW TO USE THE NYG&B LIBRARY'S CARD CATALOG,
NYGB, New York, NY.
Upon going to the library, please recall the general
rules of conduct and the procedures for searching card
catalogs as given in section 1 of this chapter. The
major finding aids in the NYGB are as follows:
__(GB-1) MAIN CARD CATALOG, NYGB, New York, NY. Search
by name, location, subject, author, title.
__(GB-2) CARD CATALOG FOR MANUSCRIPT COLLECTION AND
MICROFILMS, NAMES SECTION, NYGB, New York, NY. Search
for your progenitors' names.
__(GB-3) CARD CATALOG FOR MANUSCRIPT COLLECTION AND
MICROFILMS, PROVISIONAL CATALOGING SECTION, NYGB, New
York, NY. Search for your forebears' names.
__(GB-4) CARD CATALOG FOR MANUSCRIPT COLLECTION AND
MICROFILMS, NY TOWNS SECTION, NYGB, New York, NY.
Search for your ancestors' towns, cities, counties,
regions.
__(GB-5) CARD CATALOG FOR MANUSCRIPT COLLECTION AND
MICROFILMS, NY COUNTIES SECTION, NYGB, New York, NY.
Search for your ancestors' counties, then the pertinent
towns and cities under the counties, then look at all
NY State entries.
__(GB-6) CARD CATALOG FOR MANUSCRIPT COLLECTION AND
MICROFILMS SUBJECT SECTION, NYGB, New York, NY. Search
for subjects as recommended in section 1, this chapter.
__(GB-7) CARD CATALOG FOR MANUSCRIPT COLLECTION AND
MICROFORMS, BIBLE RECORDS SECTION, NYGB, New York, NY.
Search for your ancestors' surnames.
__(GB-8) NEW MANUSCRIPTS AND MICROFORMS NOTEBOOK, NYGB,
New York, NY. On top of Catalog for Manuscript Collec-
tion and Microforms. Search for name, location, sub-
ject, author, title.

__(GB-9) ANCESTOR EXCHANGE CARD FILE, NYGB, New York, NY. On top of Main Card Catalog cabinet. Search for your progenitors' names.

__(GB-10) FEDERAL NY CENSUS INDEXES, PRINTED FOR 1790-1860, and MICROFILM FOR 1880 AND 1900, NYGB, New York, NY. Look up all pertinent ancestors' names.

__(GB-11) MASTER INDEX TO NY STATE DAR GENEALOGICAL RECORDS, NY DAR Albany, NY, 1971, and SUPPLEMENT, 1972-8, NY DAR Albany, NY, 1978. Look up every surname and location of interest to you. Volumes to which this index refers are in NYPL, NYSL, FHL (FHC).

The above finding aids should _first_ be used to look up all your ancestral names (GB-1, 2, 3, 7, 8, 9, 10, 11), then _second_ all entries under your progenitors' places of residence (GB-1, 4, 5, 8, 10), being cautious to examine villages, towns, cities, counties, and especially looking at everything under NY (colony) and NY (state). Then, _third_, examine subject entries (GB-1, 6, 8), especially those recommended in section 1 of this chapter, plus any others in which you have a special interest. _Finally_, use the author and/or title listings (GB-1, 2, 3) to locate the large number of printed, typescript, microform, and manuscript volumes, records, abstracts, compilations, periodicals, and indexes listed in Chapter 2.

5. The NY Historical Society (NYHS)

The NY Historical Society Library (NYHS), even though not oriented primarily toward genealogical research, has excellent collections of historical materials for NY state and New York city which can be very useful to genealogists, particularly if they are interested in doing their family research with contextual historical integrity. The library, which is located at 170 Central Park West, New York, NY 10024 is open 10:00-5:00 Tuesday-Saturday for September-May and 10:00-5:00 Monday-Friday for June-August, except holidays, and the telephone number is 1-(212)-873-3400. There is a daily admission charge of $2 plus a $1 library fee. As the address indicates, the library is located along the western edge of the southern portion of Central Park in Manhattan, so hotels in the area just south of Central Park or near its southwest corner are recommended. Parking is a bad problem in Manhattan and especially so

in this area, so it is best to take subway train B, C, or
K to the 81st St. stop (then walk south) or subway train
1 to the 79th St. stop (then walk east). The library has
excellent Revolutionary War, Civil War, and Spanish-
American War collections, superb NY state and NY City
documents, directories, guides, and organization publications, the 4th largest pre-1820 US newspaper collection,
magazines and periodicals, a notable manuscript collection, and extensive holdings of maps. They charge a $5
fee for single-item mail inquiries which can be looked up
in one of their finding aids.

When you arrive at the NYHS, please remember the
general rules of conduct and the procedures for using
card catalogs which were discussed in section 1 of this
chapter. The major finding aids in the NYHS which will
permit you to work rapidly and thoroughly through their
collections to locate materials which relate to your
progenitors are:
__(HS-1) MAIN CARD CATALOG, NYHS, New York, NY. Search
 by name, location, subject, author, title.
__(HS-2) OLD GREEN CARD CATALOG, NYHS, New York, NY.
 Search by name, location, subject, author, title.
__(HS-3) COMPUTERIZED CATALOG, NYHS, New York, NY.
 Search by name, location, subject, author, title.
__(HS-4) NEWSPAPER CARD CATALOG, NYHS, New York, NY.
 Look under NY, then search by town or city.
__(HS-5) CHRONOLOGICAL NEWSPAPER CARD CATALOG, NYHS, New
 York, NY. Search by date. Not generally useful to
 genealogists.
__(HS-6) GENEALOGY SURNAME CARD FILE, NYHS, New York, NY.
 Search by name.
__(HS-7) A. J. Breton, A GUIDE TO MANUSCRIPT COLLECTIONS
 OF THE NYHS, Greenwood Press, Westport, CT, 1972, 2
 volumes, 2nd volume index.
__(HS-8) MAIN MANUSCRIPT CARD CATALOG (TO MAY 1984),
 NYHS, New York, NY. Search by name, location, subject.
__(HS-9) NEW MANUSCRIPT CARD CATALOG, NYHS, New York, NY.
 Search by name, location, subject.
__(HS-10) CALENDARS, LISTINGS, INVENTORIES, AND DESCRIP-
 TIONS OF MANY SPECIAL MANUSCRIPT COLLECTIONS, NYHS, New
 York, NY. Search for names, locations, subjects.

Now, using a procedure very similar to that for the
NYGB, you can make an exhaustive survey of these NYHS
finding aids which will reveal to you all of their re-

sources which might pertain to your forebear(s). First,
look up all your NY ancestral names in HS-1, 2, 3, 6, 7,
8, 9, 10.   Then, second, proceed to examine all entries
under each of your NY progenitors' locations, being
careful to look under NY (colony), NY (state), regions,
counties, cities, towns, and villages. For this, use HS-
1, 2, 3, 4, 7, 8, 9, 10. Your third set of searches will
involve looking under the subjects mentioned in section 1
of this chapter plus other pertinent subjects that you
might have a special interest in.   These should be employed for this: HS-1, 2, 3, 7, 8, 9, 10. Then, finally,
look up author and/or title entries in order to locate
the numerous printed, typescript, microform, and manuscript volumes, records, abstracts, compilations,
periodicals, and indexes listed in Chapter 2. For this
purpose, use HS-1, 2, 3.

6. NY Public Library (NYPL)

The main installation of the NY (City) Public
Library (NYPL) is known as the Research Libraries and is
located at 5th Ave. and 42nd St., New York, NY 10018.
The information telephone number is 1-(212)-930-0828, and
the times are 10:00-9:00 Tuesday, closed Sunday, and
10:00-6:00 all other days, with the exception of holidays. Being one of the largest libraries in the US, it
holds an exceptionally large collection of NY genealogical source materials, particularly printed, typescript,
and microform, but there is also a good manuscript collection.   By staying at a hotel just south of Central
Park, as was recommended for the NYGB and the NYHS, this
library is also readily accessible.   Parking in all of
Manhattan is a problem, so it is advisable to take subway
D, F, or S to the 42nd St. stop (a block away) or subway
7 to the 5th Ave. stop (right at the Library). There are
five areas in this immense library which are important
for genealogical research: the US History, Local History,
and Genealogical Division (Room 315N), the Public Catalog
Room (315), the Microfilm Reading Room (315M), the Manuscript and Archives Room (324), and the Map Division
(117).   In the NY Public Library Annex at 521 West 43rd
St. are storage facilities where much of the Newspaper
Collection is held.   Detailed descriptions of the holdings of the NYPL are available in this volume:
__S. P. Williams, GUIDE TO THE RESEARCH COLLECTIONS OF

THE NYPL, American Library Association, Chicago, IL, 1975.

The major finding aids at NYPL and the areas in which they are most easily accessible are as follows. It is to be noted that much of the NYPL catalog is in printed form, and is available in over 1000 volumes. In the US History, Local History, and Genealogical Division (Room 315N) are to be found the following printed catalogs along with most of the historical and genealogical works to which they refer:

__(PL-1) NYPL, DICTIONARY CATALOG OF THE LOCAL HISTORY AND GENEALOGY DIVISION THROUGH 1971, Hall and Co., Boston, MA, 1974, 18 volumes.

__(PL-2) NYPL, US LOCAL HISTORY CATALOG, Hall and Co., Boston, MA, 1974, 2 volumes.

__(PL-3) NYPL, DICTIONARY CATALOG OF MATERIALS ON NY CITY, Hall and Co., Boston, MA, 1977, 3 volumes.

__(PL-4) NYPL, DICTIONARY CATALOG OF THE RESEARCH LIBRARIES, 1972-80, NYPL, New York, NY, 1980, 64 volumes.

__(PL-5) NYPL, SUPPLEMENT TO THE DICTIONARY CATALOG OF THE RESEARCH LIBRARIES, 1972-81, NYPL, New York, NY, 1981, 12 volumes.

__(PL-6) NYPL, THE RESEARCH LIBRARIES, INTERIM LIST: INDEX, 1981-5, NYPL, New York, NY, 1985, 25 volumes.

Most of these catalogs are duplicated in the very large Public Catalog Room (315) and, in addition, there are two further catalogs, one printed, one computer, of relevance to family history investigators:

__(PL-7) NYPL, THE NYPL CATALOG, PRE-1972, Hall and Co., Boston, MA, 1972, 800 volumes. All books and periodicals in NYPL, not just genealogy and history volumes.

__(PL-8) NYPL, COMPUTER CATALOG TO THE NYPL RESEARCH LIBRARIES (abbreviated CATNYP) FOR POST-1971 MATERIALS, NYPL, New York, NY, 1972-present.

__(PL-9) NYPL, US NEWSPAPER CARD INDEX, at desk, Room 315, NYPL, New York, NY. Newspapers available at the Annex.

In the Manuscripts and Archives Room (324) these finding aids are available for locating manuscripts pertinent to your research:

__(PL-10) NYPL, DICTIONARY CATALOG OF THE MANUSCRIPT DIVISION, Hall and Co., Boston, MA, 1967, 2 volumes.

__(PL-11) NYPL, CARD CATALOG TO MANUSCRIPTS IN THE MANUSCRIPT DIVISION, Room 324, NYPL, New York, NY.

__(PL-12) NYPL, CARD CATALOG OF NEWSPAPERS IN THE RARE
BOOK ROOM, Room 324, NYPL, New York, NY. Newspapers in
original printed form, many before 1800.
__(PL-13) NYPL, MANUSCRIPT LETTERS CARD CATALOG, Room
324, NYPL, New York, NY. Mostly Revolutionary and the
years just before and after.
__(PL-14) NYPL, INVENTORIES, CALENDARS, SURVEYS OF FILES,
AIDS TO LARGER COLLECTIONS, AND ACCESSION RECORDS OF
NEW ACQUISITIONS, Room 324, NYPL, New York, NY.
The Map Division in Room 117 also has a couple of finding
aids for the location of maps which relate to your fore-
bears' areas:
__(PL-15) NYPL, DICTIONARY CATALOG OF THE MAP DIVISION,
Hall and Co., Boston, MA, 1970, 10 volumes. Maps and
atlases up through 1970.
__(PL-16) NYPL, NEW AND INTERMEDIATE MAP CATALOGS, Room
117, NYPL, New York, NY.

The 16 major genealogically-oriented finding aids
listed above for the NYPL reflect the tremendous size of
their collection. A thorough survey of the holdings can
be readily done if the following systematic approach is
followed. First, you should go to the US History, Local
History, and Genealogy Division in room 315N. Start your
search by looking for all your NY surnames in the printed
catalogs PL-1, 4, 5, 6, and PL-3 if you had an ancestor
in NY. Then go out into the Public Catalog Room and use
PL-8 (the Computer Catalog) to look up the same surnames.
Instructions for use of PL-8 are beside each computer,
and library personnel will be glad to help. All of these
catalogs will lead you to printed materials which can be
obtained for you by librarians in the US History, Local
History, and Genealogy Division (315N). When you run
across references to microfilms, you obviously will need
to go to the Microfilm Reading Room where you can request
the film, take it to an assigned reader, and read it.
Now, second, look in PL-1, 2, 4, 5, 6, (in 315N) and PL-8
(in 315) for all locations where your NY ancestors lived,
remembering to examine all listings under NY colony, NY
state, region, county, city, town, and village. The
examination of the numerous listings under NY state may
seem to be a formidable task, but you will discover that
large numbers of entries under certain sub-headings (such
as geology) can be quickly eliminated. If your ancestor
was a NY City resident, you should also examine PL-3.
Again, most materials which you find to be of value can

be requested in Room 315N (US History, Local History, and
Genealogy Division).   Microfilms, as before, can be
obtained and read in 315M.

Your next step, the third one, will be to use PL-1,
4, 5, 6, 8 (and PL-3 if called for) to look up subjects
which you think may have been missed in the previous two
steps. Section 1 of this chapter listed a number of
subjects which might be applicable. Then, fourth, employ
these same catalogs (PL-1, 3, 4, 5, 6, 8) to locate
volumes and microfilms mentioned in Chapter 2 by searching for authors and/or titles. These first four searches
will lead you to almost everything available in NYPL
which pertains to your family lines except newspapers,
manuscripts, and maps.   As you work through these
searches, you will find that as you search from names to
locations to subjects to authors/titles you will see
certain references two or more times.   In other words,
you will in a way be going over the same ground a couple
or more times. This will give you confidence in the
thoroughness of your search.

Now, let us look for the newspapers, manuscripts,
and maps. Your fifth step will involve going to the desk
in 315 (Public Catalog Room) and asking them to look in
PL-9 (US Newspaper Card Index) for newspapers in your
ancestors' towns, cities, or nearest cities. They will
usually send you to the Annex (521 West 43rd St.) to look
at the newspapers. Your sixth step will be an excursion
to the Manuscripts and Archives room (324) to examine
their catalogs. Start by looking in PL-10, 11, 13 for
your surnames, then in PL-10, 11, 12 for progenitors'
locations (note that PL-12 is for early newspapers), then
in PL-10, 11 for subjects.   In the course of your
searches, you may come across special collections, but
even if you don't, ask the archivist if any of the materials of PL-14 could be pertinent.   Your final visit
should be to Room 117 (Map Division), where you can look
into PL-15, 16 under the locations (counties, cities,
towns, and villages mostly, since state maps will usually
not be of too much help) for maps of the ancestors'
areas. You will notice that we have not mentioned use of
the 800-volumed NYPL CATALOG (PL-7) in these search
procedures. The reason is that the other catalogs ordinarily cover what you need. But there are exceptions,

and so there may be special instances when the librarian
or archivist will suggest that you use it.

7. Family History Library (FHL) and Its Branches (FHC)

The largest genealogical library in the world is the
Family History Library of the Genealogical Society of
Utah (FHL), often referred to as the Mormon Library or
the LDS Library. This repository holds well over 1.8
million rolls of microfilm plus a vast number of books,
containing over 1.5 billion name entries. It is located
at 35 North West Temple St., Salt Lake City, UT 84150.
The library opens every day except Sunday and holidays at
7:30 am. It closes at 5:00 pm Saturday, 6:00 pm Monday,
and at 10:00 pm Tuesday through Friday. The general
telephone number is 1-(801)-521-0130. The basic key to
the library is a massive index called the Family History
Library Catalog (four sections: surname, locality, subject, author-title) (FHLC). In addition to the main
library, the Society maintains a large number of branches
called Family History Centers (FHC) all over the world.
Each of these has microfiche copies of the Family History
Library Catalog (FHLC), plus several other major indexes,
plus forms for borrowing microfilm copies of the records
at FHL. This means that the astonishingly large holdings
of the FHL are available on loan through each of its
numerous FHC (Family History Centers or Branch Libraries
of the FHL).

The History Centers (FHC) in NY state are:
__Albany NY Stake, PO Box 11251, Loudonville, NY 12211.
__Buffalo NY Stake, 5074 Clearview Dr., Williamsville, NY
14221.
__Ithaca NY Stake, 3805 Pembroke Ln., Vestal, NY 13850.
__Yorktown NY Stake, 12 Green Meadow Ln., New Canaan, CT
06840.
__New York NY Stake, 3rd Floor, Two Lincoln Square, New
York, NY 10023.
__Plainview NY Stake, 168 Ontario Ave., Massapequa, NY
11758.
__Rochester NY Stake, 635 Blue Spruce Rd., Webster, NY
14580.
__Syracuse NY Stake, PO Box 5, Syracuse, NY 13205-0005.
When you get ready to visit one of the centers, write
them inquiring about open hours and exact location.

Other FHC are to be found in the cities listed below. They may be located by looking in the local telephone directories under the listing CHURCH OF JESUS CHRIST OF LATTER DAY SAINTS - GENEALOGY LIBRARY or in the Yellow Pages under CHURCHES - LATTER DAY SAINTS.

__In AL: Birmingham, Huntsville, in AK: Anchorage, Fairbanks, in AZ: Campe Verde(Cottonwood), Flagstaff, Globe, Holbrook, Mesa, Page, Phoenix, Prescott, St. David, Safford, St. Johns, Show Low, Snowflake, Tucson, Winslow, Yuma, in AR: Little Rock,

__In CA: Anaheim, Bakersfield, Barstow, Blythe(Needles), Camarillo, Cerritos(Santa Fe Springs, Lakewood), Covina (West Covina), Cypress(Buena Park), El Centro, Escondido, Eureka, Fairfield, Fresno, Garden Grove, Glendale, Gridley, Hacienda Heights, Hemet, La Crescenta(La Canada), Lancaster, Long Beach, Los Angeles(Alhambra, Canyon Country), Menlo Park, Mission Viejo, Modesto, Monterey(Seaside), Napa, Newbury Park, Oakland, Orange, Palmdale, Palm Springs(Cathedral City), Pasadena(East Pasadena), Redding, Ridgecrest, Riverside, Sacramento-(Carmichael), San Bernardino, San Diego, San Jose, San Luis Obispo, Santa Barbara(Goleta), Santa Clara, Santa Maria, Santa Rosa, Simi Valley, Southern CA(Los Angeles), Stockton, Upland, Ventura, Whittier,

__In CO: Arvada, Boulder, CO Springs, Columbine(Littleton), Cortez, Denver(Northglenn), Durango, Ft. Collins, Grand Junction, LaJara, Littleton, Meeker(Glenwood Springs), Montrose, Pueblo, in CT: Hartford, in DE: Wilmington(Newark), in FL: Cocoa, Gainesville(Alachua), Hialeah/Ft. Lauderdale, Jacksonville(Orange Park), Lakeland, Marianna, Miami, Orlando(Fern Park), Pensacola, St. Petersburg, Tallahassee, Tampa, West Palm Beach(Boca Raton), in GA: Macon, Marietta(Powder Spring), Sandy Springs(Dunwoody), in HI: Hilo, Honolulu, Kaneohe, Kona(Kailua), Laie,

__In ID: Bear Lake(Montpelier), Blackfoot(Moreland), Boise, Burley, Caldwell, Driggs, Firth, ID Falls, Iona, Lewiston, Malad, Meridian(Boise), Moore(Arco), Nampa, Pocatello, Post Falls, Salmon, Shelley, Twin Falls, Upper Snake River(Rexburg), in IL: Champaign, Chicago Heights(Lossmoor), Naperville(Downers Grove), Rockford, Wilmette, in IN: Fort Wayne, Indianapolis(Greenwood), in IA: Cedar Rapids, Davenport, Des Moines, in KS: Topeka, Wichita, in KY: Hopkinsville(Benton), Lexington, Louisville, in LA: Baton Rouge, Shreveport,

In ME: Augusta(Hallowell), in MD: Silver Spring, in MA: Boston(Natick), in MI: Bloomfield Hills, Grand Blanc, Grand Rapids, Lansing(East Lansing), Midland, Westland, in MN: Minneapolis(Richfield), St. Paul, in MS: Hattiesburg, in MO: Columbia, Kansas City(Shawnee Mission), Liberty, Springfield, St. Louis(Berkeley), in MT: Billings, Bozeman, Butte, Great Falls, Helena, Kalispell, Missoula, in NE: Omaha,

In NV: Elko, Ely, Fallon, Las Vegas, Logandale, Reno, Sparks, in NJ: East Brunswick, Morristown(Chatham), in NH: Nashua, in NM: Albuquerque(Los Alamos), Farmington, Gallup, Grants, Los Cruces, Roswell, Santa Fe, in NC: Asheville(Arden), Charlotte, Fayetteville, Hickory, Kinston, Raleigh(Bailey Road), Wilmington(Hampstead), in OH: Cincinnati, Cleveland(North Olmstead), Columbus-(Reynoldsburg), Dayton(Jettering), Kirtland, Toledo-(Maumee), in OK: Norman, Oklahoma City, Tulsa,

In OR: Beaverton, Bend, Coos Bay, Corvallis, Eugene, Grants Pass, Gresham(Fairview), Klamath Falls, La-Grande, Lake Oswego(West Linn), Medford, Nyssa(Ontario), Oregon City, Portland, Prineville, Roseburg, Salem, The Dallas, in PA: Philadelphia(Broomall), Pittsburgh, Reading, State College, York, in SC: Charleston(Hanahan), Columbia(Hopkins), Greenville, in TN: Chattanooga, Kingsport, Knoxville(Bearden), Memphis, Nashville(Madison), in TX: Austin(Georgetown), Beaumont(Nederland), Corpus Christi, Dallas, El Paso, Hurst, Friendswood, Houston(Bellaire), Longview, Lubbock, Odessa, Plano(Richardson), San Antonio,

In UT: Beaver, Blanding, Bountiful, Brigham City, Cache(Logan), Castledale(Orangeville), Cedar City, Delta, Duchesne, Fillmore, Heber City, Hurricane, Kanab, Lehi(Salt Lake City), Loa, Moroni, Mount Pleasant, Nephi, Ogden, Parowan, Price, Richfield, Roosevelt, Rose Park(Salt Lake City), Sandy, Santaquin, South Jordan(Riverton), St. George, Springville, Tremonton, UT Valley(Provo), Uintah(Vernal), in VA: Annandale, Charlottesville, Fairfax(Springfield), Norfolk(VA Beach), Oakton, Richmond, Roanoke,

In WA: Bellevue, Bellingham(Ferndale), Bremerton, Ephrata(Quincy), Everett, Kennewick, Longview, Moses Lake, Mount Vernon, Olympia, Pasco, Pullman, Puyallup-(Sumner), Richland, Seattle, Spokane, Tacoma, Vancouver, Walla Walla, Wenatchee(East Wenatchee), Yakima, in WI: Appleton, Beloit(Belvidere), Milwaukee, in WY: Afton, Casper, Cody, Evanston, Gillette(Sheridan),

Green River, Kemmerer, Lovell, Rock Springs, Worland,
Wyoming(Cheyenne).
The FHL is constantly adding new branches, so this list
will probably be out-of-date by the time you read it. An
SASE and a $2 fee to the FHL (address in the 1st para-
graph above) will bring you the most-recent listing of
FHC.

When you go to a FHC, you need to first look up the
NY surnames of interest to you in the following indexes:
the NY section of the International Genealogical Index
(IGI), the surname listings in the Family History Library
Catalog (FHLC), the Family Register, and the AIS Integrated Census Indexes for 1790/1800/10, for 1820, for
1830, for 1840, and for the 1850 Eastern States. When
using the FHLC, don't fail to look under Family Group
Records for desired surnames. The second set of index
investigations you should make is to look at all entries
under NY and then all entries under the NY counties of
interest to you in the locality portion of the Family
History Library Catalog (FHLC). You will find extensive
listings of these type of records: administrative, business, census, church, county histories, court, family
histories, genealogical collections, land, military,
newspaper, probate, tax, town, vital record (birth,
marriage, death), and will. The only other place that
many of these records are available is the county itself,
so this is an exceptionally useful source. When you find
entries which you think are applicable to your progeni-
tor(s), copy down the reference numbers and names of the
records. These data will permit the branch librarian to
borrow the microfilm(s) containing the detailed information from the FHL. The cost is only a few dollars per
roll, and when your microfilms arrive (usually 3-6
weeks), you will be notified so that you can return and
examine them. A third action you should take is to ask
the branch librarian for a form (Temple Ordinance Indexes
Request) to request from the FHL an examination of the
Temple Records Index Bureau and the Family Group Records
Archive. The above three actions will lead you to many
of the materials mentioned in Chapter 2 and many of the
records listed under the counties in Chapters 4-5.
Should you happen to visit FHL in Salt Lake City,
UT, you should proceed by examining all the above indexes
plus the Computer-Assisted Catalog(s), looking under both
surnames and localities. Pertinent records can be re-

quested or found on the open shelves. The main and second floors of the building are where most of the NY records can be found.

8. The National Archives (NA) and Its Branches (NAFB)

The National Archives and Records Service (NA), located at Pennsylvania Ave. and 8th St., Washington, DC 20408, is the national repository for federal records, many being of importance to genealogical research. The NA does not concern itself with colonial records (pre-1776), state, county, city, or town records. Among the most important NA records which pertain to NY are the following: federal census 1790–1910, emigration and immigration, military, and naturalization. Details on these have been given in the appropriate sections of Chapter 2. Please recall that there are many types of records under the military category (military service, bounty land, pension, claims, civilian). Extensive detail on NA records is provided in:
 __NA Staff, GENEALOGICAL RESEARCH IN THE NATIONAL AR-
  CHIVES, National Archives and Records Service, Washing-
  ton, DC, 1982.

The numerous records of the NA may be examined in Washington in person or by a hired researcher. Microfilm copies of many of the major records and/or their indexes may also be seen in Field Branches of the National Archives (NAFB) which are located in or near Atlanta (1557 St. Joseph Ave., East Point, GA 30344), Boston (380 Trapelo Rd., Waltham, MA 02154), Chicago (7358 S. Pulaski Rd., Chicago, IL 60629), Denver (Bldg. 48, Federal Center, Denver, CO 80225), Fort Worth (4900 Hemphill St., Ft. Worth, TX 76115), Kansas City (2306 E. Bannister Rd., Kansas City, MO 64131), Los Angeles (24000 Avila Rd., Laguna Niguel, CA 92677), New York (Bldg. 22-MOT, Bayonne, NJ 07002), Philadelphia (5000 Wissahickon Ave.), San Francisco (1000 Commodore Dr., San Bruno, CA 94066), and Seattle (6125 Sand Point Way, NE, Seattle, WA 98115).

Many of the NA records pertaining to NY are also available at NYSA and NYPL, and some are available at NYGB, LGL, and RL. In addition, practically any local library in the US can borrow NA microfilms for you from AGLL (American Genealogical Lending Library, PO Box 244, Bountiful, UT 84010). Or you may borrow from them directly. Included are census records (1790-1910), military records (Revolutionary War, War of 1812, Indian Wars, Mexican War, Civil War), and ship passenger lists (NY City 1820-1902). Many NA microfilms are also available from FHL through FHC.

9. Regional libraries (RL)

In the state of NY there are a number of regional libraries (RL) and larger city and county libraries which have good genealogical collections. Their holdings are larger than those of most local libraries (LL), but are smaller than the holdings of NYSL, NYPL, NYGB, and NYHS. As might be expected, the materials in each RL are best for the immediate and the surrounding counties. Among the better of these RL for genealogical research are the following (listed in order of the cities where they are found):

__(Brooklyn, Kings County) Brooklyn Historical Society, 128 Pierrepont St., Brooklyn, NY 11201. Strong on Long Island records.

__(Buffalo, Erie County) Buffalo and Erie County Public Library, Lafayette Square, Buffalo, NY 14203. Strong on western NY.

__(Cooperstown, Otsego County) NY State Historical Association, Fenimore House, Lake Road, Cooperstown, NY 13326. Strong on upstate NY.

__(Fonda, Montgomery County) Montgomery County Department of History and Archives, Old Courthouse, Fonda, NY 12068. Strong on east central NY.

__(Ithaca, Onondaga County) NY Historical Resources Center, Olin Library, Cornell University, Ithaca, NY 14853. Strong on state-wide historical sources.

__(Rochester, Monroe County) Rochester Public Library, 115 South Ave., Rochester, NY 14604. Strong on west central NY.

__(Syracuse, Onondaga County) Onondaga County Public Library, 335 Montgomery St., Syracuse, NY 13202. Strong on central NY.

__(Watertown, Jefferson County) Flower Memorial Library, Watertown, NY 13601. Strong on north central NY.

When a visit is made to any of these libraries, your first endeavor is to search the card catalog. You can remember what to look for with the acronym SLANT (standing for Subject, Locality, Author, Name, and Title) and

by searching the categories out in the order: name-local-
ity-subject-author-title. This procedure should give you
very good coverage of the library holdings which are
indexed in the card catalog. The second endeavor at any
of these libraries is to ask about any special indexes,
catalogs, collections, lists, finding aids, or materials
which might be pertinent to your search. You should make
it your aim particularly to inquire about Bible, cemetery, church, map, manuscript, military, mortuary, and
newspaper materials. In some cases, microform (microfilm, microfiche, microcard) records are not included in
the regular card catalog but are separately indexed. It
is important that you be alert to this possibility.

In addition to the RL mentioned above, there are
several college and university libraries in NY (in addition to Cornell's) which have notable collections of
historical materials, some of which have genealogical
import. Among the colleges and universities with such
libraries are:
__Columbia University, New York, NY 10027.
__Fordham University, Bronx, NY 10458.
__Long Island University, Greenvale, NY 11548.
__City University of NY, various branches, New York, NY
10021, 10036, 10037.
__State University of NY at Albany (12246), Binghamton
(13901), Buffalo (14214), Stony Brook (11794), Oneonta
(13820).
__NY University, New York, NY 10003.
__University of Rochester, Rochester, NY 14627.
__St. John's University, Jamaica, NY 11439.
__Syracuse University, Syracuse, NY 13210.

10. Large genealogical libraries (LGL)

Spread around the US there are a number of large
genealogical libraries (LGL) which have at least some NY
genealogical source materials. In general, those libraries nearest NY (CT, MA, NJ, PA, VT) are the ones that
have the better NY collections. The thirteen libraries
of this type which have the largest overall collections
are:
__Family History Library of the Genealogical Society of
UT, 35 North West Temple St., Salt Lake City, UT 84150.
__Public Library of Fort Wayne and Allen County, 301 West
Wayne St., Fort Wayne, IN 46802.

__New England Historic Genealogical Society Library, 101
Newbury St., Boston, MA 02116.
__NY Public Library, 5th Avenue and 42nd St., New York,
NY 10016.
__Library of Congress, First and Second Sts. at East
Capitol St. and Independence Ave., Washington, DC
20540.
__NY Genealogical and Biographical Society Library, 122–
126 East 58th St., New York, NY 10022.
__Library of the National Society of the Daughters of the
American Revolution, 1776 D St., Washington, DC 20006.
__Western Reserve Historical Society Library, 10825 East
Blvd., Cleveland, OH 44106.
__Detroit Public Library, 5201 Woodward Ave., Detroit, MI
48202.
__Newberry Library, 60 West Walton St., Chicago, IL
60610.
__State Historical Society of WI Library, 816 State St.,
Madison, WI 53703.
__Dallas Public Library, 1515 Young St., Dallas, TX
75201.
__Los Angeles Public Library, 630 West 5th St., Los
Angeles, CA 90071.

Among other large libraries which have good genea-
logical collections are the following:
__In AL: Birmingham Public Library, Davis Library at
Samford University in Birmingham, AL Department of
Archives and History in Montgomery, in AZ: Tucson
Public Library, in AR: AR State Library in Little Rock,
Central AR Library in Little Rock, in CA: see above,
Sutro Branch of the CA State Library in San Francisco,
San Diego Public Library, San Francisco Public Library,
__In CO: Denver Public Library, in CT: CT Historical
Society Library in Hartford, CT State Library in Hart-
ford, Godfrey Memorial Library in Middletown, in DE:
Dover Public Library, Historical Society of DE in
Wilmington, in DC: see above, in FL: Miami-Dade Public
Library, State Library of FL in Tallahassee, Tampa
Public Library, in GA: Atlanta Public Library, GA
Department of Archives and History in Atlanta, Wash-
ington Memorial Library in Macon, in ID: ID State His-
torical Society Library in Boise, in IL: see above, in
IN: see above, IN State Library in Indianapolis, in IA:
IA State Historical Department Library in Des Moines,

IA State Historical Department Library in Iowa City, in KS: KS State Historical Society Library in Topeka,

In KY: KY Department for Libraries and Archives in Frankfort, KY Historical Society Library in Frankfort, Filson Club Library in Louisville, in LA: LA State Library in Baton Rouge, in ME: ME State Library in Augusta, ME Historical Society Library in Portland, in MD: MD State Archives Library in Annapolis, MD Historical Society Library in Baltimore, in MA: see above, Boston Public Library, in MI: see above, Library of MI in Lansing, in MN: Minneapolis Public Library, MN Historical Society Library in St. Paul, in MS: MS Department of Archives and History in Jackson, in MO: Kansas City Public Library, St. Louis Public Library, in MT: MT Historical Society Library and Archives in Helena,

In NE: NE State Historical Society Library in Lincoln, Omaha Public Library, in NV: Las Vegas Branch of the FHL, NV Historical Society Library in Reno, in NH: NH Historical Society Library in Concord, in NJ: NJ Historical Society Library in Newark, NJ State Library in Trenton, in NM: Albuquerque Public Library, University of NM Library in Albuquerque, in NC: NC State Library in Raleigh, in ND: ND State Library in Bismarck, in OH: see above, State Library of OH in Columbus, Public Library of Cincinnati, OH Historical Society in Columbus, in OK: OK Historical Society in Oklahoma City, in OR: Genealogical Forum of Portland Library, Library Association of Portland, in PA: State Library of PA in Harrisburg, Historical Society of PA Library in Philadelphia, Historical Society of Western PA Library in Pittsburgh,

In RI: RI Historical Society Library in Providence, in SC: South Caroliniana Library in Columbia, in SD: SD Department of Cultural Affairs Historical Center and SD State Library in Pierre, in TN: Knox County Library in Knoxville, Memphis Public Library, TN State Library in Nashville, in TX: see above, TX State Library in Austin, Fort Worth Public Library, Clayton Library for Genealogical Research in Houston, in UT: see above, Brigham Young University Library in Provo, in VT: VT Historical Society Library in Montpelier, in VA: VA State Library in Richmond, VA Historical Society Library in Richmond, in WA: Seattle Public Library, Spokane Public Library, in WV: WV Archives and History

Library in Charleston, in WI: see above, Milwaukee
Public Library, in WY: WY State Library in Cheyenne.

11. Local libraries (LL)

Listed under the NY counties in Chapters 4 and 5 are
the most important local libraries (LL) in the state.
There are several types of local libraries: system libraries (serving several counties), county libraries, city
libraries, town libraries, village libraries, county
historian libraries, local historical society libraries,
local college and university libraries, a few county
historical center libraries, local genealogical society
libraries, and private libraries. These libraries are of
a very wide variety, some having sizeable genealogical
materials, some having practically none. Many of the LL
(particularly the town and village ones) are affiliates
of a nearby larger library (usually a system or county
library), which have much greater holdings. What is of
importance, however, is that you not overlook any LL in
your ancestor's county, city, town, and/or village.
Often they have local records or collections available
nowhere else. This is particularly true for Bible,
cemetery, church, manuscript, and newspaper records. It
is also sometimes the case that the counties, towns, and
villages have turned older records over to LL, especially
the county historical societies. You will usually find
local librarians to be very knowledgeable concerning
genealogical sources in their areas. Further, they are
also usually acquainted with the people in the county
(city, town, village) who are experts in the region's
history and genealogy. Thus, both local libraries and
local librarians can be of inestimable value to you.

When you visit a LL, the general procedure described
previously should be followed. First, search the card
catalog or catalogs. Look under the headings summarized
by SLANT: Subject, Location, Author, Name, Title, doing
them in the order N-L-S-A-T. Then, second, inquire about
special indexes, catalogs, collections, materials, finding aids, and microforms. Third, ask about any other
local sources of data such as cemetery records, church
records, maps and atlases, genealogical and historical
societies, mortuary records, and old newspapers, plus
indexes to all of these. Also do not forget to visit
appropriate offices related to these types of records:

offices of cemeteries, churches, societies, mortuaries, and newspapers.

If you choose to write to a LL, please remember that the librarians are very busy people. Always send them an SASE and confine your questioning to one brief straightforward item. Librarians are usually glad to help you if they can employ indexes to answer your question, but you must not expect them to do research for you. In case research is required, they can often supply you with a list of researchers which you may hire.

Abbreviations

A	Agricultural Census
AGLL	American Genealogical Lending Library, Bountiful, UT
C	Union Civil War Veteran Census
CH	Court House(s) and County Archives
DAR	Daughters of the American Revolution
E	Early Pre-1790 Census-Like Lists
FHC	Family History Center(s), Genealogical Society of UT
FHL	Family History Library, Genealogical Society of UT, Salt Lake City, UT
I	Industrial Censuses
LGL	Large Genealogical Libraries
LL	Local Library(ies) and Other Local Repositories
M	Mortality Censuses
NA	National Archives, Washington, DC
NAFB	National Archives Field Branch(es)
NYSA	New York State Archives, Albany, NY
NYGB	New York Genealogical and Biographical Society, New York, NY
NYHS	New York Historical Society, New York, NY
NYPL	New York City Public Library, New York, NY
NYSL	New York State Library, Albany, NY
P	Pensioner Census, Revolutionary War
R	Regular Federal Censuses
RL	Regional Library(ies)
S	NY State Censuses

Chapter 4

RESEARCH PROCEDURE AND NY CITY

1. <u>Introduction</u> <u>to</u> <u>county</u> <u>records</u>

Now that you have read Chapters 1-3, you should have a good idea of NY history, its genealogical records, and the locations and availabilities of these records. The emphasis in the first three chapters was on records at levels higher than the county. Detailed information on national, state-wide, and regional records was given, but county records were treated only in general. We now will turn our focus upon the county records, and those of lower levels, namely, city, town, and village records. We will also emphasize non-governmental records available at or below the county level (Bible, biography, cemetery, directories, histories, DAR, ethnic, maps, periodicals, genealogies, manuscripts, mortuary, newspaper). The reason for all this attention to county records is that these records are likely to contain more information on your ancestors than any other type. Such records were generally recorded by people who knew your forebears, and they relate to the personal details of his/her life.

In general, as we have mentioned before, county, city, town, and village records are ordinarily kept in the following places. The <u>office</u> <u>of</u> <u>the</u> <u>county</u> <u>clerk</u> keeps some vital records (birth, marriage, death), civil and criminal court records, some federal and state census records, land records, naturalization records, some military service and militia records, tax assessment records, county administration records, registers of professions, coroner's inquests, homestead exemptions, and business licenses. The <u>city,</u> <u>town,</u> <u>and</u> <u>village</u> <u>clerk's</u> <u>offices</u> sometimes hold a few vital records, some court records, some early land records (especially the town clerk), tax records, some naturalization records, a few military records, a few militia records, administrative records, and school records. The <u>office</u> <u>of</u> <u>the</u> <u>county</u> <u>surrogate</u> <u>court</u> keeps records of estates, wills, and guardianships. The <u>office</u> <u>of</u> <u>the</u> <u>chief</u> <u>county</u> <u>fiscal</u> <u>officer</u> (several titles) holds tax and assessment records. The <u>office</u> <u>of</u> <u>the</u> <u>county</u> <u>health</u> <u>department</u> maintains vital records. The offices of <u>county,</u> <u>city,</u> <u>town,</u> <u>and</u> <u>village</u> <u>historians</u> must not be overlooked, as

is the case for <u>county</u> <u>and</u> <u>city</u> <u>archives</u> or <u>historical</u>
<u>centers,</u> since they often have collections of both gov-
ernmental and non-governmental records, especially the
older ones. There are minor differences in the above
(especially for NY City), but the pattern generally
holds.

In the state of NY, the vast majority of the <u>origi-</u>
<u>nal</u> governmental records of the counties, cities, towns,
and villages remain within the counties. Many of these
original governmental records and some non-governmental
records have been <u>microfilmed</u> by the FHL, and the microfilms are available at FHL and by interlibrary loan
through the many FHC throughout the US. Some of these
original governmental records and numerous non-governmental records have been <u>published</u> in either printed
volumes or as typescripts. Most of these publications
are available in NYSL, NYPL, NYGB, and NYHS. Some are
available in LGL, and those pertinent to their regions
are available in RL and LL.

Chapters 4 and 5 will deal with county records in
detail. In Chapter 4, we will <u>first</u> discuss procedures
for finding the county in which your NY progenitor(s)
lived. This is important because knowing that your
ancestors were simply from NY is not enough to permit
genealogical research. You need to know the county since
many genealogically-applicable records were kept on the
county basis, and since you will often find more than one
person in NY state bearing the name of your forebear. In
such a case, the county location will often let you tell
them apart. After discussing ways to find the county, we
will <u>second</u> suggest approaches for doing genealogy in NY
state, recommending the order in which the various repositories should be used. Then <u>thirdly</u> (in Chapter 4),
we will treat in detail the county and city records of NY
City. The City, which consists of 5 counties (Bronx,
Kings, NY, Queens, Richmond), has now and has had a
population larger than many states of the US. This
warrants some detail on this notable section of the state
of NY.

In Chapter 5, space will be devoted to the county
(city, town, village) records of the remaining 57 counties of NY state. Particular attention will be paid to

microfilmed and published records which are available
without having to go to the county.

2. Locating the county

As you will recall from Chapter 1, the original ten
counties of the colony of NY were set up in 1683, just 74
years after the sailing of Hudson into the NY harbor
(1609), and just 59 years after the colonization of New
Amsterdam (NY City) and Fort Orange (Albany) by the Dutch
West India Company (1624). Locating your ancestor in NY
during the years 1624-83 is usually not a problem because
practically all records were kept at the colony level,
although there are some that are specific either to New
Amsterdam or Albany. Please remember that the Dutch
started this period, then were displaced by the English
in 1664. There are numerous indexed records during this
time (before 1683), particularly those listed in section
10 of Chapter 2 [colonial records], but also some listed
in sections 6 [early lists of inhabitants], 7 [early
religious groups], 11 [early court records], 12 [the
extensive DAR typescripts], 15 [early immigration
records], 18 [genealogical indexes], 21 [colonial land
grant applications and surveys, early land conveyances,
deeds, and mortgages], 23 [colonial NY marriages], 24
[colonial military records], 29 [early oaths of alleg-
iance], and 34 [early wills and probates].

For the period from the formation of counties onward
(1683-), knowledge that your ancestor was simply from NY
is usually not sufficient to permit you to proceed with
the research. You need to know the county because many
genealogically-applicable records after 1683 were kept by
the county. If you happen to know your forebear's county, you may skip the remainder of this section. If not,
your first priority must be a search for the county. The
most efficient method for discovering the county depends
on the time period in which your progenitor lived in NY.
We will discuss county finding techniques for three more
basic periods in NY history: (1) 1683-1782, (2) 1782-
1900, (3) after 1900.

Should your ancestor's time period by 1683-1782, the
major resources for locating the county are the indexed
colonial records of the colony of NY. For these see

section 10, Chapter 2. If these should not tell you what
you seek, then try:
___Large name indexes for the US, sections 18 and 31,
    Chapter 2.
___Large name indexes for NY, section 18, Chapter 2.
___Indexes to NY land grant application files, section 21,
    Chapter 2.
___Surname listings in card, computer, and microfilm
    catalogs of NYSL, NYPL, NYGB, NYHS, and FHL[FHC].
___Will and estate record indexes, section 34, Chapter 2.
___Indexes to colonial militia and to Revolutionary War
    service, bounty land, and pension records, sections 24-
    25, Chapter 2.
___Indexes to other colonial records, sections 6-7, 11,
    15, 23, and 29, Chapter 2.
If after all of this you are still having trouble, it is
well to recall that by 1772 there were only twelve counties and by 1791 only twenty. Hence, a county-by-county
search in the records of the counties would not be an
exceptionally arduous task.

If your ancestor was somewhere in NY state during
1782-1900, the major finding aids are the indexes to the
1790/1800/10/20/30/40/50/60, 1880/1900 censuses. For
these see section 6, Chapter 2. If these do not locate
your ancestor for you, try:
___Large name indexes for the US, sections 18 and 31,
    Chapter 2.
___Large name indexes for NY, section 18, Chapter 2.
___Revolutionary War, War of 1812, Mexican War, Civil War,
    Spanish-American War service, bounty land, and pension
    records, sections 25-27, Chapter 2.
___Surname listings in card, computer, and microfilm
    catalogs in NYSL, NYPL, NYGL, NYHS, and FHL(FHC).
___City directories for cities, section 8, chapter 2.

In case your ancestor was in NY state after 1900, it
is usually the situation that the key item is family
information. If this does not give you the county location, use the state-wide birth, marriage, and death
records. Check sections 4, 13, and 23, Chapter 2. Now
let us summarize. The key items for the 1624-83 period
are the indexed published colonial records. These are
available in NYSL, NYPL, NYGB, and NYHS, and some of them
can often be found in FHL[FHC], LGL, and RL. The key
items for the 1683-1792 period are also the indexed

published colonial records, found in the places just
mentioned. The key items for <u>1782-1900</u> are the federal
census indexes. These are available at NYSL, NYPL, NYGB,
NYHS, FHL[FHC], NA, NAFB, and in some LGL and RL. They
may also be searched and/or borrowed through AGLL. The
key items for the years <u>after 1900</u> are family information
and the state-wide vital records. Many of these can be
obtained through the NY State Department of Health or
county or city health offices (see sections 4, 13, and
23, Chapter 2).

The work of locating your NY ancestor can generally
be done from where you live or nearby. This is because
the key items are either indexes or indexed records which
means that they can be scanned rapidly. Also many are in
published form which means that they are in numerous LGL
outside of NY as well as being available through FHC.
Some can be borrowed from AGLL. Therefore, you should
not have to travel too far to find many of the indexes
that you need. If however, it is more convenient, you
may hire a researcher in Albany to delve into the records
at NYSL to locate your progenitor. This should not cost
too much because you can instruct your searcher to look
into the indexes which are noted above in this section.

3. Research approaches

Having identified the county of your forebear's
residence, you are in position to ferret out the details.
This means that you need to identify what non-governmental, federal, state(colonial), county, city, town, and
village records are available, then to locate them, and
finally to examine them in detail. The most useful non-
governmental records have been discussed in Chapter 2
(sections 2-3, 5, 7-9, 12, 16-19, 22, 28, 30-32, 35).
The federal records which are most important for consideration also have been treated in Chapter 2 (sections
6, 15, 25-27, 30). State records of the greatest utility
for genealogical research are examined in certain sections of Chapter 2 (4, 6, 11, 13-14, 21, 23, 25-27, 29,
34). Colonial governmental records were listed prin-
cipally in section 10 of Chapter 2, but other sections
also deal with them (6, 11, 14-15, 21, 24, 34). The
types of records which were generated by NY counties,
cities, towns, and villages are listed in chapter 1
(section 9) and this chapter (section 1), and they are

discussed in various sections of Chapter 2 (4, 11, 13-14, 21, 23, 29, 33-34). County, city, town, and village records which have been microfilmed are in FHL (available through FHC), and county, city, town, and village records which have been published (printed and typescript) are in NYSL, NYPL, NYGB, and NYHS. Some of these published materials are also located in LGL, RL, and LL. Both the major microfilmed records and the major published records are listed in detail in later sections of this chapter and in Chapter 5.

The general approach for doing an utterly thorough job of researching a NY ancestor is to follow this pattern:

_1st, check all family sources (oral, records, mementos, Bible)

_2nd, locate your forebear's county (section 2, this chapter)

_3rd, use the nearest LGL (indexes, publications, microfilms)

_4th, use the nearest FHC or FHL (surname and locality indexes, integrated census indexes, borrow microfilmed records)

_5th, borrow any major federal records you haven't seen from AGLL (census, military, passenger lists)

_6th, use the NYSL (original, microfilmed, and published federal, state, colony, and non-governmental records; published county, city, town, and village records)

_7th, use the NYSA (manuscripts, original state documents)

_8th, use the NYPL, NYGB, and NYHS (published and microfilmed federal, state, colony, and non-governmental records; published county, city, town, and village records; manuscripts)

_9th, use LL (indexes, manuscripts, local records), visit offices of cemeteries, churches, mortuaries, newspapers, organizations, use RL (if LL directs you there)

_10th, use court houses and offices of city, town, and village record keepers (local records not seen)

_11th, use NAFB and NA (further federal, military, census, passenger list, and court materials)

_12th, use Church Archives (if church records still not found)

The precise way in which you use this scheme is chiefly determined by how far you are from Albany, NY, and NY

City, NY where NYSL, NYSA, NYPL, NYGB, and NYHS are located. It is in these five repositories that the best total collection of NY genealogical materials in the whole world exists (even though they are all short on county record microfilms). This county record shortage means that a visit to the county is also essential. Therefore the major idea that you must recognize is that eventually you will have to go to Albany, NY City, and the county, or to hire a researcher to go for you. In short, research in these repositories is an absolute necessity if your ancestor quest is to be complete.

If you live <u>very</u> <u>far</u> from Albany and NY City, you should follow the research procedure essentially as it is. In the 3rd, 4th, and 5th steps (LGL, FHC, FHL, AGLL), just as many items as possible should be examined, since this will reduce what remains to be done at the rest of the repositories (6th through 12th), but espe-cially at the county, city, town, and village offices. It is preferable to visit FHL rather than FHC, so you should elect that option if you are near enough to Salt Lake City, UT (where FHL is). You then need to hire a researcher to go to NYSL, NYSA, NYPL, NYGB, and NYHS, or go there yourself. Be sure and explain to your hired researcher exactly what records you have seen so that your money will not be wasted on duplicated work. Once the 6th, 7th, and 8th steps have been done, a hired researcher or a personal visit will again be involved for the 9th and 10th steps (LL and county, city, town, and villages offices). The 11th step can be done at the NAFB in your region, and the 12th can be conducted by mail.

If you live <u>within</u> <u>range</u> of NY, the 12-step pattern can be modified substantially. By "within range" is meant that you deem a personal visit to NY workable within the near future. In such a case, you can skip the 3rd and 4th steps, then do the 5th by mail, then the 6th through the 10th by personal visit, and finally the 11th at the nearest NAFB (or the NA) and the 12th by mail.

In selecting a research approach, whether it be one of the above or a modified one which you design, you need to think about three items. The <u>first</u> is expense. You need to balance the cost of a <u>hired</u> researcher over against the cost of personal visits (to Albany, NY City, and the county): travel, lodging, meals. Also do not

forget the costs of borrowing microfilms from your nearest FHC (a few dollars per roll). Of course, your desire
to look at the records for yourself (rather than have a
researcher do it) may be an important consideration.

The second item is a reminder about interlibrary
loans. With the exceptions of the microfilms of FHL
(available through FHC) and those of AGLL (available
personally or through your local library), very few
libraries and practically no archives will lend out
genealogical materials. The third item is also a reminder. Correspondence with librarians, governmental
officials, and archivists is of very limited use. The
reason is that these helpful and hard-working state,
local, and private employees do not have time to do any
detailed work for you because of the demanding duties of
their offices. In some cases, these people will have
time to look up one specific item for you (a land grant,
a deed record, a will, a military pension) if an overall
index is available. Please don't ask them for detailed
data, and please don't write them a long letter. If you
do write them, enclose a long SASE, a check for $5 with
the payee line left blank, and a brief request (no more
than one-third page) for one specific item in an index or
catalog. Ask them to use the check if there is a charge
for their services or for copying, and if they do not
have the time to look themselves, that they hand the
check and your letter to a researcher who can do the
work.

4. Format of the county listings

The remainder of this chapter and all of the following chapter, Chapter 5, will be devoted to detailed
listings of record and research information for the 62 NY
counties. These records are largely county-wide in their
coverage, previous treatment having been given in Chapter
2 to regional, state, and federal records. Let us
emphasize this: the records to be listed subsequently are
largely county-wide records. And further, these are
county-wide records which are available in central
repositories outside the counties themselves. Each
listing will consist of the following items, which can be
easily seen if you will look at a sample listing from
this or the next chapter. (1) First, the name of the
county is listed, with the year it was formed, the county

or area from which it originated, the county seat, the
county seat's zip code, and, if necessary, some notes
about the county's history or its records. (2) Second,
if any special reference guides are available, they are
listed. Some of these guides were published many years
ago, which means that they are outdated. Nonetheless, if
used with caution, they can be useful in alerting you to
what records were available at the time of publication.
Sometimes the records are not where they were at that
time, and sometimes they have been lost, but you will at
least know what to look for. (3) Third, the census
records which are available on microfilm in places like
the NA, AGLL, NAFB, NYSL, NYPL, FHL, and FHC are listed.
These censuses may not all be available in all the above
repositories, but by combining the resources of two or
more, they may all be accessed. The various types of
census records will be indicated by the abbreviations
which were introduced in section 6, Chapter 2. They are
E: early lists, R: regular federal, S: NY state, A:agri-
cultural, I:industrial, M: mortality, P: Revolutionary
pension, C: Civil War veteran.

(4) Fourth, the microfilmed governmental records
available at FHL and obtainable through every FHC are set
out. Most of these are available nowhere else, except in
the original forms in the counties. (5) Fifth, the
microfilmed non-governmental records available at FHL and
obtainable through every FHC are listed. (6) Sixth,
there is a listing of published and/or microfilmed county
records, most available in such large libraries as NYSL
and NYPL, with many available at NYGB and NYHS. Some of
these are also available in LGL, and those pertaining to
certain counties may be found in nearby RL and in their
own LL. You must not assume that these records are
necessarily complete. Most are not since they represent
records for a restricted number of years or for a restricted number of institutions. For example, if the
word Baptist appears it means only the records for some
Baptist churches are available, not all. And if the word
mortgage appears, it does not necessarily mean that all
the county mortgage records are available in published
form. It usually means only that some of the years have
been printed or microfilmed. Quite a few of the referenced records (particularly Bible, cemetery, and church)
are ones published in the DAR compilations. And others
are published in major NY genealogical periodicals. At

the end of this heading, references to volumes of NYGBR,
TT, and ESNY are given. NYGBR stands for the NY Genealogical and Biographical Record, TT for Tree Talks, and
ESNY for Early Settlers of NY. (7) Seventh, the major
repositories in the county are given. They may include
libraries, archives, museums, and record offices. These
are by no means all of the repositories in the county,
especially since many towns have at least a small library. However, the larger repositories will refer you to
the others if there are materials there you need to use.
(8) Eighth, some of the larger societies in the county
are shown. These generally have genealogical interests
or at least have some members who have. Often there are
other societies in the county which can help you, and
these larger ones can refer you to them.

Finally, carefully review the regional and local
genealogical periodicals listed in section 19 of Chapter
2. Those relating to the various NY counties and regions
must by no means be overlooked. They are often loaded
with excellent genealogical information.

5. NY city-county-borough history

Today the City of NY is a combination of five counties which are called boroughs of the city, and which
maintain some degree of autonomy, but which are all under
the supervening governance of the City. These boroughs
(counties) are: New York County (Manhattan Borough),
Kings County (Borough of Brooklyn), Queens County (Borough of Queens), Richmond County (Borough of Staten
Island), and Bronx County (Bronx Borough). The first
four were original counties which were established in
1683. The expansion of NY City, as was pointed out
previously, began in 1873 when 13,000 acres of southern
Westchester County were annexed. More of Westchester was
added in 1895 (East Chester, West Chester, Pelham, and
Wakefield), and then in 1897, the NY legislature authorized Greater NY City which was made up of a combination
of New York (Manhattan), Kings (Brooklyn), Queens, and
Richmond (Staten Island). Then in 1914, the northern
section of New York County was made into Bronx County.

Some of the records of Greater NY City are kept
by the city and some of the records rest with the separate counties. These divisions will be made clear in

the sections that follow. In this chapter, the five counties making up NY City will be treated. Extra comments will be added, especially for NY County (Manhattan), since it has been so very central to all of the state (the capital until 1796), to the southeastern region, and to the counties that surround it. And a very large fraction of the population of NY State has always been within the area encompassed by the boundaries of the five boroughs (counties) of NY City. In addition, recall the critical importance of NY harbor as the entry-way through which many immigrants came. In the fifth Chapter, which follows this one, the other 57 NY counties will be listed and their records will be noted according to the layout discussed in the previous section.

6. NEW YORK County [Manhattan Borough], formed 1683 as an original County, County Seat NY City (10007). Guides: Historical Records Survey, GUIDE TO PUBLIC VITAL STATISTICS, INCLUDING NY CITY, WPA, Albany, NY, 1942; Historical Records Survey, GUIDE TO VITAL STATISTICS RECORDS IN THE CITY OF NY, CHURCHES, WPA, New York, NY, 1942; Historical Records Survey, INVENTORY OF THE CHURCH ARCHIVES OF NY CITY, WPA, New York, NY, 1939-41; R. F. Bailey, GUIDE TO GENEALOGICAL AND BIOGRAPHICAL SOURCES FOR NY CITY, The Author, New York, NY, 1954; I. N. P. Stokes, THE ICONOGRAPHY OF MANHATTAN ISLAND, Dodd, New York, NY, 1928, 6 volumes, index in Volume 6, pages 285-677, bibliography of sources, Volume 6, pages 181-281, street maps, Volume 2, pages 452 ff, newspapers, Volume 2, pages 431 ff; B. Kronman, GUIDE TO NEW YORK CITY PUBLIC RECORDS, Public Interest Clearinghouse, New York, NY, 1984. Censuses: Pre-1790E, 1790R, 1800R, 1810R, 1820RI, 1830R, 1840RP, 1850RAIM, 1855S, 1860RAIM, 1870RAIM, 1880RAIM, 1890C, 1900R, 1905S, 1910R, 1915S, 1925S [1855S in NYPL, 1890 Police Census and 1905S/15S/25S in County Clerk's Office].
    FHL governmental microfilms: administrations (1743-1910), chamberlains bonds (1752-1821), chancery court (1700-1910), comptrollers vouchers (1795-1803), coroner (1795-1830, 1862-1918), corporation certificates (1818-1920), county court (1686-1934), court of common pleas (1821-1917), death (1798-1865), deed (1654-1866), estate accounts (1803-88), federal census (1790-1910), general sessions court (1683-1742), guardian (1802-1910), inventories (1709-1834), lis pendens (1864-1901), marriage (1686-1702, 1830-54), mayor's court (1670-1821), mortgage

(1665-75, 1754-1890), naturalization (1784-1906), poll list (1761, 1768-9), probate (1662-1910), state census (1915-25), superior court (1828-95), supreme court (1704-1910), town, will (1662-1910). FHL non-governmental microfilms: Baptist, Bible, Dutch Reformed, Evangelical Lutheran, Episcopal, Friends, German Church, Jewish, Lutheran, Methodist, Moravian, newspaper, Presbyterian, Reformed.

Published and microfilmed works (NYPL, NYSL, NYGB, NYHS): administrations index (1743-1875), apprentices, atlas (1867-99 and Stokes), Baptist, Bible, biography, birth index (August 1888-), burgomasters court (1653-74), cemetery, church, city directory (annually 1786-), court of quarter sessions (1722-42), colonial (many volumes), common council (1675-1831), Congregational, court of quarter sessions (1684-1797), DAR, death index (August 1888-), Dutch records (1630-64), Dutch Reformed, Evangelical Lutheran, Episcopal, federal census (1790-1910), Friends, guides to manuscript repositories, guides to vital statistics in public records, guides to vital statistics in church records, history (1853/72/77-80/-1909), Huguenot, immigration indexes, immigration lists, Jewish, jury, land indexes, Lutheran, marriage, marriage index (August 1888-1937), marriages by mayor (1830-54), mayors court (1674-5), Methodist, newspaper abstracts, newspaper indexes, notarial (1661-2), obituaries (1858-1968), orphanmasters (1655-63), passenger lists, Presbyterian, probate administration bonds, Reformed, slave births, state census (1855, 1915-25), supreme court (1797-1847), telephone directory (1925-), vital records indexes (1888-1937), will abstracts (1665-1892), will calendars, will indexes (1653-1875). See NYGBR 3-20, 36, 42, 46, 55, 68, 71, 73, 79-89, 93, 95-97, 103, 105-106, 110, 112; National Genealogical Society Quarterly 70-71, 221.

Repositories: NYPL; NYGB; NYHS; Municipal Archives, 52 Chambers St., New York, NY 10007 [birth 1847-9, 1853-1909, death 1798-1804, 1812-1929, marriage 1847-8, 1853-1937, tax assessment books 1789-1854, coroners' records]; Bureau of Vital Records, NY City Department of Health, 125 Worth St., New York, NY 10013 [birth 1910-, death 1930-]; Office of the City Clerk, Municipal Building, Chambers and Centre Sts., New York, NY 10007 [marriage 1938-]; NY County Surrogate's Court, 31 Chambers St., New York, NY 10007 [wills 1665-, administrations, guardians, dower, inventories]; NY County Clerk, 60 Centre St., New

York, NY 10007 [1905/15/25 State Censuses]; NY County Clerk, 31 Chambers St., New York, NY 10007 [1890 Police Census, naturalization 1907-25, divorce available up to 1888, chancery court, supreme court, court of common pleas, superior court]; NY Field Branch, National Archives, Building 22, Military Ocean Terminal, Bayonne, NJ 07002 [naturalizations 1792-1906]; City Register, Rooms 203, 205, and 209, 31 Chambers St., New York, NY 10007 [conveyances and deeds 1683-, mortgages 1754-, maps]; other city and county repositories listed in guidebook by Kronman; Friends Haviland Record Room, 15 Rutherford Pl., New York, NY 10003; Lutheran Council Archives, 145 W. 15th St., New York, NY 10010; Columbia University Libraries, 535 W. 114th St., New York, NY 10027; General Theological (Episcopal) Seminary Library, 175 Ninth Ave., New York, NY 10011.

Societies: NYGB; NYHS; Huguenot Society of America, 122 E. 58th St., New York, NY 10022; Holland Society of NY, 122 E. 58th St., New York, NY 10022; Jewish Historical Society of NY, 8 W. 70th St., New York, NY 10023; Sons of the Revolution in NY, 54 Pearl St., New York, NY 10004; Jewish Genealogical Society, PO Box 6398, New York, NY 10128.

7. Special notes on NY County

Because of its importance throughout the history of NY, some special notes on NY County need to be called to your attention. The guides that are referenced in the section preceding this one are all out-of-date except the last one by Kronman. Even so, they are still of value, especially the volumes by Bailey and by Stokes. Some of the records which they mention are now in different repositories listed above. Hence, as listings of what is available and as what you should look for, the guides are indispensible. Of exceptional import are the indexes in the 6th Volume of the works by Stokes. Be sure to look under these headings: Associations, Cemeteries, Churches, Courts, Grants and Farms, Newspapers, Streets. Now, in the paragraphs to follow, we will comment on each of the types of records listed in Chapter 2, paying particular notice to NY City.

Bible records. Use the DAR compilation indexes and check the surname and manuscript indexes at NYPL, NYGB, and NYHS. Also remember to seek genealogical periodical

articles. Biographies. Utilize the index by Pohl, take
a look at the large number of specialized biography works
listed by Bailey, and look in the catalogs of NYPL, NYGB,
and NYHS under NY-Biography. Birth records. NY City
kept birth records from 1847 onward, but the earlier ones
are somewhat incomplete. There are indexes to many of
these records in NYPL, NYGB, and NYHS. The records from
1847-97 are available in the Municipal Archives, and
those afterwards are obtainable through the Department of
Health. The records at both places are partially indexed. Cemetery records. Consult the DAR compilations
and the NYPL, NYGB, and NYHS catalogs, as well as the
churches affiliated with earlier cemeteries. Also consult Bailey and Stokes (Index in Volume 6). Census
records. Review section 6, Chapter 2. Take special note
of the availability of the 1855S census in the NYPL, and
the 1890 Police Census in the County Clerk's Office.
Remember that the census records are complemented by the
year-to-year listings in the city directories (1786-).
Church records. Consult Bailey and Stokes, also the
catalogs in NYPL, NYGB, and NYHS. In Stokes, consult the
heading Churches (also Cemetery and Clergymen) in the
Index in Volume 6. City directories. Available almost
every year from 1786. They are the most valuable locator
resource for NY County.

City and county histories. Use the resources recommended in section 9, Chapter 2, and the card catalogs in
NYPL, NYGB, and NYHS. Colonial records. Consult the
numerous materials given in section 10, Chapter 2. All
of the volumes which refer to the colony of NY carry
references to NY County. Be sure and look at the colonial resources suggested in other sections of Chapter 2:
6-7, 11-12, 15, 21-25, 29-30, and 34. Court records.
Check the NY County court records mentioned in section
11, Chapter 2. NY County court records, other than
probate, are mostly located in the Office of the County
Clerk. See Kronman for details. DAR records. Review
section 12, Chapter 2. Death records. Kept in NY County
1795 onward. Early records are incomplete. For records
1795-1919, go to Municipal Archives. The records after
1919 are in the Department of Health. Partial indexes
are available at both places. Partial indexes from 1888
are at NYPL, NYGB, and NYHS. Divorce records. County
Clerks Office. Emigration and Immigration. Check passenger lists and special immigrant volumes given in

section 15, Chapter 2. Ethnic records. Consult section 16, Chapter 2. Gazetteers, atlases, and maps. Of utter import is the set of 6 volumes by Stokes. Consult the index in Volume 6 for references to Manhattan maps. Genealogical indexes. See section 18, Chapter 2. Genealogical periodicals. See section 19, Chapter 2. Genealogical and historical societies. See section 20, Chapter 2, and section 6, Chapter 4.

Land records. Do not overlook the valuable material in Stokes. Deeds, conveyances, and mortgages are at the City Register's Office, 31 Chambers St., New York, NY 10007. Tax records are at the Bureau of City Collections, 1 Centre St., New York, NY 10007. Assessment records are at the Real Property Assessment Bureau, 1 Centre St., New York, NY 10007. Indexes to conveyances up to 1857 are in 17 volumes at NYPL, NYGB, and NYHS. Manuscripts. Principal repositories in NY County are NYPL, NYGB, NYHS, Municipal Archives, Baeck Jewish Institute, Episcopal Archives, Friends Haviland Records room, Holland Society. Consult the guides to manuscripts in NY City mentioned in section 22, Chapter 2. Marriage records. Kept in NY County since 1847. Early records are incomplete. For records 1847-65, go to the Municipal Archives. Records after that are located at the Office of the City Clerk. Partial indexes are available at these locations. Partial indexes for 1888-1937 are in NYPL, NYGB, and NYHS. Military records. Review sections 24-27, Chapter 2.

Mortuary records. Consult NY County mortuaries and use catalogs in NYPL, NYGB, and NYHS. Naturalization records. Make use of the references in section 29, Chapter 2. Pay special attention to the NY City Naturalization Photocopies and Index at the Federal Archives Center in Bayonne, NJ. Newspapers. Excellent collections in NYHS and NYPL. Checklists in French and in Stokes. Regional publications. See section 32, Chapter 2. Tax lists. NY County tax office is given in land section just above. Will and intestate records. Recall that most probate matters for the entire colony/state were handled by the NY County Court until 1787. Since then, NY County probate records have been kept in the Surrogate's Court. Most records prior to 1787 have been transcribed, abstracted, indexed, and published. See section 34, Chapter 2. Will indexes 1662-1875 are in

NYPL, NYGB, and NYHS, as are indexes to letters of administration 1743-1875.

8. BRONX County [Bronx Borough], formed 1914 from NY County, County Seat Bronx (10451). What is now Bronx County was once part of Westchester County. In 1874, the portion west of the Bronx River was attached to NY County, then in 1895 the portion east of the Bronx River was added to NY County. In 1898, the attached areas became the Borough of the Bronx of NY City of NY County. Then in 1914, the borough also became Bronx County. Guides: L. Tosi and J. Butler, GENEALOGY IN THE BRONX, Bronx County Historical Society, Bronx, NY, 1986; Historical Records Survey, GUIDE TO PUBLIC VITAL STATISTICS, WPA, Albany, NY, 1942; Historical Records Survey, GUIDE TO VITAL STATISTICS IN THE CITY OF NY, CHURCHES, WPA, New York, NY, 1939-41; Historical Records Survey, INVENTORY OF THE COUNTY ARCHIVES OF NY CITY, BRONX COUNTY, WPA, New York, NY, 1939-42; B. Kronman, GUIDE TO NYC PUBLIC RECORDS, Public Interest Clearinghouse, New York, NY, 1984. Censuses: 1915S, 1925S.

FHL governmental microfilms: state censuses. FHL non-governmental microfilms: Presbyterian, Reformed. Published and microfilmed works (NYPL, NYSL): atlas (1890/93/97/1907), Bible, biography (1898), birth index (1911-33), cemetery, church, DAR, death index (1904-33), Dutch Reformed, history (1906/12/27/62), marriage index (1904-33), state census, vital records index.

Repositories: NYPL; NYGB; NYHS; Bronx County Historical Society Library, 3309 Bainbridge Ave., Bronx, NY 10467; Bronx County Register, 1932 Arthur Ave., Bronx, NY 10457 (land 1684-); Department of Health, 125 Worth St., New York, NY 10013 (birth 1898-), County Clerk's Office, 851 Grand Concourse, Bronx, NY 10451 (civil and criminal courts, naturalization); Queens College Library, Flushing, NY 11367; Marriage License Bureau, 1780 Grand Concourse, Bronx, NY 10457 (marriage 1899-); Surrogate's Court, 851 Grant Concourse, Bronx, NY 10451 (probate); Fordham Library Center of NYPL, 2556 Bainbridge Ave., Bronx, NY 10458; Fordham University Library, Bronx, NY 10458. Societies: Bronx County Historical Society, 3309 Bainbridge Ave., Bronx, NY 10467; Eastchester Historical Society, 388 California Rd., Bronxville, NY 10708.

9. KINGS County [Borough of Brooklyn], formed 1683 as an original County, County Seat Brooklyn (11201). Guides:

Historical Records Survey, GUIDE TO PUBLIC VITAL STATIS-
TICS, WPA, Albany, NY, 1942; Historical Records Survey,
GUIDE TO VITAL STATISTICS RECORDS IN THE CITY OF NY,
CHURCHES, WPA, New York, NY, 1942; Historical Records
Survey, INVENTORY OF THE CHURCH ARCHIVES OF NY CITY, WPA,
New York, NY, 1939-41; Historical Records Survey, INVEN-
TORY OF THE COUNTY ARCHIVES OF KINGS COUNTY, WPA, New
York, NY, 1939-42; B. Kronman, GUIDE TO NYC PUBLIC
RECORDS, Public Interest Clearinghouse, New York, NY,
1984. Censuses: Pre-1790E, 1790R, 1800R, 1810R, 1820RI,
1830R, 1840RP, 1850RAIM, 1855S, 1860RAIM, 1865S, 1870
RAIM, 1875S, 1880 RAIM, 1890C, 1892S, 1900R, 1905S,
1910R, 1915S, 1925S.

FHL governmental microfilms: birth (1869), death
(1847-61), federal census (1790-1910), guardian (1814-
68), probate (1787-1923), state census (1915-25), town,
will (1787-1881). FHL non-governmental microfilms:
Congregational, Dutch Reformed, Episcopal, Jewish, Methodist, newspaper, Presbyterian, Reformed. Published and
microfilmed works (NYPL, NYSL): atlas (1869/74/80/86/90/-
94/98), Baptist, Bible, biography (1925), birth index
(1888-), cemetery, church, city directory (1796, 1802/11,
1822-), DAR, death index (1888-), deed, Dutch Reformed,
early settlers (to 1700), estate (1683), federal census
(1790-1910), Friends, genealogy (1925), history (1840/-
49/67-70/81/84/1938), marriage index (1888-1937), newspaper, Presbyterian, Reformed, residence (1702), Revolutionary War, slave, state census (1915-25), supervisors,
tax (1675-6), vital records index (1888-), will and
probate index (1650-1850). See NYGBR 47, 55.

Repositories: NYPL; NYGB; NYHS; Brooklyn Public
Library, Grand Army Plaza, Brooklyn, NY 11238; St. Fran-
cis College Library, 180 Remsen St., Brooklyn, NY 11201;
Brooklyn Historical Society Library, 128 Pierrepont St.,
Brooklyn, NY 11201; Municipal Archives, 52 Chambers St.,
New York, NY 10007 (birth 1866-97, death 1847-1919,
marriage 1847-51 incomplete); City Department of Health,
125 Worth St., New York, NY 10013 (birth 1898-, death
1920-); Office of the City Clerk, 208 Joralemon St.,
Brooklyn, NY 11201 (marriage 1866-); Surrogate's Court, 2
Johnson St., Brooklyn, NY 11201; County Clerk, 360 Adams
St., Brooklyn, NY (Censuses 1855S, 1865S, 1875S, 1892S,
1905S, 1915S, 1925S); City Register's Office, 210 Joralemon St., Brooklyn, NY 11201 (deeds, mortgages); Bureau of
City Collections, 210 Joralemon St., Brooklyn, NY 11201
(tax); Federal Archives Center, Building 22, Military

Ocean Terminal, Bayonne, NJ 07002 (naturalization 1792–1906). Society: Brooklyn Historical Society, 128 Pierrepont St., Brooklyn, NY 11201.

10. QUEENS County [Borough of Queens], formed 1683 as an original County, County Seat Jamaica (11435). Guides: Historical Records Survey, GUIDE TO PUBLIC VITAL STATISTICS, WPA, Albany, NY, 1942; Historical Records Survey, GUIDE TO VITAL STATISTICS RECORDS IN THE CITY OF NY, CHURCHES, WPA, New York, NY, 1942; Historical Records Survey, INVENTORY OF THE CHURCH ARCHIVES OF NY CITY, WPA, New York, NY, 1939–41; B. Kronman, GUIDE TO NYC PUBLIC RECORDS, Public Interest Clearinghouse, New York, NY, 1984. Censuses: Pre-1790E, 1790R, 1800R, 1810R, 1820R, 1830R, 1840RP, 1850RAIM, 1860RAIM, 1870RAIM, 1880RAIM, 1890C, 1892S, 1900R, 1910R, 1925S.
    FHL governmental microfilms: chancery court (1701–1802, 1846–7), deed (1683–1765), federal census (1790–1910), guardian (1787–1899), military (1861–86), naturalization (1888–98), probate (1787–1922), state census (1915–25), supreme court (1868–70), tax (1790/92/99/–1802/07/10/20–21/77), town, vital records (1847–49/77), will (1680–1922). FHL non-governmental microfilms: Bible, Dutch Reformed, Episcopal, genealogy, Methodist, Presbyterian. Published and microfilmed works (NYPL, NYSL): atlas (1891), Bible, biography (1882/96/1925), birth index (1888–), Catholic, cemetery, church, DAR, death index (1888–), deed, Dutch Reformed, Episcopal, federal census (1790–1910), Friends, genealogy (1925), history (1856/82/96/1908), landowners, land record index, Lutheran, marriage index (1888–1937), Methodist, military, Presbyterian, probate index, Reformed, Revolutionary War, state census (1915–25), tax, vital records index (1888–), will and probate index (1680–1835), will. See NYGBR 54, 65.
    Repositories: NYPL; NYGB; NYHS; Queens College Library, 65–30 Kissena Rd., Flushing, NY 11367; Queens Borough Public Library, 89–11 Merrick Rd., Jamaica, NY 11432; Municipal Archives, 52 Chambers St., New York, NY 10007 (birth 1847–97, death 1847–9, 1881–1919, marriage 1881–); Department of Health, 125 Worth St., New York, NY 10013 (birth 1898–, death 1920–); Office of the City Clerk, 120–55 Queens Blvd., Kew Gardens, NY 11424 (marriage 1881–); Surrogate's Court, 88–11 Sutphin Blvd., Jamaica, NY 11435 (probate, census 1892S, 1915S, 1925S); Federal Records Center, Building 22, Military Ocean

Terminal, Bayonne, NJ 07002 (naturalization 1792–1906);
City Register's Office, 90–27 Sutphin Blvd., Jamaica, NY
11435 (deeds, mortgages); Bureau of City Collections, 90–
15 Sutphin Blvd., Jamaica, NY 11435 (tax). Society:
Queens County Historical Society, 169–08 Grand Central
Parkway, Jamaica, NY 11432.

11. RICHMOND County [Borough of Staten Island], formed
1683 as an original County, County Seat St. George
(10301). Guides: Historical Records Survey, GUIDE TO
PUBLIC VITAL STATISTICS, WPA, Albany, NY, 1942; Histori-
cal Records Survey, GUIDE TO VITAL STATISTICS RECORDS IN
THE CITY OF NY, CHURCHES, WPA, New York, NY, 1942; Historical Records Survey, INVENTORY OF THE CHURCH ARCHIVES
OF NY CITY, WPA, New York, NY, 1939–41; B. Kronman, GUIDE
TO NYC PUBLIC RECORDS, Public Interest Clearinghouse, New
York, NY, 1984; NY Historical Resources Center, GUIDE TO
HISTORICAL RESOURCES IN RICHMOND COUNTY, The Center,
Ithaca, NY, 1985. Censuses: Pre-1790E, 1790R, 1800R,
1810R, 1820RI, 1830R, 1840RP, 1850RAIM, 1855S, 1860RAIM,
1865S, 1870RAIM, 1890C, 1900R, 1910R, 1915S, 1925S.
    FHL governmental microfilms: circuit court (1847–
61), court of common pleas (1711–1847), court of oyer and
terminer (1847–62), deed (1630–1972), federal census
(1790–1910), general sessions court (1847–63), homestead
(1851–1911), guardian (1802–66), land (1800–99), military
(1866, 1917), mortgage (1756–1973), naturalization (1820–
1924), probate (1787–1967), road (1758–1888), school
(1896), state census (1855–75, 1915–25), supreme court
(1847–81), tax (1800–99 scattered), town (1678–1813),
will (1787–1967). FHL non-governmental microfilms:
Bible, Dutch Reformed, Episcopal, genealogy, Methodist,
Moravian, newspaper, Reformed. Published and microfilmed
works (NYPL, NYSL): atlas (1874/87/94/98), Bible, birth
index (1888–), cemetery, census (1706), church, DAR, city
directory (1886–), death index (1888–), Dutch Reformed,
Episcopal, federal census (1790–1910), history (1877/87/–
98/1930), marriage index (1888–1937), state census (1855–
75, 1915–25), United Brethren. See NYGBR 25, 38, 60.
    Repositories: NYPL, NYGB, NYHS, Staten Island His-
torical Society Library, 441 Clark Ave., Staten Island,
NY 10306; Municipal Archives, 52 Chambers St., New York,
NY 10007 (birth 1847–53, 1881–97, death 1847–52, 1881–97,
marriage 1848–97); Department of Health, 125 Worth St.,
New York, NY 10013 (birth 1898–, death 1898–), Office of
City Clerk, Borough Hall, Staten Island, NY 10301 (mar-

riage 1898-); Surrogate's Court, County Court House,
Staten Island, NY 10301 (probate, wills); County Clerk,
County Court House, Staten Island, NY 10301 (census
1915S, 1925S); Federal Records Center, Building 22,
Military Ocean Terminal, Bayonne, NJ 07002 (naturaliza-
tion 1792-1906); City Register's Office, 18 Richmond
Terrace, Staten Island, NY 10301 (deed, mortgage); Bureau
of City Collections, 350 St. Mark's Place, Staten Island,
NY 10301 (tax). <u>Society</u>: Staten Island Historical Socie-
ty, 441 Clark Ave., Staten Island, NY 10306.

Abbreviations

A	Agricultural Census
AGLL	American Genealogical Lending Library, Bountiful, UT
C	Union Civil War Veteran Census
CH	Court House(s) and County Archives
DAR	Daughters of the American Revolution
E	Early Pre-1790 Census-Like Lists
FHC	Family History Center(s), Genealogical Society of UT
FHL	Family History Library, Genealogical Society of UT, Salt Lake City, UT
I	Industrial Censuses
LGL	Large Genealogical Libraries
LL	Local Library(ies) and Other Local Repositories
M	Mortality Censuses
NA	National Archives, Washington, DC
NAFB	National Archives Field Branch(es)
NYSA	New York State Archives, Albany, NY
NYGB	New York Genealogical and Biographical Society, New York, NY
NYHS	New York Historical Society, New York, NY
NYPL	New York City Public Library, New York, NY
NYSL	New York State Library, Albany, NY
P	Pensioner Census, Revolutionary War
R	Regular Federal Censuses
RL	Regional Library(ies)
S	NY State Censuses

Chapter 5

OTHER NY COUNTY LISTINGS

1. Introduction

In this chapter, the listings of records for NY counties will be continued. The later sections of the previous chapter were devoted to the records of the five counties (New York, Bronx, Kings, Queens, Richmond) which make up NY City. The remaining 57 counties of the State of NY will be dealt with in this chapter.

The format of the listings will remain the same. First, the name of the county, its date of creation, its county seat and zip code, and sometimes some historical notes will be given. Then, second, pertinent reference guides will be listed. Third, both federal and state census records which are available will be noted. Fourth, the microfilmed governmental records which are at FHL and are available on interlibrary loan from FHC are set out. Fifth, the non-governmental microfilms available from that same source are shown. Sixth, there is a listing of published and microfilmed county records available in such large libraries as NYSL and NYPL. Remember that some of these are in periodicals. Pertinent volumes of NYGBR (NY Genealogical and Biographical Record), TT (Tree Talks), and ESNY (Early Settlers of NY) are listed at the end of this category. Seventh, the major record repositories in the county are given. And eighth, one or more of the pertinent societies in the county are shown.

There are a couple of reference guides which are pertinent to all the 57 counties to be treated in this chapter. Rather than list them under each county, they will be noted here. However, you must not forget to consult them for every county.
__Historical Records Survey, GUIDE TO PUBLIC VITAL STATISTICS, WPA, Albany, NY, 1942, Volume 1 births, Volume 2 marriages, Volume 3 deaths.
__Historical Records Survey, GUIDE TO VITAL STATISTICS OF RECORDS OF CHURCHES IN NY STATE, WPA, Albany, NY, 1942, Volume 1 Albany to Montgomery Counties, Volume 2 Nassau to Yates Counties.

In addition, there are major repositories of certain
types which will be found in every county. These are the
county, city, town, and village offices, including the
very important Offices of the County, City, Town, and
Village Clerks, the Office of the Surrogate Court, the
Office of the county fiscal officer, and the Offices of
the County, City, Town, and Village Historians. These
may be found in county court houses, city halls, town
halls, municipal buildings, and other governmental buildings called by similar names. All of these will be
called local repositories and they will be collectively
abbreviated as LR. This abbreviation LR will appear
under each county to remind you of these utterly essential record-keeping agencies.

2. ALBANY County, formed 1683 as an original county,
County Seat Albany (12207). Guides: W. B. Melius and F.
H. Burnap, INDEX TO THE PUBLIC RECORDS OF THE COUNTY OF
ALBANY, 1630-1894, Argus Co., Albany, NY, 1902-17, 37
volumes; Historical Records Survey, INVENTORY OF THE
COUNTY ARCHIVES OF ALBANY COUNTY, WPA, Albany, NY, 1939;
D. A. Franz, A DESCRIPTIVE INVENTORY OF ALBANY'S MUNICI-
PAL ARCHIVES, The Archives, Albany, NY, 1974; M. L.
Bailey and S. M. Sweeney, GUIDE TO HISTORICAL RECORDS IN
THE OFFICE OF THE ALBANY COUNTY CLERK, National Histori-
cal Publications and Records Commission, Albany, NY,
1979; R. W. Arnold, HANDBOOK FOR USING THE ALBANY COUNTY
HALL OF RECORDS, County Clerk, Albany, NY, 1983; NY
Historical Resources Center, GUIDE TO HISTORICAL RE-
SOURCES IN ALBANY COUNTY, The Center, Ithaca, NY, 1986.
Censuses: Pre-1790E, 1790R, 1800R, 1810R, 1820RI, 1830R,
1835S, 1840RP, 1850RAIM, 1855S, 1860RAIM, 1865S,
1870RAM, 1875S, 1880RAIM, 1890C, 1892S, 1900R, 1905S,
1910R, 1915S, 1925S.
　　FHL governmental microfilms: burial, chancery court,
commissioners (1676-80), county court (1652-1782, 1849-
80), court of oyer and terminer (1825-34), deed (1630-
1966), federal census (1790-1910), incorporation (1784-
1880), justice of peace (1665-85, 1811-20), lis pendens
(1630-1904), mortgage (1630-1894), notarial (1660-95),
probate (1787-1902), state census (1835, 1855-1925), tax,
town (1658-1764), treasurer (1702-12, 1808-49), vital
records (1824-34, 1847-81), will (1656-1774). FHL non-
governmental microfilms: Bible, Dutch Reformed, Evangelical Lutheran, Episcopal, Friends, genealogy, Lutheran,
Methodist, newspaper (1818-25), Presbyterian, Reformed,

Revolutionary War. Published and microfilmed works (NYSL, NYPL): atlas (1866), Baptist, Bible, biography, cemetery, city, city directory (1813-), colonial, court (1652-1702), court of common pleas (1766-1850), court of sessions (1685-9, 1717-23, 1763-82), DAR, deed, Dutch Reformed, early records, Evangelical Lutheran, Episcopal, federal census (1790-1910), Friends, first settlers, genealogy, history (1850-9/1865-71/72/86/97), Lutheran, Methodist, military, mortgage, newspaper, Presbyterian, Reformed, Revolutionary War, road, settlers (1630-1800), state census (1835, 1855-1925), town, vital records, voter, will index (1780-1895), wills and will calendars (1626-1836). See TT 3, 12, 16; NYGBR 94; ESNY 3; National Genealogical Society Quarterly 48, 63, 68.

Repositories: NYSL; NYSA; LR; Albany Public Library, 161 Washington Ave., Albany, NY 12210; Albany County Hall of Records, 27 Western Ave., Albany, NY 12203. Societies: Capital District Genealogical Society, PO Box 2175, Empire State Plaza Station, Albany, NY 12220; Dutch Settlers Society of Albany, 6 DeLucia Terrace, Albany, NY 12211; Franco-American Genealogical Association, RFD 2, Albany, NY 12186; Shaker Heritage Society, Albany-Shaker Rd., Albany, NY 12211; Albany County Historical Association, 9 Ten Broeck Pl., Albany, NY 12210.

3. ALLEGANY County, formed 1806 from Genesee County, County Seat Belmont (14813). Guide: NY Historical Resources Center, GUIDE TO HISTORICAL RESOURCES IN ALLEGANY COUNTY, The Center, Ithaca, NY, 1980. Censuses: 1810R, 1820RI, 1830R, 1840RP, 1850RAIM, 1855S, 1860RAIM, 1865S, 1870RAM, 1875S, 1880RAIM, 1890C, 1892S, 1900R, 1905S, 1910R, 1915S, 1925S.

FHL governmental microfilms: county court (1850-1903), court of common pleas (1807-50), court of oyer and terminer (1815-95), deed (1807-1940), federal census (1810-1910), guardian (1807-1952), marriage (1908-55), mortgage (1807-1961),naturalization (1866-1930), probate (1807-1952), state census (1855-1925), supreme court (1820-1967), will (1831-1906). FHL non-governmental microfilms: Bible, genealogy, Presbyterian. Published and microfilm works (NYSL, NYPL): atlas (1869), Baptist, Bible, biography, cemetery, DAR, federal census (1810-1910), gazetteer (1875), genealogy, history (1879/96/1981), marriage, naturalization, state census (1855-1925), town, vital records (1847-9), will. See TT 3-5, 12-14, 22; ESNY 6-7.

Repositories: LR; Allegany County Historical Museum Library, Court House, Belmont, NY 14813; Belmont Free Library, Park Pl., Belmont, NY 14813; State University of NY at Alfred, NY 14802. Society: Allegany County Historical Society, 20 Willets Ave., Belmont, NY 14813.

4. BROOME County, formed 1806 from Tioga County, County Seat Binghamton (13901). Guides; Historical Records Survey, INVENTORY OF THE COUNTY ARCHIVES OF BROOME COUNTY, WPA, Albany, NY, 1938; NY Historical Resources Center, GUIDE TO HISTORICAL RESOURCES IN BROOME COUNTY, The Center, Ithaca, NY, 1982. Censuses: 1810R, 1820RI, 1825S, 1830R, 1835S, 1840RP, 1845S, 1850RAIM, 1855S, 1860RAIM, 1865S, 1870RAM, 1875S, 1880RAIM, 1890C, 1892S, 1900R, 1905S, 1910R, 1915S, 1925S.
    FHL governmental microfilms: county court (1808-1951), court of common pleas (1806-61), court of oyer and terminer (1807-56), death (1816-65), deed (1791-1961), election (1821-85), federal census (1810-1910), general sessions court (1818-48), guardian (1830-1917), incorporation (1811-88), justice court (1819-57), lis pendens (1850-1900), marriage (1816-65, 1908-35), military (1806-32, 1962/4), mortgage (1791-1895), naturalization (1820-1920), patent (1790-1926), probate (1806-1951), road (1806-1940), school, state census (1825-1925), tax (1837/40, 1869-70), vital records (1847-50, 1865-75) will (1806-1906). FHL non-governmental microfilms: business, Congregational, newspaper, Presbyterian. Published and microfilm works (NYSL, NYPL): atlas (1866/76/86), Baptist, Bible, biography (1885/94), cemetery, church, city directory (1857-), Congregational, DAR, Dutch Reformed, Episcopal, federal census (1810-1910), gazetteer (1872-), genealogy, history (1885/94/1924/81), Methodist, newspaper, Presbyterian, Revolutionary War, state census (1915-25), tax, vital records (1847-9), will. See TT 1, 3, 14-15, 20, 22; ESNY 4.
    Repositories: LR; Broome County Historical Library, 30 Front St., Binghamton, NY 13905; Broome County Public Library, 78 Exchange St., Binghamton, NY 13901; State University of NY, Vestal Parkway E, Binghamton, NY 13903. Society: Broome County Historical Society, 30 Front St., Binghamton, NY 13901.

5. CATTARAUGUS County, formed 1808 from Genesee County, County Seat Little Valley (14755). Guides: Historical Records Survey, INVENTORY OF THE COUNTY ARCHIVES OF

CATTARAUGUS COUNTY, WPA, Albany, NY, 1939; NY Historical Resources Center, GUIDE TO HISTORICAL RESOURCES IN CATTARAUGUS COUNTY, The Center, Ithaca, NY, 1980; J. W. Palmer, A GUIDE TO LOCAL HISTORY IN CATTARAUGUS AND CHAUTAUQUA COUNTIES, Buffalo, NY, 1985. Censuses: 1810R, 1820RI, 1825S, 1830R, 1835S, 1840RP, 1845S, 1850RAIM, 1855S, 1860RAIM, 1865S, 1870RAM, 1875S, 1880RAIM, 1890C, 1892S, 1900R, 1905S, 1910R, 1915S, 1925S.

FHL governmental microfilms: county court (1817-54), court of common pleas (1817-54), deed (1800-1968), federal census (1810-1910), guardian (1870-1922), lis pendens (1835-1907), marriage (1908-35), mortgage (1800-77), naturalization (1847-1954), probate (1800-1956), state census (1825-1925), vital records (1908-21, 1926-35), will (1830-1906). FHL non-governmental microfilms: Baptist, Congregational, genealogy, Methodist, Presbyterian. Published and microfilm works (NYSL, NYPL): atlas (1868/9), Baptist, Bible, biography (1893), cemetery, church, Congregational, DAR, death, Episcopal, federal census (1810-1910), gazetteer (1893), history (1857/79/-93/1979), Lutheran, marriage, Methodist, newspaper, pioneer, Revolutionary War, state census (1915-25), town, vital records (1847-9), will (1808-51). See TT 3-4, 7, 9-10, 14, 20.

Repositories: LR; Cattaraugus County Memorial and Historical Museum Library, Court St., Little Valley, NY 14755. Society: Cattaraugus Area Historical Society, 23 Main St., Cattaraugus, NY 14719.

6. CAYUGA County, formed 1799 from Onondaga County, County Seat Auburn (13021). Guide: NY Historical Resources Center, GUIDE TO HISTORICAL RESOURCES IN CAYUGA COUNTY, The Center, Ithaca, NY, 1980. Censuses: 1800R, 1810R, 1820RI, 1830R, 1840RP, 1850RAIM, 1855S, 1860RAIM, 1865S, 1870RAM, 1875S, 1880RAIM, 1890C, 1892S, 1900R, 1905S, 1910R, 1915S, 1925S.

FHL governmental microfilms: county court (1845-1919), court (1794-1905), court of common pleas (1799-1846), court of oyer and terminer (1830-45), election (1799-1817), deed (1793-1956), federal census (1800-1910), homestead (1851-1966), lis pendens (1864-1903), marriage (1847, 1908-35), mortgage (1794-1906), naturalization (1831-1972), probate (1799-1952), state census (1865-1925), supreme court (1855-1912), town (1796-1823), vital records (1908-17), will (1799-1902). FHL non-governmental microfilms: Baptist, Dutch Reformed, newspaper, Presbyterian. <u>Published</u> <u>and</u> <u>microfilm</u> <u>works</u> (NYSL, NYPL): atlas (1875), Baptist, Bible, biography (1894), Catholic, cemetery, church, city directory (1857-), Congregational, DAR, early county records, election, Episcopal, federal census (1800-1910), Friends, gazetteer (1868), genealogy, history (1879/94/1941/58), naturalization, newspaper, Presbyterian, Reformed, Revolutionary War, school, state census (1915-25), town, Universalist, vital records (1847-50), will (1799-1834). See TT 1, 6, 21.

    <u>Repositories</u>: LR; Cayuga County Historian, County Office Building, Genesee St., Auburn, NY 13021; Cayuga Community College Library, Franklin St., Auburn, NY 13021. <u>Society</u>: Cayuga County Historical Society, 203 Genesee St., Auburn, NY 13021; Cayuga-Owasco Lakes Historical Society, PO Box 241, Moravia, NY 13118; Cayuga County Genealogical Society, 3 Seymour St., Auburn, NY 13021.

7. CHAUTAUQUA County, formed 1808 from Genesee County, County Seat Mayville (14757). <u>Guides</u>: Historical Records Survey, INVENTORY OF THE COUNTY ARCHIVES OF CHAUTAUQUA COUNTY, WPA, Albany, NY, 1938; NY Historical Resources Center, GUIDE TO HISTORICAL RESOURCES IN CHAUTAUQUA COUNTY, The Center, Ithaca, NY, 1982; J. W. Palmer, A GUIDE TO LOCAL HISTORY IN CATTARAUGUS AND CHAUTAUQUA COUNTIES, Buffalo, NY, 1985. <u>Censuses</u>: 1810R, 1820RI, 1825S, 1830R, 1835S, 1840RP, 1845S, 1850RAIM, 1855S, 1860RAIM, 1865S, 1870RAM, 1875S, 1880RAIM, 1890C, 1892S, 1900R, 1905S, 1910R, 1915S, 1925S.

    <u>FHL</u> <u>governmental</u> <u>microfilms</u>: deed (1811-1917), federal census (1810-1910), naturalization (1837-1972), probate (1811-1962), state census (1825-1925), vital records (1908-35), will (1830-1901). <u>FHL</u> <u>non-government</u><u>al</u> <u>microfilms</u>: newspaper (1857-8). <u>Published</u> <u>and</u> <u>microfilmed</u> <u>works</u> (NYSL, NYPL): atlas (1869/81), Baptist, Bible, biography (1891/1904), cemetery, church, Civil War, Congregational, DAR, Episcopal, federal census (1810-1910), gazetteer (1873), genealogy, history (1846/75/91/94/1904/21/80), marriage (1830-7), Methodist, newspaper (1823-40), Presbyterian, Revolutionary War, state census (1825-1925), town, will. See TT 5, 21.

    <u>Repositories</u>: LR; Chautauqua County Historical Society Library, E. Main St., Westfield, NY 14787; State University of NY College Library, Fredonia, NY 14063; Fenton Historical Society Library, 67 Washington St.,

Jamestown, NY 14701.   Societies: Chautauqua County Historical Society, E. Main St., Westfield, NY 14787; Fenton
Historical   Society,   67 Washington St., Jamestown, NY
14701; Chautauqua Genealogical Society, PO Box 97, Dun-
kirk, NY 14048.

8. CHEMUNG County, formed 1836 from Tioga County, County
Seat Elmira   (14901).   Guides: Historical Records Survey,
INVENTORY OF THE ARCHIVES OF CHEMUNG COUNTY, WPA, Albany,
NY, 1939; NY Historical Resources Center, GUIDE TO HIS-
TORICAL RESOURCES IN CHEMUNG COUNTY, The Center, Ithaca,
NY, 1986.   Censuses: 1840RP, 1850RAIM, 1855S, 1860RAIM,
1865S, 1870RAM, 1875S, 1880RAIM, 1890C, 1892S, 1900R,
1905S, 1910R, 1915S, 1925S.
     FHL governmental microfilms: county court (1836-
1906), deed (1791-1942), federal census (1840-1910), lis
pendens (1837-1903), marriage (1908-26), mortgage (1791-
1888), naturalization (1859-1955), probate (1836-1932),
state census (1855-1925), supreme court (1836-1906),
vital records (1908-36), will (1836-1923).   FHL non-
governmental microfilms: Baptist, Presbyterian. Published and microfilmed works (NYSL, NYPL): atlas (1869),
Bible, biography (1902), cemetery, church, city directory
(1857-), Congregational, DAR, early settlers, Episcopal,
federal census (1840-1910), gazetteer (1868), history
(1879/85/91/1902/07/61/76), marriage, pioneers, Revolutionary War, state census (1855-1925), will. See TT 3-4,
8, 21.
     Repositories: LR; Chemung County Historical Society
Library, 1 Library Plaza, Elmira, NY 14901. Societies:
Chemung County Historical Society, 415 E. Water St.,
Elmira, NY 14901; Twin Tiers Genealogical Society, 230
Devonshire Dr., Elmira, NY 14903.

9. CHENANGO County, formed 1798 from Tioga and Herkimer
Counties, County Seat Norwich (13815).   Guide: NY Historical Resources Center, GUIDE TO HISTORICAL RESOURCES
IN CHENANGO COUNTY, The Center, Ithaca, NY, 1982. Censuses: 1800R, 1810R, 1820RI, 1830R, 1840RP, 1850RAIM,
1855S, 1860RAIM, 1865S, 1870RAM, 1875S, 1880RAIM, 1890C,
1900R, 1905S, 1910R, 1915S, 1925S.
     FHL governmental microfilms: circuit court (1799-
1835), court (1799-1895), court of common pleas (1821-
58), court of oyer and terminer (1798-1858), deed (1798-
1969), federal census (1800-1910), general sessions court
(1820-5), incorporation (1799-1855), justice court (1798-

1844), lis pendens (1798–1858), marriage (1830–73, 1908–35), military (1851–66), mortgage (1798–1899), naturalization (1859–1929), probate (1798–1970), school (1827–81), state census (1855–75, 1905–25), supervisors (1798–1891), supreme court (1819–47), tax (1851–65), town (1795–1876), vital records (1847–75), will (1792–1970). FHL non-governmental microfilms: Baptist, Bible, business, Christian Church, Congregational, Episcopal, Methodist, newspaper (1847–56, 1864–1900), Presbyterian, Universalist. Published and microfilmed works: (NYSL, NYPL): atlas (1875), Baptist, Bible, biography (1880/98), cemetery, Christian Church, church, Congregational, DAR, Episcopal, federal census (1800–1910), gazetteer (1869), genealogy, guardian (1814–68), history (1850/80/98), jury, marriage, Methodist, military, newspaper, Revolutionary War, school, state census (1915–25), tax (1817–65), town, Universalist, vital records (1847–51), will. See TT 8–9, 11, 20, 22.

Repositories: LR; Guernsey Memorial Library, 3 Court St., Norwich, NY 13815. Society: Chenango County Historical Society, 45 Rexford St., Norwich, NY 13815.

10. CLINTON County, formed 1788 from Washington County, County Seat Plattsburgh (12901). Guide: NY Historical Resources Center, GUIDE TO HISTORICAL RESOURCES IN CLINTON COUNTY, The Center, Ithaca, NY, 1984. Censuses: 1790R, 1800R, 1810R, 1820RI, 1830R, 1840RP, 1850RAIM, 1860RAIM, 1870RAM, 1880RAIM, 1890C, 1892S, 1900R, 1905S, 1910R, 1915S, 1925S.

FHL governmental microfilms: court of common pleas (1789–1847), deed (1788–1966), federal census (1800–1910), guardian (1830–1969), lis pendens (1824–1900), marriage (1908–36), mortgage (1788–1855), probate (1790–1969), state census (1892–1925), vital records (1908–35), will (1807–1908). FHL non-governmental microfilms: Baptist, Catholic. Published and microfilmed works (NYSL, NYPL): atlas (1869/85), Baptist, Bible, biography (1896), cemetery, church, citizens (1825), circuit court (1796–1827), court of common pleas (1789–1819), court of oyer and terminer (1796–1839, 1847–61), DAR, federal census (1800–1910), Friends, gazetteer (1862), history (1880/85/96), Methodist, poor, Presbyterian, state census (1915/25), town, will. See TT 18, 22; NYGBR 113.

Repositories: LR; Plattsburgh Public Library, 15 Oak St., Plattsburgh, NY 12901; State University Library, Draper Ave., Plattsburgh, NY 12901. Societies: Clinton

County Historical Association, City Hall, Plattsburgh, NY
12901; Northern NY American-Canadian Genealogical Society, PO Box 1256, Plattsburgh, NY 12901.

11. <u>COLUMBIA</u> County, formed 1786 from Albany County,
County Seat Hudson (12534). <u>Guide</u>: M. S. Maynard, A
GUIDE TO LOCAL HISTORY AND GENEALOGICAL RESOURCES IN
COLUMBIA COUNTY, The Author, Brookville, NY, 1979.
<u>Censuses</u>: 1790R, 1800R, 1810R, 1820RI, 1830R, 1840RP,
1845S, 1850RAIM, 1855S, 1860RAIM, 1865S, 1870RAM, 1875S,
1880RAIM, 1890C, 1900R, 1905S, 1910R, 1915S, 1925S.
  <u>FHL governmental microfilms</u>: federal census (1790–
1910), state census (1855–75, 1905–25). <u>FHL non-governmental microfilms</u>: business, Congregational, Dutch Reformed, Evangelical Lutheran, German Reformed, Lutheran,
map, newspaper, Presbyterian, Reformed. <u>Published and
microfilmed works</u> (NYSL, NYPL): atlas (1873/88), Baptist,
Bible, biography (1894), cemetery, church, civil list
(1786–1886), Congregational, DAR, Dutch Reformed, Evangelical Lutheran, federal census (1790–1910), Friends,
genealogy, history (1851/78/94/1900), Lutheran, Methodist, newspaper, Presbyterian, Reformed, Revolutionary
War, state census (1845–75, 1905–25), town. See TT 10,
23; NYGBR 60, 81, 94: ESNY 3.
  <u>Repositories</u>: LR; Columbia County Historical Society
Library, 5 Albany Ave., Kinderhook, NY 12106; Hudson Area
Association Library, 400 State St., Hudson, NY 12534.
<u>Society</u>: Columbia County Historical Society, 5 Albany
Ave., Kinderhook, NY 12106.

12. <u>CORTLAND</u> County, formed 1808 from Onondaga County,
County Seat Cortland (13045). <u>Guide</u>: NY Historical
Resources Center, GUIDE TO HISTORICAL RESOURCES IN CORT-
LAND COUNTY, The Center, Ithaca, NY, 1981. <u>Censuses</u>:
1820RI, 1825S, 1830R, 1835S, 1840RP, 1845S, 1850RAIM,
1855S, 1860RAIM, 1865S, 1870RAM, 1875S, 1880RAIM, 1890C,
1892S, 1900R, 1905S, 1910R, 1915S, 1925S.
  <u>FHL governmental microfilms</u>: county court (1856–
1908), court (1830–1919), court of common pleas (1808–
80), court of oyer and terminer (1856–95), deed (1808–
1962), electors (1859–80), federal census (1820–1910),
general sessions court (1853–95), guardian (1832–1970),
justice of peace (1797–1816), lis pendens (1865–1908),
marriage (1908–35), military (Revolution), mortgage
(1808–77), naturalization (1816–1965), overseer (1856–
80), probate (1808–1970), school (1829–80), state census

(1825-1925), supreme court (1808-1910), tax (1839), town (1794-1895), vital records (various), will (1809-1908). FHL non-governmental microfilms: Baptist, business, Congregational, genealogy, history, Methodist, newspaper, Presbyterian, Seventh-Day Baptist. Published and microfilmed works (NYSL, NYPL): atlas (1876), Baptist, Bible, business, cemetery, Christian Church, church, Civil War, Congregational, DAR, early settlers, federal census (1820-1910), gazetteer (1869), genealogy, historical records (36 volumes), history (1859/85/1932/52), justice of peace, marriage, Methodist, military, naturalization, newspaper, overseer, pioneers, Presbyterian, residents (1800-10), Revolutionary War, school, state census (1825-45, 1915-25), supervisors, tax, town, Universalist, vital records (1847-9), voter, will. See TT 1, 4, 9, 11-12, 14, 16-18, 21.

Repositories: LR: Cortland County Historical Society Library, 25 Homer Ave., Cortland, NY 13045; Cortland Free Library, 32 Church St., Cortland, NY 13045. Society: Cortland County Historical Society, 25 Homer Ave., Cortland, NY 13045.

13. DELAWARE County, formed 1797 from Ulster and Otsego Counties, County Seat Delhi (13753). Guide: NY Historical Resources Center, GUIDE TO HISTORICAL RESOURCES IN DELAWARE COUNTY, The Center, Ithaca, NY, 1986. Censuses: 1800R, 1810R, 1820RI, 1830R, 1840RP, 1850RAIM, 1855S, 1860RAIM, 1865S, 1870RAM, 1875S, 1880RAIM, 1890C, 1892S, 1900R, 1905S, 1910R, 1915S, 1925S.

FHL governmental microfilms: circuit court (1810-97), court (1804-95), court of common pleas (1797-1860), deed (1792-1962), federal census (1800-1910), guardian (1797-1965), incorporation (1842-93), maps (1797-1969), military (1862-4), mortgage (1797-1913), probate (1797-1963), state census (1855-1925), supreme court (1847-1905), town (1793-1900), vital records (1847-8, 1908-35), will (1797-1963). FHL non-governmental microfilms: Dutch Reformed, Episcopal, newspaper, Presbyterian. Published and microfilmed works (NYSL, NYPL): administration (1797-1875), atlas (1869), Baptist, Bible, biography (1894), cemetery, church, Congregational, DAR, Dutch Reformed, Episcopal, federal census (1800-1910), history (1856/80/97/1949), Methodist, Presbyterian, Reformed, Revolutionary War, state census (1915-25), town, vital records (1847-9), will. See TT 3, 6-7, 10, 18; ESNY 5.

Repositories: LR; Cannon Free Library, 40 Elm St., Delhi, NY 13753; Delaware County Historical Association Library, RD 2, Delhi, NY 13753. Society: Delaware County Historical Association, RD 2, Delhi, NY 13753.

14. DUTCHESS County, formed 1683 as an original County, County Seat Poughkeepsie (12601). Many records in the journal THE DUTCHESS. Censuses: Pre-1790E, 1790R, 1800R, 1810R, 1820RI, 1830R, 1840RP, 1850RAIM, 1860RAIM, 1865S, 1870RAM, 1875S, 1880RAIM, 1890C, 1892S, 1900R, 1910R, 1915S, 1925S.

FHL governmental microfilms: circuit court (1851-70), city court (1840-1), Civil War (1861-5), county court (1847-1951), court (1721-1862), court of common pleas (1721-1889), court of oyer and terminer (1787-1895), deed (1718-1950), election (1799-1848), federal census (1790-1910), general sessions court (1721-1889), guardian (1800-1972), homestead (1851-1952), incorporation (1796-1973), indenture (1831), jury (various), justice court (1785-92), land (1697-1907), loan office (1771-1882), maps (1750-1917), marriage (1785-1801), military (1777-1919), mortgage (1754-1950), naturalization (1878-1906), overseer (1807-15, 1827-38), probate (1751-1934), property (1798-1860), road (1744-1813), state census (1865-92, 1915-25), supervisors (1771-94), surveys (1739-1913), tax (1717-79, 1803-90), town (1769-1850), treasurer (1821-33), will (1751-1905). FHL non-governmental microfilms: Baptist, business, Catholic, Congregational, Dutch Reformed, Episcopal, Friends, genealogy, German Reformed, Lutheran, Methodist, newspaper (1778-1871), Presbyterian, Reformed. Published and microfilmed works (NYSL, NYPL): atlas (1876), Baptist, Bible, biography (1897, 1909/12), business, cemetery, census (1702/14/20), Christian Church, church, city directory (1843-), Civil War, tax, colonial, DAR, death (1868-1918), deed (1789-1854), Dutch Reformed, Evangelical Lutheran, Episcopal, federal census (1790-1919), Friends, genealogy, German Church, history (1877/82/97/1909/12/31/56/75), justice of peace, land documents, Lutheran, marriage, Methodist, militia, naturalization, newspaper abstracts, Presbyterian, Reformed, Revolutionary War, school, state census (1915-25), supervisors, surname index, tax, town, will. See NYGBR 33, 37, 39, 65-69, 73, 78, 83-84, 101, 114.

Repositories: LR; Adriance Memorial Library, 93 Market St., Poughkeepsie, NY 12601. Societies: Dutchess

County Genealogical Society, PO Box 708, Poughkeepsie, NY 12602; Dutchess County Historical Society, PO Box 88, Poughkeepsie, NY 12602.

15. ERIE County, formed 1821 from Niagara County, County Seat Buffalo (14202). Guide: NY Historical Resources Center, GUIDE TO HISTORICAL RESOURCES IN ERIE COUNTY, The Center, Ithaca, NY, 1983. Censuses: 1830R, 1840RP, 1850RAIM, 1855S, 1860RAIM, 1865S, 1870RAM, 1875S, 1880-RAIM, 1890C, 1892S, 1900R, 1905S, 1910R, 1915S, 1925S.

FHL governmental microfilms: court (1808-1907), deed (1808-1912), federal census (1830-1910), guardian (1810-98), mortgage (1808-77), naturalization (1831-1906), probate (1800-1929), state census (1855-1925). FHL nongovernmental microfilms: Baptist, Congregational, Evangelical Lutheran, Friends, Presbyterian. Published and microfilmed works (NYSL, NYPL): atlas (1866/80/93), Baptist, biography (1906-8), Catholic, cemetery, church, city directory (1828-), Civil War, Congregational, DAR, Evangelical Lutheran, Episcopal, federal census (1830-1910), Friends, German Church, guide to manuscripts, history (1876/84/98/1906-8/19), land, Lutheran, military, militia, newspaper abstracts, Presbyterian, school, state census (1915-25), vital records. See TT 4, 11, 20.

Repositories: LR; Buffalo and Erie County Historical Society Library, 25 Nottingham Ct., Buffalo, NY 14216; Buffalo and Erie County Public Library, Lafayette Sq., Buffalo, NY 14203. Societies: Buffalo and Erie County Historical Society, 25 Nottingham Ct., Buffalo, NY 14216; Western NY Genealogical Society, PO Box 338, Hamburg, NY 14075.

16. ESSEX County, formed 1799 from Clinton County, County Seat Elizabethtown (12932). Guide: NY Historical Resources Center, GUIDE TO HISTORICAL RESOURCES IN ESSEX COUNTY, The Center, Ithaca, NY, 1986. Censuses: 1800R, 1810R, 1820RI, 1830R, 1840RP, 1850RAIM, 1855S, 1860RAIM, 1865S, 1870RAIM, 1875S, 1880RAIM, 1890C, 1892S, 1900R, 1905S, 1910R, 1915S, 1925S.

FHL governmental microfilms: court (1799-1879), deed (1799-1873), federal census (1800-1910), guardian (1847-1910), land (1820-94), lis pendens (1827-76), marriage (1908-22), mortgage (1799-1867), probate (1803-1938), state census (1855-1925), will (1803-1938). FHL nongovernmental microfilms: Catholic, Dutch Reformed, Episcopal, Methodist, Presbyterian. Published and microfilmed works (NYSL, NYPL): atlas (1876), Baptist, biography (1896), business, cemetery, church, Civil War, DAR, Episcopal, federal census (1800-1910), history (1869/85/96), justice of peace, Methodist, military, Revolutionary War, state census (1915-25), town, vital records (1847), will. See TT 12, 22.

Repositories: LR; Essex County Historical Society, Court St., Elizabethtown, NY 12932. Societies: Essex County Historical Society, Court St., Elizabethtown, NY 12932; Adirondack Genealogical-Historical Society, 100 Main St., Saranac Lake, NY 12983.

17. FRANKLIN County, formed 1808 from Clinton County, County Seat Malone (12953). Guide: NY Historical Resources Center, GUIDE TO HISTORICAL RESOURCES IN FRANKLIN COUNTY, The Center, Ithaca, NY, 1986. Censuses: 1810R, 1820RI, 1830R, 1840RP, 1850RAIM, 1860RAIM, 1870RAIM, 1875S, 1880RAIM, 1890C, 1900R, 1905S, 1910R, 1915S, 1925S.

FHL governmental microfilms: deed (1808-1965), federal census (1810-1910), guardian (1842-1913), lis pendens (1858-1903), marriage (1908-30), mortgage (1808-73), probate (1809-1927), state census (1875, 1905-25), vital records (1908-35), will (1908-1900). FHL nongovernmental microfilms: newspaper. Published and microfilmed works (NYSL, NYPL): atlas (1876), Bible, biography (1918), cemetery, church, citizens (1825), DAR, federal census (1810-1910), gazetteer (1862), history (1853/80/1918), marriage, military, Revolutionary War, state census (1915-25), will. See TT 8, 18, 20.

Repositories: LR; Wead Library, 64 Elm St., Malone, NY 12953. Societies: Franklin County Historical and Museum Society, 51 Milwaukee St., Malone, NY 12953: Adirondack Genealogical-Historical Society, 100 Main St., Saranac Lake, NY 12983.

18. FULTON County, formed 1838 from Montgomery County, County Seat Johnstown (12095). Guide: NY Historical Resources Center, GUIDE TO HISTORICAL RESOURCES IN FULTON COUNTY, The Center, Ithaca, NY, 1984. Censuses: 1840RP, 1845S, 1850RAIM, 1855S, 1860 RAIM, 1865S, 1870RAIM, 1875S, 1880RAIM, 1890C, 1900R, 1905S, 1910R, 1915S, 1925S.

FHL governmental microfilms: deed (1772-1910), federal census (1840-1910), guardian (1838-1907), marriage (1848-79, 1908-19), probate (1838-1967), state census (1845–75, 1905–25), vital records (some 1887–1907, 1908–19), will (1789–1967). FHL non-governmental microfilms: Baptist, Dutch Reformed, Episcopal, Presbyterian. Published and microfilmed works (NYSL, NYPL): atlas (1868), Baptist, Bible, cemetery, church, Congregational, DAR, Dutch Reformed, Episcopal, federal census (1840–1910), gazetteer (1870), history (1878/92), Lutheran, Methodist, newspaper, Presbyterian, Revolutionary War, state census (1845–75), 1905–25), town, vital records (1847–9), will. See TT 3–4, 12, 15.

Repositories: LR; Gloversville Free Library, 58 E. Fulton St., Gloversville, NY 12078; Johnstown Historical Society Library, 17 N. William St., Johnstown, NY 12095. Society: Fulton County Historical Society, 168 E. State St., Gloversville, NY 12078.

19. GENESEE County, formed 1802 from Ontario County, County Seat Batavia (14020). Guide: NY Historical Resources Center, GUIDE TO HISTORICAL RESOURCES IN GENESEE COUNTY, The Center, Ithaca, NY, 1982. Censuses: 1810R, 1820RI, 1830R, 1840RP, 1850RAIM, 1860RAIM, 1870RAIM, 1875S, 1880RAIM, 1890C, 1892S, 1900R, 1905S, 1910R, 1915S, 1925S.

FHL governmental microfilms: Civil War (1861–5), deed (1792–1901), federal census (1810–1910), guardian (1810–1906), justice of peace (1835–43, 1850–85), lis pendens (1865–1904), marriage (1908–36), mortgage (1804–1912), probate (1805–1920), school (1837–44), state census (1875–1925), town, vital records (1908–26), will (1805–1920). FHL non-governmental microfilms: Baptist, business, Catholic, newspaper, Presbyterian. Published and microfilmed works (NYSL, NYPL): atlas (1866/76), Baptist, Bible, biography (1890), cemetery, church, DAR, Episcopal, federal census (1810–1910), gazetteer (1869/-90), history (1890/1952), Lutheran, marriage, Methodist, newspaper, Presbyterian, Revolutionary War, state census (1912–25), Universalist, will. See TT 4, 19.

Repositories: LR; Genesee County Historical Department Library, 131 W. Main St., Batavia, NY 14020; Richmond Memorial Library, 19 Ross St., Batavia, NY 14020. Society: Holland Purchase Historical Society, 131 W. Main St., Batavia, NY 14020.

20. GREENE County, formed 1800 from Albany and Ulster Counties, County Seat Catskill (12414). Censuses: 1800R, 1810R, 1820RI, 1830R, 1840RP, 1850RAIM, 1855S, 1860RAIM,

1865S, 1870RAIM, 1875S, 1880RAIM, 1890C, 1892S, 1900R, 1905S, 1910R, 1915S, 1925S.

FHL governmental microfilms: deed (1800-1922), federal census (1800-1910), guardian (1816-1912), justice of peace (1808-17), marriage (1908-23), probate (1800-1930), state census (1855-1925), will (1800-1902). FHL non-governmental microfilms: Dutch Reformed, Evangelical Lutheran, Episcopal, Lutheran, newspaper, Presbyterian. Published and microfilmed works (NYSL, NYPL): atlas (1867), Baptist, Bible, biography (1884/99), cemetery, church, DAR, Dutch Reformed, Evangelical Lutheran, Episcopal, federal census (1800-1910), Friends, history (1884/1927/63), justice of peace, Lutheran, marriage, Methodist, newspaper, Presbyterian, Reformed, Revolutionary War, state census (1855-1925), supervisors, will. See NYGBR 73, 86, 88.

Repositories: LR; Greene County Historical Society, Vedder Memorial Library, Coxsackie, NY 12051. Society: Greene County Historical Society, Coxsackie, NY 12051.

21. HAMILTON County, formed 1816 from Montgomery County, County Seat Lake Pleasant (12108). Guide: NY Historical Resources Center, GUIDE TO HISTORICAL RESOURCES IN HAMILTON COUNTY, The Center, Ithaca, NY, 1984. Censuses: 1820RI, 1830R, 1840RP, 1850RAIM, 1860RAIM, 1870RAIM, 1880RAIM, 1890C, 1892S, 1900R, 1905S, 1910R, 1915S, 1925S.

FHL governmental microfilms: deed (1797-1959), federal censuses (1820-1910), guardian (1878-1920), lis pendens (1880-1902), marriage (1908-36), mortgage (1797-1953), probate (1861-1934), state census (1892-1925), will (1861-1934). Published and microfilmed works (NYSL, NYPL): Bible, cemetery, church, DAR, federal census (1820-1910), history (1965), state census (1892-1925), vital records (1847-9), will. See TT 23.

Repositories: LR; county and town historians; Indian Lake Public Library, Main St., Indian Lake, NY 12842.

22. HERKIMER County, formed 1791 from Montgomery County, County Seat Herkimer (13350). First court house burned with loss of some 1798-1804 records. Many of the 1791-8 records are in Oneida County. Guide: NY Historical Resources Center, GUIDE TO HISTORICAL RESOURCES IN HERKIMER COUNTY, The Center, Ithaca, NY, 1986. Censuses: 1800R, 1810R, 1820RI, 1825S, 1830R, 1840RP, 1845S, 1850RAIM, 1855S, 1860RAIM, 1865S, 1870RAIM, 1875S,

1880RAIM, 1890C, 1892S, 1900R, 1905S, 1910R, 1915S, 1925S.

FHL governmental microfilms: county court (1847–1920), court (1882–1901), court of oyer and terminer (1804–28), deed (1804–1952), federal census (1800–1910), guardian (1800–1926), lis pendens (1864–1902), marriage (1908–27), mortgage (1804–56), naturalization (1818–1955), probate (1792–1970), Revolutionary veterans, state census (1825–1925), supreme court (1847–59, 1896–1922), tax (1817), town, vital records (1847–9), 1908–35), will (1792–1912). FHL non-governmental microfilms: Dutch Reformed, Episcopal, genealogy, Reformed. Published and microfilmed works (NYSL, NYPL): atlas (1868), Baptist, bible, biography (1856/93), business, cemetery, church, Civil War, Congregational, DAR, Dutch Reformed, Episcopal, federal census (1800–1910), gazetteer (1869), history (1856/79/93), justice court, justice of peace, Lutheran, marriage, Methodist, military, newspaper, Presbyterian, Reformed, Revolutionary War, school, state census (1915–25), tax, town, will. See TT 4, 18.

Repositories: LR; Basloe Library of Herkimer, 245 N. Maine St., Herkimer, NY 13350; Herkimer County Historical Society Library, 400 N. Main St., Herkimer, NY 13350. Society: Herkimer County Historical Society, 400 N. Main St., Herkimer, NY 13350.

23. JEFFERSON County, formed 1805 from Oneida County, County Seat Watertown (13601). Guide: NY Historical Resources Center, GUIDE TO HISTORICAL RESOURCES IN JEFFERSON COUNTY, The Center, Ithaca, NY, 1985. Censuses: 1810R, 1820RI, 1825S, 1830R, 1835S, 1840RP, 1845S, 1850RAIM, 1855S, 1860RAIM, 1865S, 1870RAIM, 1875S, 1880RAIM, 1890C, 1892S, 1900R, 1905S, 1910R, 1915S, 1925S.

FHL governmental microfilms: county court (1817–35, 1859–1909), court (1857–1903), court of common pleas (1817–34), court of oyer and terminer (1829–94), death (1846–1903 incomplete), deed (1795–1966), federal census (1810–1910), general sessions court (1855–94), guardian (1831–1900), lis pendens (1864–1907), marriage (1846–1903 incomplete), 1908–35), military, mortgage (1805–88), naturalization (1805–1945), probate (1805–1945), state census (1825–75, 1905–25), supreme court (1847–1905), town, vital records (1908–35), will (1830–1900). FHL non-governmental microfilms: Baptist, mortuary (1881–1933), newspaper, Presbyterian, Reformed. Published and microfilmed works (NYSL, NYPL): atlas (1864/88), Baptist, Bible, biography (1878/94/98/1905), cemetery, church, DAR, federal census (1810-1910), gazetteer (1866/90), genealogy, history (1854/78/90/94/98/1905), Methodist, newspaper, Presbyterian, Reformed, Revolutionary War, state census (1915-25), supervisors, tax, town, Universalist, vital records (1847-9), will. See TT 1, 5; ESNY 3.

Repositories: LR; Flower Memorial Library, 229 Washington St., Watertown, NY 13601; Jefferson County Historical Society Library, 228 Washington St., Watertown, NY 13601. Societies: Jefferson County Historical Society, 228 Washington St., Watertown, NY 13601; Flower Memorial Library, Genealogical Committee, Watertown, NY 13601.

24. LEWIS County, formed 1805 from Oneida County, County Seat Lowville (13367). Guide: NY Historical Resources Center, GUIDE TO HISTORICAL RESOURCES IN LEWIS COUNTY, The Center, Ithaca, NY, 1986. Censuses: 1810R, 1820RI, 1825S, 1830R, 1835S, 1840RP, 1850RAIM, 1855S, 1860RAIM, 1865S, 1870RAIM, 1875S, 1880RAIM, 1890C, 1892S, 1900R, 1905S, 1910R, 1915S, 1925S.

FHL governmental microfilms: county court (1886-1901), court (1805-1901), deed (1788-1873), federal census (1810-1910), guardian (1806-55), lis pendens (1805-73), marriage (1908-34), mortgage (1794-1870), naturalization (1808-1955), probate (1805-1940), state census (1825-35, 1855-1925), supreme court (1847-65), vital records (1849-1935), will (1805-1940). FHL nongovernmental microfilms: genealogy, newspaper (1821-59), Presbyterian. Published and microfilmed works (NYSL, NYPL): atlas (1875), Bible, biography (1883), cemetery, church, DAR, federal census (1810-1910), Friends, gazetteer (1872), history (1860/83/1970), Lutheran, military, newspaper, Revolutionary War, state census (1915-25), supervisors, Universalist, vital records (1847-9), will. See TT 3, 8-9, 13, 15.

Repositories: LR; Lowville Free Library, 5387 Dayan St., Lowville, NY 13367. Society: Lewis County Historical Society, High St., Lyons Falls, NY 13368.

25. LIVINGSTON County, formed 1821 from Genesee and Ontario Counties, County Seat Geneseo (14454). Guide: NY Historical Resources Center, GUIDE TO HISTORICAL RESOURCES IN LIVINGSTON COUNTY, The Center, Ithaca, NY,

1981.   Censuses: 1830R,   1840RP, 1850RAIM, 1855S, 1860
RAIM, 1865S, 1870RAIM, 1875S, 1880RAIM, 1890C, 1900R,
1910R, 1915S, 1925S.

FHL governmental microfilms: court   of common pleas
(1820-1910), court of oyer and terminer (1840-71), deed
(1820-1921), federal census (1830-1910), guardian (1823-
70, 1876-1915), marriage (1848-80 incomplete, 1908-35),
mortgage (1821-1906), naturalization (1853-1936), probate
(1821-1969), state census (1855-75, 1915-25), will (1821-
1905).   FHL non-governmental microfilms: Presbyterian.
Published and microfilmed works (NYSL, NYPL): atlas
(1872), Bible, biography (1876/81/95), cemetery, cemetery
record index, church, DAR, Evangelical Lutheran, federal
census (1830-1910), gazetteer (1868), genealogy, history
(1876/81/95/1905),   Lutheran,   military,   Presbyterian,
Revolutionary War, state census (1915-25), tax (1824),
town, will. See TT 4, 9, 13, 22-23.

Repositories: LR; Wadsworth Library, 24 Center St.,
Geneseo, NY 14454; State University of NY Library, Geneseo, NY, 14454; Livingston County Historical Collection
30 Center St., Geneseo, NY 14454. Societies: Livingston
County Historical Society, 30 Center St., Geneseo, NY
14454; Livingston County Genealogical Society, Nunda, NY
14517.

26. MADISON County, formed 1806 from Chenango County,
County Seat Wampsville (13163). Guide: NY Historical
Resources Center, GUIDE TO HISTORICAL RESOURCES IN MADI-
SON COUNTY, The Center, Ithaca, NY, 1982. Censuses:
1810R, 1820RI, 1830R, 1840RP, 1850RAIM, 1855S, 1860RAIM,
1865S, 1870RAIM, 1875S, 1880RAIM, 1890C, 1892S, 1900R,
1905S, 1910R, 1915S, 1925S.

FHL governmental microfilms: court of oyer and
terminer (1808-35, 1841-54, 1874-93), deed (1806-1900),
federal census (1810-1910), guardian (1806-1927), marriage (1908-20), military (1815), naturalization (1835-
1924), overseer, probate (1806-1927), Revolutionary
veterans, state census (1855-1925), tax (1805/12), vital
records (1926-35), will (1806-1900). FHL non-governmental microfilms: Baptist, Congregational, Dutch Reformed, genealogy, Masonic (1817-8), Methodist, newspaper
(1801-1906), pioneer (1790-1840), Presbyterian, veterans.
Published and microfilmed works (NYSL, NYPL): atlas
(1875), Baptist, Bible, biography (1880/94), business,
cemetery, church, Congregational, DAR, Episcopal, federal
census (1810-1910), genealogy, history (1872/80/94/99/-

1943), marriage, Methodist, newspaper, pioneers, poor, Presbyterian, state census (1855-1925), supervisors, town, vital records (1847-9), will. See TT 2, 4, 6, 8, 10, 14, 17-18, 22-23; ESNY 8.

Repositories: LR; Oneida Library, 220 Broad St., Oneida, NY 13421; Madison County Historical Society Library, 435 Main St., Oneida, NY 13421. Society: Madison County Historical Society, 435 Main St., Oneida, NY 13421.

27. MONROE County, formed 1821 from Genesee and Ontario Counties, County Seat Rochester (14614). Guides: NY Historical Resources Center, GUIDE TO HISTORICAL RESOURCES IN MONROE COUNTY, The Center, Ithaca, NY, 1984; R. T. Halsey, GENEALOGICAL GUIDE TO MONROE COUNTY, Rochester Genealogical Society, Rochester, NY 1985; D. K. Clark, THE IDEA GUIDE FOR MONROE COUNTY, Ancestor Publishers, Arvada, CO, 1985; D. K. Clark, MONROE COUNTY GENEALOGICAL DIRECTORY OF RECORDS, Ancestor Publishers, Arvada, CO, 1987; D. K. Clark, MONROE COUNTY FIELD TRIP GUIDE, Ancestor Publishers, Arvada, CO, 1987. Censuses: 1830R, 1840RP, 1850RAIM, 1855S, 1860RAIM, 1865S, 1870 RAIM, 1875S, 1880RAIM, 1890C, 1892S, 1900R, 1905S, 1910R, 1915S, 1925S.

FHL governmental microfilms: court (1821-1923), deed (1821-1975), federal census (1830-1910), guardian (1826-1901), marriage (1908-35), mortgage (1821-71), naturalization (1821-1929), probate (1824-1970), state census (1855-1925), will (1829-1901). FHL non-governmental microfilms: business, Congregational, newspaper, Presbyterian. Published and microfilmed works (NYSL, NYPL): atlas (1872), Baptist, Bible, biography (1877/95/1902/8), cemetery, church, city directory (1827-), Congregational, DAR, ear marks, estate, Episcopal, federal census (1830-1910), Friends, gazetteer (1869), genealogy, history (1860/77/95/1902/8), marriage, Methodist, newspaper, pioneers, Presbyterian, Revolutionary War, state census (1855, 1915-25), tax, town, treasurer (1821-41), will index (1821-74). See TT 3, 13, 22-23; ESNY 6.

Repositories: LR; Office of the City Historian, 115 South Ave., Rochester, NY 14604; Rochester Historical Society Library, 485 East Ave., Rochester, NY 14607; Rochester Public Library, 115 South Ave., Rochester, NY 14604. Societies: American Baptist Historical Society, 1106 S. Goodman St., Rochester, NY 14620; Rochester Historical Society, 485 East Ave., Rochester, NY 14607;

Kodak Genealogical Club, Eastman Kodak Company, Rochester, NY 14650; Rochester Genealogical Society, PO Box 92553, Rochester, NY 14692.

28. MONTGOMERY County, formed 1772 from Albany County, County Seat Fonda (12068), known as Tryon County 1772-84. Guides: NY Historical Resources Center, GUIDE TO HISTORICAL RESOURCES IN MONTGOMERY COUNTY, The Center, Ithaca, NY, 1983; Montgomery County Department of History and Archives, CATALOG OF GENEALOGICAL MATERIAL IN THE ARCHIVES, The Department, Fonda, NY, 1978; many records in THE MOHAWK. Censuses: Pre-1790E, 1790R, 1800R, 1810R, 1820RI, 1830R, 1840RP, 1850RAIM, 1855S, 1860RAIM, 1865S, 1870RAIM, 1875S, 1880RAIM, 1890C, 1892S, 1900R, 1905S, 1910R, 1915S, 1925S.
   FHL governmental microfilms: court of common pleas (1772-1806), deed (1777-1935), federal census (1790-1910), general sessions court (1772-1806), guardian (1825-1903), marriage (1803-35 incomplete), probate (1787-1906), school (1796), state census (1855-1925), tax (1795-6 incomplete). FHL non-governmental microfilms: Baptist, Christian Church, Dutch Reformed, Evangelical Lutheran, Lutheran, Methodist, newspaper, Presbyterian, Reformed. Published and microfilmed works (NYSL, NYPL): administration, atlas (1868), Baptist, Bible, cemetery, Christian Church, church, court of common pleas (1789-1850), DAR, deed (1792-1851), Dutch Reformed, Evangelical Lutheran, Episcopal, federal census (1790-1910), Friends, gazetteer (1870), history (1831/78/92), Lutheran, marriage, Methodist, military, militia, newspaper, Presbyterian, Reformed, Revolutionary War, school, state census (1865-1925), supervisors, town, vital records (1847-9), will (1787-1831). See TT 2, 4, 12; NYGBR 49-50, 56, 107; National Genealogical Society Quarterly 53.
   Repositories: LR; Montgomery County Department of History and Archives, Old Court House, Fonda, NY 12068. Societies: Heritage and Genealogical Society of Montgomery County, Old Court House, Fonda, NY 12068; Montgomery County Historical Society, Old Fort Johnson, Route 5, Fort Johnson, NY 12070; Palatine Heritage Society, 78 W. Main St., St. Johnsville, NY 13452.

29. NASSAU County, formed 1899 from Queens County, County Seat Mineola (11501). Censuses: 1900R, 1910R, 1915S, 1925S.

FHL governmental microfilms: Civil War (1861-5), federal census (1900-10), state census (1915-25). FHL non-governmental microfilms: Baptist, business, Dutch Reformed, Episcopal, Friends, genealogy, Methodist, Presbyterian. Published and microfilmed works (NYSL, NYPL): atlas (1906), Bible, biography, cemetery, church, DAR, Dutch Reformed, Episcopal, federal census (1900-10), Friends, history (1949), marriage, Methodist, Presbyterian, state census (1915-25), town, vital records. See NYGBR 16.

Repositories: LR; the numerous libraries of the Nassau Library System, 900 Jerusalem Ave., Uniondale, NY 11553. Society: Nassau County Historical Society, PO Box 207, Garden City, NY 11530; Nassau Genealogical Workshop, 245 Main St., Port Washington, NY 11050.

30. NIAGARA County, formed 1808 from Genesee County, County Seat Lockport (14094). Guide: NY Historical Resources Center, GUIDE TO HISTORICAL RESOURCES IN NIAGARA COUNTY, The Center, Ithaca, NY, 1982. Censuses: 1810R, 1820RI, 1830R, 1840RP, 1850RAIM, 1860RAIM, 1870 RAIM, 1880RAIM, 1890C, 1892S, 1900R, 1905S, 1910R, 1915S, 1925S.

FHL governmental microfilms: deed (1800-1962), federal census (1810-1910), guardian (1822-1972), land (1800-1972), marriage (1847-8, 1908-34), mortgage (1800-1917), naturalization (1830-1906), probate (1822-1932), state census (1892-1925), vital records (1908-35), will (1822-1932). FHL non-governmental microfilms: genealogy, town history. Published and microfilmed works (NYSL, NYPL): atlas (1875), Baptist, Bible, biography (1892/7), cemetery, church, Civil War, DAR, federal census (1810-1910), Friends, gazetteer (1869), history (1878/92/97/1902/21), Methodist, military, probate (1813-56), Presbyterian, Revolutionary War, state census (1892-1925), supervisors, tax, will. See TT 3, 5, 7, 19-20.

Repositories: LR; Niagara County Historical Society Library, 215 Niagara St., Lockport, NY 14094; Niagara Falls Public Library, 1425 Main St., Niagara Falls, NY 14305; Sanborn Free Library, West St., Sanborn, NY 14132. Societies: Niagara County Historical Society, 215 Niagara St., Lockport, NY 14094; Niagara County Genealogical Society, 2650 Hess Rd., Appleton, NY 14008.

31. ONEIDA County, formed 1798 from Herkimer County, County Seat Utica (13501). Guides: NY Historical Re-

sources Center, GUIDE TO HISTORICAL RESOURCES IN ONEIDA
COUNTY, The Center, Ithaca, NY, 1983; Oneida Historical
Society, CATALOG OF THE MANUSCRIPT HOLDINGS AT THE ONEIDA
HISTORICAL SOCIETY, The Society, Utica, NY, 1959. Censuses: 1800R, 1810R, 1820RI, 1830R, 1840RP, 1850RAIM,
1860RAIM, 1870RAIM, 1880RAIM, 1890C, 1900R, 1905S, 1910R,
1915S, 1925S.

FHL governmental microfilms: deed (1790-1912),
federal census (1800-1910), guardian (1830-1933), marriage (1908-25), naturalization (1805-1964), probate
(1798-1909), state census (1915-25), vital records (1908-
35), will (1798-1909). FHL non-governmental microfilms:
Congregational, Dutch Reformed, Episcopal, newspaper,
Presbyterian, Reformed. Published and microfilmed works
(NYSL, NYPL): atlas (1874), Baptist, Bible, biography
(1878/96/1900/12), cemetery, church, city directory (Rome
1857-, Utica 1817, 1828-), Civil War, Congregational,
DAR, Episcopal, federal census (1800-1910), Friends,
gazetteer (1869), genealogy, history (1851/78/96/1909/
12/77), marriage, Methodist, newspaper, Presbyterian,
Reformed, Revolutionary War, state census (1915-25),
supervisors, tax, town, Universalist, vital records
(1847-9), will. See TT 4, 11, 14-15, 18-19, 21-22; NYGBR
67.

Repositories: LR; Oneida Historical Society Library,
318 Genesee St., Utica, NY 13502; Utica Public Library,
303 Genesee St., Utica, NY 13501; Rome Historical Society
Library, 112 Spring St., Rome, NY 13440; Jervis Public
Library, 613 N. Washington St., Rome, NY 13440. Socie-
ties: Oneida Historical Society, 318 Genesee St., Utica,
NY 13502; Rome Historical Society, 112 Spring St., Rome,
NY 13440; Oneida County Genealogical Club, 318 Genesee
St., Utica, NY 13502.

32. ONONDAGA County, formed 1794 from Herkimer County,
County Seat Syracuse (13202). Guide: NY Historical
Resources Center, GUIDE TO HISTORICAL RESOURCES IN ONON-
DAGA COUNTY, The Center, Ithaca, NY, 1986. Censuses:
1800R, 1810R, 1820RI, 1830R, 1840RP, 1850RAIM, 1855S,
1860RAIM, 1865S, 1870RAIM, 1875S, 1880RAIM, 1890C, 1892S,
1900R, 1905S, 1910R, 1915S, 1925S.

FHL governmental microfilms: bounty land (1798-
1802), court of common pleas (1807-53), court of oyer and
terminer (1846-89), deed (1784-1870), federal census
(1800-1910), guardian (1821-52), homestead (1851-1971),
justice of peace (1809-11), lis pendens (1838-91), mar-

riage (1908-34), military (1812 incomplete), mortgage (1794-1870), naturalization (1799-1927), patent (1823-82), petition (1794), probate (1796-1923), Revolutionary veterans, state census (1855-1925), tax (1827 incomplete), will (1796-1867. FHL non-governmental microfilms: Baptist, business, Congregational, Episcopal, genealogy, newspaper, Presbyterian. Published and microfilmed works (NYSL, NYPL): atlas (1874), Baptist, Bible, cemetery, Christian Church, church, city directory (1844, 1851-), Civil War, Congregational, DAR, deed, Episcopal, federal census (1800-1910), gazetteer (1868), genealogy, guardian (1815-24), history (1849/78/96/1904/8), marriage, Methodist, military, naturalization (1802-59), newspaper, Presbyterian, Revolutionary War, school, state census (1915-25), town, will (1796-1829). See TT 1, 4-5, 7, 10-12, 21; NYGBR 53.

Repositories: LR; Onondaga County Public Library, 327 Montgomery St., Syracuse, NY 13202; Onondaga Historical Association Library, 311 Montgomery St., Syracuse, NY 13202. Societies: Onondaga Historical Association, 311 Montgomery St., Syracuse, NY 13202; Central NY Genealogical Society, PO Box 104, Colvin Station, Syracuse, NY 13205.

33. ONTARIO County, formed 1789 from Montgomery County, County Seat Canandaigua (14424). Guide: NY Historical Resources Center, GUIDE TO HISTORICAL RESOURCES IN ONTARIO COUNTY, The Center, Ithaca, NY, 1982. Censuses: 1790R, 1800R, 1810R, 1820RI, 1830R, 1840RP, 1850RAIM, 1855S, 1860RAIM, 1865S, 1870RAIM, 1875S, 1880RAIM, 1890C, 1892S, 1900R, 1905S, 1910R, 1915S, 1925S.

FHL governmental microfilms: Civil War (1862), county court (1794-1916), court (1790-1915), court of common pleas (1794-1847), court of oyer and terminer (1793-1881), deed (1789-1958), federal census (1790-1910), general sessions court (1794-1850), guardian (1821-52), lis pendens (1864-1902), marriage (1908-35), mortgage (1789-1899), naturalization (1803-1956), oaths of office (1830-56), probate (1789-1965), road (1798-1865), school (1817), state census (1855-92, 1915-25), tax (1813-22), vital records (1908-35), will (1789-1965). FHL non-governmental microfilms: Congregational, Dutch Reformed, genealogy, Methodist, newspaper, Presbyterian. Published and microfilmed works (NYSL, NYPL): atlas (1874), Baptist, Bible, biography (1876/93/1911), business, business directory (1867-8), cemetery, church, city directory (1857-), Congregational, DAR, federal census (1790-1910), Friends, gazetteer (1867), history (1876/93/1911), military (1790-1806), Presbyterian, Revolutionary War, school, state census (1915-25), supervisors, tax, town, vital records (1847-8), will. See TT 3, 10-11, 19, 22; ESNY 1.

Repositories: LR; Ontario County Historical Society Library, 55 N. Main St., Canandaigua, NY 14424; Wood Library, 134 N. Main St., Canandaigua, NY 14424; Geneva Free Library, 244 Main St., Geneva, NY 14456. Societies: Ontario County Historical Society, 55 N. Main St., Canandaigua, NY 14424; Canandaigua Genealogical Society, Clifton Springs, NY 14432.

34. ORANGE County, formed 1683 as an original County, County Seat Goshen (10924). Guide: D. K. Clark, ORANGE COUNTY GENEALOGICAL FIELD TRIP GUIDE, Ancestor Publishers, Arvada, CO, 1987. Censuses: Pre-1790E, 1790R, 1800R, 1810R, 1820RI, 1825S, 1830R, 1835S, 1840RP, 1845S, 1850RAIM, 1855S, 1860RAIM, 1865S, 1870RAIM, 1875S, 1880RAIM, 1890C, 1900R, 1910R, 1915S, 1925S.

FHL governmental microfilms: court of common pleas (1727-1856), deed (1703-1965), federal census (1790-1910), guardian (1823-1906), lis pendens (1824-1900, marriage (1908-32), military (1780/2), mortgage (1703-1869), probate (1787-1941), state census (1825-75, 1915-25), tax (1798, 1803-4), vital records (1908-33), will (1830-1901). FHL non-governmental microfilms: Baptist, Congregational, Dutch Reformed, genealogy, German Church, history, Methodist, newspaper, Presbyterian, Reformed. Published and microfilmed works (NYSL, NYPL): atlas (1875), Baptist, Bible, biography (1875/81/95/1908), cemetery, census (1702/14/20), church, city directory (1856-), DAR, deed, directory (1870), Dutch Reformed, federal census (1790-1810), genealogy (1875), German church, history (1846/67/75/81/95/1908/28/68), inhabitants (1767), land, marriage, Methodist, mortuary (1852-75), newspaper, pioneers, Presbyterian, Revolutionary War, school, state census (1915-25), tax, town, will. See NYGBR 42, 62-64; ESNY 2-3, 8.

Repositories: LR; Goshen Public Library and Historical Society, 203 Main St., Goshen, NY 10924; Orange County Museum, 240 Main St., Goshen, NY 10924. Societies: Goshen Historical Society, 203 Main St., Goshen, NY 10924; Orange County Genealogical Society, 101 Main St., Goshen, NY 10924.

35. ORLEANS County, formed 1824 from Genesee County, County Seat Albion (14411). Guide: NY Historical Resources Center, GUIDE TO HISTORICAL RESOURCES IN ORLEANS COUNTY, The Center, Ithaca, NY, 1982. Censuses: 1830R, 1840RP, 1850RAIM, 1855S, 1860RAIM, 1865S, 1870RAIM, 1875S, 1880RAIM, 1890C, 1892S, 1900R, 1905S, 1910R, 1915S, 1925S.

FHL governmental microfilms: deed (1810-1950), federal census (1830-1910), guardian (1830-1911), land (1825-1902), lis pendens (1864-1912), marriage (1908-35), mortgage (1825-52), naturalization (1830-1955), probate (1825-1926), state census (1855-1925), town, vital records (1847-9), will (1823-1926). FHL non-governmental microfilms: Baptist, Catholic, marriage, Presbyterian. Published and microfilmed works (NYSL, NYPL): atlas (1875), Baptist, Bible, biography (1871/79/94), birth, business, cemetery, church, Civil War, DAR, early settlers, federal census (1830-1910), genealogy (1894), history (1871/79/94/1939), justice of peace, marriage, Methodist, newspaper, pioneers, Presbyterian, school (1839-53, 1877-92), state census (1855-1925), supervisors, town, will (1824-97). See TT 3, 8, 10, 14.

Repositories: LR; Lee-Whedon Memorial Library, 620 West Ave., Medina, NY 14103; Swan Library, 4 N. Main St., Albion, NY 14411. Society: Orleans County Historical Association, 13979 Allen Rd., Albion, NY 14411.

36. OSWEGO County, formed 1816 from Oneida and Onondaga Counties, County Seat Oswego (13126). Guide: NY Historical Resources Center, GUIDE TO HISTORICAL RESOURCES IN OSWEGO COUNTY, The Center, Ithaca, NY, 1984. Censuses: 1820RI, 1830R, 1840RP, 1850RAIM, 1855S, 1860RAIM, 1865S, 1870RAIM, 1875S, 1880RAIM, 1890C, 1892S, 1900R, 1905S, 1910R, 1915S, 1925S.

FHL governmental microfilms: court (1816-66), deed (1791-1948), federal census (1820-1910), guardian (1831-1916), lis pendens (1864-1908), marriage (1908-35), mortgage (1816-75), naturalization (1868-1956), probate (1816-1971), state census (1855-1925), vital records (1908-35), will (1816-1971). FHL non-governmental microfilms: Congregational, genealogy, history, Methodist, Presbyterian. Published and microfilmed works (NYSL, NYPL): atlas (1867), Bible, biography (1877/95), cemetery, church, city directory (1852-), Congregational, DAR, deed, early settlers, Episcopal, federal census

(1820-1910), gazetteer (1866), history (1877/95), Methodist, military, newspaper, Presbyterian, Revolutionary War, state census (1915-25), supervisors, town, vital records (1847-9), will. See TT 1-2, 3, 6, 11, 16, 22.

Repositories: LR; Oswego City Library, 120 E. Second St., Oswego, NY 13126. Society: Oswego County Historical Society, 135 E. Third St., Oswego, NY 13126.

37. OTSEGO County, formed 1791 from Montgomery County, County Seat Cooperstown (13326). Guide: NY Historical Resources Center, GUIDE TO HISTORICAL RESOURCES IN OTSEGO COUNTY, The Center, Ithaca, NY, 1982. Censuses: 1800R, 1810R, 1820RI, 1825S, 1830R, 1840RP, 1850RAIM, 1855S, 1860RAIM, 1865S, 1870RAIM, 1875S, 1880RAIM, 1890C, 1892S, 1900R, 1905S, 1910R, 1915S, 1925S.

FHL governmental microfilms: court of oyer and terminer (1792-1893), deed (1791-1949), federal census (1800-1910), guardian (1803-1918), lis pendens (1865-1901), marriage (1847-1908-26), military (1866-1919), mortgage (1791-1899), naturalization (1806-1956), probate (1791-1934), Revolutionary veterans, state census (1825, 1855-1925), vital records (1908-35), will (1792-1923). FHL non-governmental microfilms: Baptist, business, Congregational, Dutch Reformed, Episcopal, Friends, genealogy, history, newspaper, Presbyterian. Published and microfilmed works (NYSL, NYPL): atlas (1868), Baptist, Bible, biography (1893), business, cemetery, church, DAR, early settlers, Evangelical Lutheran, Episcopal, federal census (1800-1910), Friends, gazetteer (1872), genealogy, guardian (1803-30), history (1852/78/93/1902/21), justice of peace, land patents, marriage, Methodist, newspaper, Presbyterian, Revolutionary War, state census (1892, 1915-25), town, vital records, voter, will. See TT 7, 11, 22; NYGBR 61; ESNY 5.

Repositories: LR; NY State Historical Association, Lake Rd., Cooperstown, NY 13326; State University of NY Library, Oneonta, NY 13820. Society: NY State Historical Association, Lake Rd., Cooperstown, NY 13326.

38. PUTNAM County, formed 1812 from Dutchess County, County Seat Carmel (10512). Censuses: 1820RI, 1830R, 1840RP, 1850RAIM, 1860RAIM, 1870RAIM, 1880RAIM, 1890C, 1900R, 1910R, 1915S, 1925S.

FHL governmental microfilms: deed (1812-1963), federal census (1820-1910), guardian (1812-1936), lis pendens (1824-94), marriage (1908-35), mortgage (1812-

1970), state census (1915-25), will (1816-1901). FHL
non-governmental microfilms: newspaper. Published and
microfilmed works (NYSL, NYPL): atlas (1867), Baptist,
Bible, biography (1886), business, cemetery, church,
Civil War, DAR, early settlers, Evangelical Lutheran,
federal census (1820-1910), genealogy, history (1849/86/-
1912), Methodist, newspaper, Presbyterian, Revolutionary
War, state census (1915-25), tax, town. See ESNY 8.

Repositories: LR; Reed Memorial Library, 2 Brewster
Ave., Carmel, NY 10512; Putnam County Historical Society
Library, 63 Chestnut St., Cold Spring, NY 10516. Soci-
ety: Putnam County Historical Society, 63 Chestnut St.,
Cold Spring, NY 10516.

39. RENSSELAER County, formed 1791 from Albany County,
County Seat Troy (12180). Guide: NY Historical Resources
Center, GUIDE TO HISTORICAL RESOURCES IN RENSSELAER
COUNTY, The Center, Ithaca, NY, 1983. Censuses: 1800R,
1810R, 1820RI, 1830R, 1840RP, 1850RAIM, 1855S, 1860RAIM,
1865S, 1870RAIM, 1875S, 1880RAIM, 1890C, 1900R, 1905S,
1910R, 1915S, 1925S.

FHL governmental microfilms: deed (1791-1960),
federal census (1800-1910), mortgage (1791-1866), probate
(1802-1906), state census (1855-75, 1905-25), vital
records (1846-51, 1874-81). FHL non-governmental microfilms: Baptist, business, Dutch Reformed, Evangelical
Reformed, Episcopal, Methodist, Presbyterian, Reformed.
Published and microfilmed works (NYSL, NYPL): atlas
(1876), Baptist, Bible, biography (1880/97/1925), Catholic, cemetery, church, city directory (1829-), DAR, deed,
Dutch Reformed, earmarks, Evangelical Lutheran, Episcopal, federal census (1800-1910), Friends, gazetteer
(1870),history (1880/97/1925), justice of peace, Lutheran, marriage, Methodist, naturalization, newspaper,
Presbyterian, Revolutionary War, state census (1855-75,
1905-25, tax, town, vital records (1846-51, 1874-81).
See TT 21, 23; NYGBR 59, 108; ESNY 3.

Repositories: LR; Rensselaer County Historical
Society Library, 59 Second St., Troy, NY 12180; Troy
Public Library, 100 Second St., Troy, NY 12180. Society:
Rensselaer County Historical Society, 59 Second St.,
Troy, NY 12180.

40. ROCKLAND County, formed 1798 from Orange County,
County Seat New City (10956). Censuses: 1800R, 1810R,
1820RI, 1830R, 1840RP, 1850RAIM, 1855S, 1860RAIM, 1865S,

1870RAIM, 1875S, 1880RAIM, 1890C, 1892S, 1900R, 1905S, 1910R, 1915S, 1925S.

FHL governmental microfilms: deed (1703-1929), federal census (1800-1910), guardian (1798-1909), marriage (some 1694-1831, 1908-18), mortgage (1703-1929), probate (1798-1909), state census (1855-1925), will (1798-1901). FHL non-governmental microfilms: Dutch Reformed, history, Methodist, Presbyterian, Reformed. Published and microfilmed works (NYSL, NYPL): atlas (1875/6), Baptist, Bible, biography (1884), cemetery, church, DAR, deed, Dutch Reformed, earmarks, Evangelical Lutheran, federal census (1800-1910), genealogy, history (1884/86/1941/76), Methodist, Reformed, Revolutionary War, road, state census (1915-25), town, will. See NYGBR 61, 63, 84, 101.

Repositories: LR; New City Library, 220 N. Main St., New City, NY 10956. Society: Historical Society of Rockland County, 20 Zukor Rd., New City, NY 10956.

41. ST. LAWRENCE County, formed 1802 from Clinton County, County Seat Canton (13617). Censuses: 1800R, 1810R, 1815S, 1820RI, 1830R, 1840RP, 1845S, 1850RAIM, 1860RAIM, 1865S, 1870RAIM, 1880RAIM, 1890C, 1900R, 1905S, 1910R, 1915S, 1925S.

FHL governmental microfilms: circuit court (1848-57), county court (1847-1901), court (1844-1902), deed (1787-1955), federal census (1810-1910), general sessions court (1857-1903), guardian (1830-1913), lis pendens (1865-1901), marriage (1908-35), mortgage (1802-82), naturalization (1818-1977), probate (1830-1955), state census (1815/45/65/1905/15/25), supreme court (1857-1906), vital records (1846-1902, 1908-35), will (1830-1955). FHL non-governmental microfilms: Episcopal, Presbyterian. Published and microfilmed works (NYSL, NYPL): atlas (1865), Baptist, Bible, biography (1853/78/94), cemetery, church, city directory (1857-), Congregational, DAR, Episcopal, federal census (1810-1910), gazetteer (1873), history (1853/78/94/1974), marriage, Methodist, naturalization, Presbyterian, Revolutionary War, state census (1815/45/65/1915/25), vital records (1847-9), will. See TT 4, 6, 18, 22.

Repositories: LR; St. Lawrence County Historical Association Library, 3 E. Main St., Canton, NY 13617; St. Lawrence University Library, Park St., Canton, NY 13617. Societies: St. Lawrence County Historical Association, 3 E. Main St., Canton, NY 13617; Nyando Roots Genealogical

Society, PO Box 175, Massena, NY 13662; St. Lawrence
Valley Genealogical Society, PO Box 86, Potsdam, NY
13676.

42. SARATOGA County, formed 1791 from Albany County,
County Seat Ballston Spa (12020). Guides: Saratoga
County Historical Society, CATALOG OF THE MANUSCRIPT
COLLECTION, The Society, Ballston Spa, NY, 1979; P. F.
Horne, GENEALOGICAL GUIDE TO SARATOGA COUNTY, Saratoga
County Historical Society, Ballston Spa, NY, 1980; NY
Historical Resources Center, GUIDE TO HISTORICAL RE-
SOURCES IN SARATOGA COUNTY, The Center, Ithaca, NY, 1983;
many records in THE SARATOGA. Censuses: 1800R, 1810R,
1820RI, 1830R, 1840RP, 1850RAIM, 1855S, 1860RAIM, 1865S,
1870RAIM, 1875S, 1880RAIM, 1890C, 1892S, 1900R, 1905S,
1910R, 1915S, 1925S.

FHL governmental microfilms: chancery court (1847–
67), deed (1774–1964), federal census (1800–1910), guardian (1815–1923), lis pendens (1865–1901), map index
(1850–1), mortgage (1791–1899), probate (1791–1923),
state census (1855–1925), tax (1840), vital records
(1908–35), will (1791–1906). FHL non-governmental microfilms: Baptist, Congregational, Dutch Reformed, Episcopal, family history, genealogy, Methodist, newspaper,
Presbyterian, Reformed. Published and microfilmed works
(NYSL, NYPL): administration, atlas (1866), Baptist,
Bible, biography (1878/93/99), cemetery, church, circuit
court (1791–1824), Congregational, court of common pleas
(1791–1818), court of oyer and terminer (1791–1842),
court of general sessions (1791–1817), DAR, Dutch Reformed, Episcopal, federal census (1800–1910), Friends,
gazetteer (1871), genealogy, history (1859/78/93/99/
1974), justice of peace, land, marriage, Methodist,
military, naturalization, newspaper, Presbyterian, probate (1791–1806), Reformed, Revolutionary War, school,
state census (1845/1915/25), tax (1779), town, vital
records 1847–9), will. See TT 2, 4, 6, 10; NYGBR 34,
ESNY 8.

Repositories: LR; Ballston Spa Public Library, 21
Milton Ave., Ballston Spa, NY 12020; Saratoga County
Historical Society Library, Brookside, Fairground Ave.,
Ballston Spa, NY 12020. Societies: Saratoga County
Historical Society, Brookside, Fairground Ave., Ballston
Spa, NY 12020; Ballston Spa Genealogy Club, Ballston Spa
Library, Ballston Spa, NY 12020.

43. SCHENECTADY County, formed 1809 from Albany County, County Seat Schenectady (12307). Guides: NY Historical Resources Center, GUIDE TO HISTORICAL RESOURCES IN SCHENECTADY COUNTY, The Center, Ithaca, NY, 1983; many records in THE MOHAWK. Censuses: 1810R, 1820RI, 1830R, 1835S, 1840RP, 1850RAIM, 1855S, 1860RAIM, 1865S, 1870RAIM, 1875S, 1880RAIM, 1890C, 1892S, 1900R, 1905S, 1910R, 1915S, 1925S.

FHL governmental microfilms: court of common pleas (1834-8), deed (1809-1901), federal census (1810-1910), guardian (1809-1907), marriage (1908-20), probate (1809-1916), state census (1835, 1855-1925), will (1809-1900). FHL non-governmental microfilms: Baptist, Bible, Dutch Reformed, Episcopal, Methodist, Presbyterian, Reformed. Published and microfilmed works (NYSL, NYPL): administration, atlas (1866), Baptist, Bible, biography (1886/99/-1902), birth, cemetery, church, city directory (1841, 1857-), Civil War, DAR, Dutch Reformed, early settlers, Episcopal, federal census (1810-1910), Friends, gazetteer, genealogy, guardian, history (1873/86/99/1902), Methodist, military, newspaper, Presbyterian, Reformed, Revolutionary War, state census (1915-25), tax (1779), town, Universalist, will. See TT 2, 5, 7, 16, 18; NYGBR 73, 94; ESNY 4.

Repositories: LR; City History Center Library, City Hall, Schenectady, NY 12305; Schenectady County Historical Society Library, 32 Washington Ave., Schenectady, NY 12305; Schenectady County Public Library, Liberty and Clinton Sts., Schenectady, NY 12305. Society: Schenectady County Historical Society, 32 Washington Ave., Schenectady, NY 12305.

44. SCHOHARIE County, formed 1795 from Albany and Otsego Counties, County Seat Schoharie (12157). Guide: NY Historical Resources Center, GUIDE TO HISTORICAL RESOURCES IN SCHOHARIE COUNTY, The Center, Ithaca, NY, 1983. Censuses: 1800R, 1810R, 1820RI, 1825S, 1830R, 1835S, 1840RP, 1850RAIM, 1855S, 1860RAIM, 1865S, 1870RAIM, 1875S, 1880 RAIM, 1890C, 1892S, 1900R, 1905S, 1910R, 1915S, 1925S.

FHL governmental microfilms: court (1851-1901), court of common pleas (1796-1852), deed (1795-1940), federal census (1800-1910), guardian (1830-1901), marriage (1847-52, 1908-26), mortgage (1795-1870), probate (1795-1933), state census (1825-35, 1855-1925), vital records (1847-9), will (1795-1913). FHL non-governmental microfilms: genealogy, history, Reformed. Published and microfilmed works (NYSL, NYPL): atlas (1866), Bible, biography (1882/99), cemetery, church, DAR, directory, Dutch Reformed, early settlers, Evangelical Lutheran, federal census (1800-1910), gazetteer (1872), genealogy, German Church, history (1845/82/91/1964), Lutheran, Methodist, military, mortuary, newspaper, probate (1795-1863), Reformed, Revolutionary War, state census (1915-25), tax, town, will. See TT 8, 11, 18.

Repositories: LR; State University of NY Library, W. Main St., Cobleskill, NY 12043; Old Stone Fort Museum Complex, PO Box 69, Schoharie, NY 12157; Schoharie County Historical Society Library, N. Main St., Schoharie, NY 12157; Dibble Memorial Library, Summit, NY 12175. Society: Schoharie County Historical Society, N. Main St., Schoharie, NY 12157.

45. SCHUYLER County, formed 1854 from Chemung, Steuben, and Tompkins Counties, County Seat Watkins Glen (14891). Guide: NY Historical Resources Center, GUIDE TO HISTORICAL RESOURCES IN SCHUYLER COUNTY, The Center, Ithaca, NY, 1981. Censuses: 1855S, 1860RAIM , 1865S, 1870RAIM, 1875S, 1880RAIM, 1890C, 1900R, 1905S, 1910R, 1915S, 1925S.

FHL governmental microfilms: deed (1798-1965), federal census (1860-1910), guardian (1855-1905), lis pendens (1855-1907), marriage (1908-35), mortgage (1798-1952), naturalization (1864-1949), probate (1854-1970), state census (1855-75, 1915-25), will (1854-1901). FHL non-governmental microfilms: Baptist, history, Presbyterian. Published and microfilmed works (NYSL, NYPL): atlas (1874), Baptist, Bible, biography (1879/95/1903), cemetery, church, DAR, federal census (1860-1910), Friends, gazetteer (1868), history (1879/85/95/1903), newspaper, state census (1915-25), will. See TT 18-19.

Repositories: LR; Watkins Glen Public Library, N. Franklin St., Watkins Glen, NY 14891; Schuyler County Historical Society Museum, 108 N. Catherine St., Montour Falls, NY 14865. Society: Schuyler County Historical Society, Route 14, Montour Falls, NY 14865.

46. SENECA County, formed 1804 from Cayuga County, County Seat Waterloo (13165). Guide: NY Historical Resources Center, GUIDE TO HISTORICAL RESOURCES IN SENECA COUNTY, The Center, Ithaca, NY, 1980. Censuses: 1810R, 1820RI, 1830R, 1840RP, 1850RAIM, 1860RAIM, 1870RAIM, 1880RAIM, 1890C, 1900R, 1910R, 1915S, 1925S.

FHL governmental microfilms: court (1804-1924), county records (1817-1963), court of oyer and terminer (1875-95), deed (1804-1967), federal census (1810-1910), general sessions court (1834-40), guardian (1816-1901), homestead (1851-1902), lis pendens (1855-1907), marriage (some 1865-1900, 1908-35), military (1813-67, 1918), mortgage (1804-57), naturalization (1827-1956), poor (1876-80k1), probate (1804-1919), state census (1915-25), town, will (1804-1919). FHL non-governmental microfilms: business, early settlers, genealogy, mortuary, newspaper, Presbyterian, Reformed. Published and microfilmed works (NYSL, NYPL): atlas (1874), Baptist, Bible, biography (1895), business, cemetery, church, DAR, deed, Dutch Reformed, Episcopal, federal census (1810-1910), gazetteer (1867), history (1876/95/1976/83), inhabitants (1835), justice of peace, Methodist, military, mortgage, Presbyterian, Reformed, Revolutionary War, school, state census (1915-25), tax, town, will. See TT 3, 8-12, 23.

Repositories: LR; Waterloo Library and Historical Society, 31 E. Williams St., Waterloo, NY 13165. Societies: Waterloo Historical Society, 31 E. Williams St., Waterloo, NY 13165; Seneca Falls Historical Society, 55 Cayuga St., Seneca Falls, NY 13148; Finger Lakes Genealogical Society, PO Box 47, Seneca Falls, NY 13148; Genealogical Conference of NY, Interlaken, NY 14847.

47. STEUBEN County, formed 1796 from Ontario County, County Seat Bath (14810). Guide: NY Historical Resources Center, GUIDE TO HISTORICAL RESOURCES IN STEUBEN COUNTY, The Center, Ithaca, NY, 1981. Censuses: 1800R, 1810R, 1820RI, 1825S, 1830R, 1835S, 1840RP, 1845S, 1850RAIM, 1855S, 1860RAIM, 1865S, 1870RAIM, 1875S, 1880RAIM, 1890C, 1900R, 1905S, 1910R, 1915S, 1925S.

FHL governmental microfilms: county court (1847-1904), deed (1796-1960), federal census (1800-1910), guardian (1796-1936), lis pendens (1820-1972), marriage (1908-36), military (1862-7), mortgage (1796-1906), probate (1796-1936), state census (1825-75, 1905-25), vital records (some 1847-9, 1908-36), will (1800-69). FHL non-governmental microfilms: history, newspaper, Presbyterian. Published and microfilmed works (NYSL, NYPL): atlas (1873), Bible, biography (1879/91/96), business, Catholic, cemetery, church, DAR, deed (1847-98), federal census (1800-1910), funeral, gazetteer (1868/91), genealogy, history (1853/79/85/91/96/1911/35), Methodist, naturalization, newspaper, Presbyterian,

Revolutionary War, school, state census (1825–75, 1905–25), tax, Universalist, vital records, will. See TT 5, 19–21; NYGBR 60.

Repositories: LR; Davenport Library, Cameron Park, Bath, NY 14810. Society: Steuben County Historical Society, 6 William St., Bath, NY 14810.

48. SUFFOLK County, formed 1683 as an original County, County Seat Riverhead (11901). Guide: Suffolk County Archives and Records Service Division, ARCHIVES GUIDE, The Division, Riverhead, NY, 1981. Censuses: 1790R, 1800R, 1810R, 1820RI, 1830R, 1840RP, 1850RAIM, 1860RAIM, 1870RAIM, 1880RAIM, 1890C, 1900R, 1910R, 1915S, 1925S.

FHL governmental microfilms: deeds (a few), federal census (1790–1910), marriage (1802–56 incomplete), military (1776), state census (1915–25), town (for one town 1657–1873), will (1787–1929 incomplete). FHL non-governmental microfilms: newspaper, Presbyterian. Published and microfilmed works (NYSL, NYPL): atlas (1888), Baptist, Bible, biography (1896), cemetery, census (1778), church, Civil War, Congregational, DAR, early inhabitants, Episcopal, history (1849/74/82/96/1949), Methodist, newspaper, Presbyterian, Revolutionary War, state census (1915–25), tax, town, vital records (1847–52), will. See NYGBR 11, 24, 29, 38, 42. 47–49, 50, 53, 55–57, 64, 66.

Repositories: LR; Suffolk County Historical Society Library, 300 W. Main St., Riverhead, NY 11901; East Hampton Free Library, 159 Main St., East Hampton, NY 11937; Huntington Historical Society Library, 209 Main St., Huntington, NY 11743. Societies: Suffolk County Historical Society, 300 W. Main St., Riverhead, NY 11901; Huntington Historical Society, Genealogy Workshop, 209 Main St., Huntington, NY 11743.

49. SULLIVAN County, formed 1809 from Ulster County, County Seat Monticello (12701). Early will records burned in 1909. Censuses: 1810R, 1820RI, 1830R, 1840RP, 1850RAIM, 1855S, 1860RAIM, 1870RAIM, 1875S, 1880RAIM, 1890C, 1900R, 1910R, 1915S, 1925S.

FHL governmental microfilms: court (1850–1924), deed (1809–78), federal census (1810–1910), lis pendens (1864–1902), marriage (1908–34), mortgage (1809–77), state census (1855/75/1915/25), tax (one precinct 1776), vital records (1926–33). FHL non-governmental microfilms: Baptist, Congregational, Dutch Reformed, Methodist, Presbyterian. Published and microfilmed works (NYSL,

NYPL): atlas (1875), Bible, cemetery, church, Congregational, DAR, Dutch Reformed, federal census (1810–1910), gazetteer (1872), history (1873), Methodist, Presbyterian, Reformed, state census (1915/25), town.

Repositories: LR; Crawford Memorial Library, 189 Broadway, Monticello, NY 12701; Sullivan County Historical Museum, Bank St., Monticello, NY 12701.

50. TIOGA County, formed 1791 from Montgomery County, County Seat Owego (13827). Guide: NY Historical Resources Center, GUIDE TO HISTORICAL RESOURCES IN TIOGA COUNTY, The Center, Ithaca, NY, 1981. Censuses: 1800R, 1810R, 1820RI, 1825S, 1830R, 1835S, 1840RP, 1850RAIM, 1855S, 1860RAIM, 1865S, 1870RAIM, 1875S, 1880RAIM, 1890C, 1892S, 1900R, 1905S, 1910R, 1915S, 1925S.

FHL governmental microfilms: court (1829–1964), court of common pleas (1794–1846), court of oyer and terminer (1790–1826), deed (1791–1965), federal census (1800–1910), guardian (1840–90, 1905–47), lis pendens (1829–1910), marriage (1908–26), military (1865), mortgage (1791–1891), probate (1798–1969), road (1791), state census (1825–35, 1855–1925), vital records (1908–35). FHL non-governmental microfilms: business, history, newspaper, Presbyterian. Published and microfilmed works (NYSL, NYPL): atlas (1869), Baptist, Bible, biography (1879/97), cemetery, church, Congregational, DAR, early settlers, Episcopal, executor-administrator (1825–54), federal census (1800–1910), gazetteer (1887), history (1879/85/88/97), marriage, Methodist, Presbyterian, road, state census (1915–25), tax, town, vital records (1847–9), will. See TT 2, 4, 7, 12, 19; NYGBR 57, 59–60.

Repositories: LR; Coburn Free Library, 275 Main St., Owego, NY 13827; Tioga County Historical Society Library, 110 Front St., Owego, NY 13827. Society: Tioga County Historical Society, 110 Front St., Owego, NY 13827.

51. TOMPKINS County, formed 1817 from Seneca and Cayuga Counties, County Seat Ithaca (14850). Guide: NY Historical Resources Center, GUIDE TO HISTORICAL RESOURCES IN TOMPKINS COUNTY, The Center, Ithaca, NY, 1981. Censuses: 1820RI, 1825S, 1830R, 1835S, 1840RP, 1850RAIM, 1860RAIM, 1865S, 1870RAIM, 1875S, 1880RAIM, 1890C, 1892S, 1900R, 1905S, 1910R, 1915S, 1925S.

FHL governmental microfilms: court (1817–1905), court of common pleas (1817–22), deed (1817–1967), federal census (1820–1910), guardian (1817–1916), lis pendens (1841-1905), marriage (1844-87 some, 1908-35), mortgage (1816-1912), naturalization (1818-1976), probate (1817-1916), state census (1825-35, 1865-1925), will (1817-1903). FHL non-governmental microfilms: history. Published and microfilmed works (NYSL, NYPL): atlas (1866), Baptist, Bible, biography (1879/94), cemetery, church, DAR, deed (1794-1822), dower, Dutch Reformed, early settlers, Episcopal, Evangelical, federal census (1820-1910), gazetteer (1868), genealogy, history (1879/ 84/95), newspaper, Presbyterian, probate (1817-75), Revolutionary War, state census (1915-25), will. See TT 8, 12, 15, 17.

Repositories: LR; Cornell University Libraries, Ithaca, NY 14853; DeWitt Historical Society of Tompkins County Library, 116 N. Cayuga St., Ithaca, NY 14850; Tompkins County Public Library, 312 N. Cayuga St., Ithaca, NY 14850; Finger Lakes Library System, 314 N. Cayuga St., Ithaca, NY 14850. Society: DeWitt Historical Society of Tompkins County, 116 N. Cayuga St., Ithaca, NY 14850.

52. ULSTER County, formed 1683 as an original County, County Seat Kingston (12401). Guide: Historical Records Survey, INVENTORY OF THE COUNTY ARCHIVES OF ULSTER COUNTY, WPA, New York, NY, 1939. Censuses: Pre-1790E, 1790R, 1800R, 1810R, 1820RI, 1830R, 1840RP, 1850RAIM, 1855S, 1860RAIM, 1865S, 1870RAIM, 1875S, 1880RAIM, 1890C, 1892S, 1900R, 1905S, 1910R, 1915S, 1925S.

FHL governmental microfilms: birth (1847-9), chancery court (1830-50), circuit court (1844-78), court (1718-1814), county court (1847-81), court of common pleas (1663-84, 1707-1885), court of oyer and terminer (1684-1774, 1862-95), death (1847-50), deed (1684-1931), federal census (1790-1910), general sessions court (1693-8, 1818-95), guardian (1823-1905), homestead (1851-1940), incorporation (1784-1910), justice of peace (1704-70), land (1666-1850), lis pendens (1825-1905), maps (1746-1936), marriage (1847-50, 1908-35), mortgage (1755-1899), naturalization (1812-92), oaths of office (1866-80), probate (1662-1921), quit rent (1717-85), road (1722-95), state census (1855-1925), supervisors (1710-30, 1793-1806), supreme court (1786-1867), tax (1709-38, 1767), town (1667-1816), vital records (1847-1925), will (1787-1916). FHL non-governmental microfilms: Baptist, Catholic, Dutch Reformed, Evangelical Lutheran, Friends, Lutheran, Methodist, newspaper, Presbyterian, Reformed.

Published and microfilmed works (NYSL, NYPL): atlas
(1875), Baptist, Bible, biography (1880/96/1907), business, cemetery, church, citizens (1770), court (1661-75,
1693-1775, 1778-82), colonial, Congregational, DAR, deed,
Dutch Reformed, early settlers, Evangelical Lutheran,
federal census (1790-1910), freeholders (1798-1812),
Friends, gazetteer (1871), genealogy, history (1880/96/-
1907/23/75/77), Huguenot, jury (1750-99), land (1661-
1728), Lutheran, marriage, Methodist, naturalization
(1715), newspaper, Presbyterian, probate (1665-), Revolutionary War, state census (1915-25), tax (1709-12, 1718-
21, 1798, 1805/9/15), town, vital records (1847-50),
will. See NYGBR 11, 50, 62, 73, 87, 91, 106, 110, 113;
National Genealogical Society Quarterly 53, 57, 60, 68.
    Repositories: LR; Kingston Area Library, 55 Franklin
St., Kingston, NY 12401; Huguenot Historical Society
Library, 88 Huguenot St., New Paltz, NY 12561. Societies: Ulster County Historical Society, PO Box 3752,
Kingston, NY 12401; Huguenot Historical Society, PO Box
339, New Paltz, NY 12561; Ulster County Genealogical
Society, PO Box 333, Hurley, NY 12443.

53. WARREN County, formed 1813 from Washington County,
County Seat Lake George (12845). Guide: NY Historical
Resources Center, GUIDE TO HISTORICAL RESOURCES IN WARREN
COUNTY, The Center, Ithaca, NY, 1982. Censuses: 1820RI,
1830R, 1840RP, 1850RAIM, 1855S, 1860RAIM, 1865S, 1870
RAIM, 1875S, 1880RAIM, 1890C, 1892S, 1900R, 1905S, 1910R,
1915S, 1925S.
    FHL governmental microfilms: chancery court (1847-
62), circuit court (1834-90), county court (1800-1924),
court of common pleas (1813-65), court of oyer and terminer (1816-95), deed (1813-1901), excise (1857-69),
federal census (1820-1910), general sessions court (1813-
1933), incorporation (1853-1939), justice court (1812-
75), license (1879-1946), marriage (1908-27), mortgage
(1813-1944), notary (1904-55), oaths of office (1862-
1907), probate (1813-1955), state census (1855-1925),
supreme court (1840-1954), voter (1822-1905), will (1813-
1955). FHL non-governmental microfilms: Baptist, business, Episcopal, Methodist, newspaper. Published and
microfilmed works (NYSL, NYPL): atlas (1876), Baptist,
Bible, biography (1885), Catholic, cemetery, church,
Civil War, DAR, deed (1813-25), federal census (1820-
1910), Friends, history (1885/1942/63), Methodist, newspaper, Presbyterian, Revolutionary War, state census

(1855/1915/25), tax (1814/16), town, will. See TT 3, 5, 8, 11.

Repositories: LR; Crandall Library, City Park, Glens Falls, NY 12801. Societies: Lake George Historical Association, PO Box 391, Lake George, NY 12845; Northeastern NY Genealogical Society, Route 2, Box 3B, Lake George, NY 12845.

54. WASHINGTON County, formed 1772 from Albany County, County Seat Hudson Falls (12839), known as Charlotte County 1772-84, county clerk at Hudson Falls and surrogate at Salem. Guides: Washington County Planning Department, AN INTRODUCTION TO HISTORIC RESOURCES IN WASHINGTON COUNTY, The Department, Granville, NY, 1976; NY Historical Resources Center, GUIDE TO HISTORICAL RESOURCES IN WASHINGTON COUNTY, The Center, Ithaca, NY, 1986. Censuses: Pre-1790E, 1790R, 1800R, 1810R, 1820RI, 1825S, 1830R, 1835S, 1840RP, 1850RAIM, 1855S, 1860RAIM, 1865S, 1870RAIM, 1875S, 1880RAIM, 1890C, 1892S, 1900R, 1905S, 1910R, 1915S, 1925S.

FHL governmental microfilms: court of common pleas (1797-8), deed (1774-1959), federal census (1790-1910), mortgage (1773-1881), probate (1787-1911), state census (1825-35, 1855-1925), town, will (1788-1901). FHL nongovernmental microfilms: Dutch Reformed, Episcopal, Friends, Presbyterian. Published and microfilmed works (NYSL, NYPL): atlas (1866), Baptist, Bible, biography (1894/1901), cemetery, church, Civil War, Congregational, DAR, deed (1786-1887), Dutch Reformed, Episcopal, federal census (1790-1910), Friends, gazetteer (1849), history (1849/78/94/1901/32), marriage, Masonic, Methodist, newspaper, patent, Presbyterian, Reformed, Revolutionary War, school, state census (1825-35, 1855-1925), tax, town, vital records (1847-50, 1881-1900), will. See TT 2-3, 7, 10, 12-13, 20-21; ESNY 1, 6.

Repositories: LR; Hudson Falls Free Library, 220 Main St., Hudson Falls, NY 12839. Society: Washington County Historical Society, 167 Broadway, Ft. Edward, NY 12828.

55. WAYNE County, formed 1823 from Ontario and Seneca Counties, County Seat Lyons (14489). Guide: NY Historical Resources Center, GUIDE TO HISTORICAL RESOURCES IN WAYNE COUNTY, The Center, Ithaca, NY, 1981. Censuses: 1830R, 1840RP, 1850RAIM, 1855S, 1860RAIM, 1870RAIM,

1880RAIM, 1890C, 1892S, 1900R, 1905S, 1910R, 1915S, 1925S.

FHL governmental microfilms: county court (1847-75, 1881-4), court of oyer and terminer (1836-1905), deed (1794-1958), federal census (1830-1910), guardian (1823-90), marriage (1907-35), naturalization (1854-1959), probate (1823-1964), state census (1855, 1892-1925), town (1793-1909), vital records (1847-50), will (1823-1901). FHL non-governmental microfilms: Baptist, business, Episcopal, history, newspaper, Presbyterian. Published and microfilmed works (NYSL, NYPL): atlas (1874), Baptist, Bible, biography (1877/95), cemetery, church, Civil War, DAR, early settlers, federal census (1830-1910), gazetteer (1867), history (1877/83/95), Methodist, naturalization, Presbyterian, Revolutionary War, road, school, state census (1915-25), town, vital records (1847-9), will. See TT 4-5, 9. 18; NYGBR 55.

Repositories: LR; Lyons School District Public Library, 67 Central St., Lyons, NY 14489. Society: Wayne County Historical Society, 21 Butternut St., Lyons, NY 14489.

56. WESTCHESTER County, formed 1683 as an original County, County Seat White Plains (10601). Censuses: Pre-1790E, 1790R, 1800R, 1810R, 1820RI, 1830R, 1840RP, 1850RAIM, 1860RAIM, 1865S, 1870RAIM, 1880RAIM, 1890C, 1900R, 1905S, 1910R, 1915S, 1925S.

FHL governmental microfilms: deed (1680-1966), federal census (1790-1910), guardian (1802-1900), lis pendens (1823-1901), military (1781), mortgage (1680-1966), probate (1777-1905), Revolutionary veterans, state census (1905-25), tax (1763), town (1665-1835), vital records (1807-79 scattered), will (1787-1905). FHL non-governmental microfilms: business, Congregational, Dutch Reformed, French Reformed, Friends, Methodist, newspaper, Presbyterian, Reformed. Published and microfilmed works (NYSL, NYPL): atlas (1872/81/93), Bible, biography (1899/1925), cemetery, church, city directory (1858-), court of sessions (1675-96), Civil War, Congregational, DAR, Dutch Reformed, Episcopal, federal census (1790-1910), Friends, history (1848/55/81/86/99/1900/13/25/26/46/52), Huguenot, inhabitants (1698, 1710), land, map, marriage, Methodist, militia, newspaper, Presbyterian, Revolutionary War, state census (1915-25), tax, town, Universalist, vital records (1847-55),, will. See NYGBR 3, 31, 37, 57-60, 73, 79, 107.

Repositories: LR; White Plains Public Library, 100
Martine Ave., White Plains, NY 10601; Westchester Library
System, 285 Central Ave., White Plains, NY 10606 and its
many local libraries; Westchester County Historical
Society Library, 75 Grasslands Rd., Valhalla, NY 10505.
Societies: Westchester County Historical Society, 75
Grasslands Rd., Valhalla, NY 10595; Westchester County
Genealogical Society, PO Box 518, White Plains, NY 10603.

57. WYOMING County, formed 1841 from Genesee County,
County Seat Warsaw (14569). Guide: NY Historical Re-
sources Center, GUIDE TO HISTORICAL RESOURCES IN WYOMING
COUNTY, The Center, Ithaca, NY, 1981. Censuses: 1850
RAIM, 1860RAIM, 1870RAIM, 1875S, 1880RAIM, 1890C, 1900R,
1910R, 1915S, 1925S.

FHL governmental microfilms: court (1841-1929), deed
(1841-1964), federal census (1850-1910), guardian (1841-
1912), lis pendens (1841, 1864-1909), marriage (1843-52
some, 1908-21), mortgage (1841-99, naturalization (1841-
1954), probate (1841-1969), state census (1875, 1915-25),
vital records (1926-35), will (1841-1918).   FHL non-
governmental microfilms: Catholic, Presbyterian. Published and microfilmed works (NYSL, NYPL): atlas (1866/
1902), Baptist, Bible, biography (1880/95), cemetery,
church, Civil War, Congregational, court of general
sessions (1841-53), DAR, federal census (1850-1910),
gazetteer (1870), genealogy, history (1800/95), marriage,
mortgage (1837-64), oaths, Presbyterian, state census
(1915-25), town, vital records (1847-9), will. See TT 4,
13; NYGBR 67; ESNY 2, 5.

Repositories: LR; Warsaw Historical Society Library,
15 Perry Ave., Warsaw, NY 14569; Warsaw Public Library,
130 N. Main St., Warsaw, NY 14569. Societies: Warsaw
Historical Society, 15 Perry Ave., Warsaw, NY 14569;
Western NY Genealogical Society, PO Box 338, Hamburg, NY
14075.

58. YATES County, formed 1823 from Ontario and Steuben
Counties, County Seat Penn Yan (14527). Guide: NY Historical Resources Center, GUIDE TO HISTORICAL RESOURCES
IN YATES COUNTY, The Center, Ithaca, NY, 1982. Censuses:
1825S, 1830R, 1835S, 1840RP, 1845S, 1850RAIM, 1855S,
1860RAIM, 1865S, 1870RAIM, 1875S, 1880RAIM, 1890C, 1892S,
1900R, 1905S, 1910R, 1915S, 1925S.

FHL governmental microfilms: court (1823-1913),
court of common pleas (1823-77), court of oyer and ter-

miner (1835–95), deed (1790–1965), federal census (1830–
1910), guardian (1823–94), guardian (1823–94), homestead
(1851–1907), lis pendens (1832–1950), marriage (1908–35),
military (1863–1943), mortgage (1823–83), naturalization
(1823–1958), probate (1823–1951), state census (1825–
1925), will (1823–1903). FHL non-governmental microfilms: newspaper, Presbyterian. Published and microfilmed works (NYSL, NYPL): atlas (1876), Baptist, biography (1892), cemetery, church, Civil War, DAR, deed
(1754–1898), federal census (1830–1910), Friends, genealogy, history (1873/92/95), military, newspaper, Presbyterian, state census (1915–25), will index. See TT 3, 9–
10, 18; ESNY 3, 7.

Repositories: LR; Penn Yan Public Library, 214 Main
St., Penn Yan, NY 14527. Society: Yates County Genea-
logical and Historical Society, 200 Main St., Penn Yan,
NY 14527.

Books by George K. Schweitzer

CIVIL WAR GENEALOGY. A 78-paged book of 316 sources for tracing your Civil War ancestor. Chapters include I: The Civil War, II: The Archives, III: National
Publications, IV: State Publications, V: Local Sources,
VI: Military Unit Histories, VII: Civil War Events.

GENEALOGICAL SOURCE HANDBOOK. A 100-paged book
describing all major and many minor sources of genealogical information with precise and detailed instructions
for obtaining data from them.

GEORGIA GENEALOGICAL RESEARCH. A 235-paged book
containing 1303 sources for tracing your GA ancestor
along with detailed instructions. Chapters include I: GA
Background, II: Types of Records, III: Record Locations,
IV: Research Procedure and County Listings (detailed
listing of records available for each of the 159 GA
counties).

KENTUCKY GENEALOGICAL RESEARCH. A 154-paged book
containing 1191 sources for tracing your KY ancestor
along with detailed instructions. Chapters include I: KY
Background, II: Types of Records, III: Record Locations,
IV: Research Procedure and County Listings (detailed
listing of records available for each of the 120 KY
counties).

NEW YORK GENEALOGICAL RESEARCH. A 252-paged book containing 1426 sources for tracing your NY ancestor along with detailed instructions. Chapters include I: NY Background, II: Types of Records, III: Record Locations, IV: Research Procedure and NY City Record Listings (detailed listing of records available for the 5 counties of NY City), V: Record Listings for Other Counties (detailed listing of records available for each of the other 57 NY counties).

NORTH CAROLINA GENEALOGICAL RESEARCH. A 190-paged book containing 1233 sources for tracing your NC ancestor along with detailed instructions. Chapters include I: NC Background, II: Types of Records, III: Record Locations, IV: Research Procedure and County Listings (detailed listing of records available for each of the 100 NC counties).

PENNSYLVANIA GENEALOGICAL RESEARCH. A 225-paged book containing 1309 sources for tracing your PA ancestor along with detailed instructions. Chapters include I: PA Background, II: Types of Records, III: Record Locations, IV: Research Procedure and County Listings (detailed listing of records available for each of the 67 PA counties).

REVOLUTIONARY WAR GENEALOGY. A 110-paged book containing 407 sources for tracing your Revolutionary War ancestor. Chapters include I: Revolutionary War History, II: The Archives, III: National Publications, IV: State Publications, V: Local Sources, VI: Military Unit Histories, VII: Sites and Museums.

SOUTH CAROLINA GENEALOGICAL RESEARCH. A 190-paged book containing 1107 sources for tracing your SC ancestor along with detailed instructions. Chapters include I: SC Background, II: Types of Records, III: Record Locations, IV: Research Procedure and County Listings (detailed listing of records available for each of the 47 SC counties and districts).

TENNESSEE GENEALOGICAL RESEARCH. A 136-paged book containing 1073 sources for tracing your TN ancestor along with detailed instructions. Chapters include I: TN Background, II: Types of Records, III: Record Locations, IV: Research Procedure and County Listings (detailed listing of records available for each of the 96 TN counties).

VIRGINIA GENEALOGICAL RESEARCH. A 187-paged book containing 1273 sources for tracing your VA ancestor along with detailed instructions. Chapters include I: VA Background, II: Types of Records, III: Record Locations, IV: Research Procedure and County Listings (detailed listing of records available for each of the 100 VA counties and 41 major cities).

WAR OF 1812 GENEALOGY. A 69-paged book of 289 sources for tracing your War of 1812 ancestor. Chapters include I: History of the War, II: Service Records, III: Bounty Land and Pension Records, IV: National and State Publications, V: Local Sources, VI: Military Unit Histories, VII: Sites and Events.

All of the above books may be ordered from Dr. George K. Schweitzer at the address given on the title page. Or send a long SASE for a FREE descriptive leaflet on any or all of the books.